Corporate
Operational
Analysis

Corporate Operational Analysis

A Procedure for Evaluating Key Factors in Internal Operations, Acquisitions, and Takeovers

Jerry W. Anderson, Jr.
and
John B. Camealy

QUORUM BOOKS
New York • Westport, Connecticut • London

Library of Congress Cataloging-in-Publication Data

Anderson, Jerry W.
    Corporate operational analysis : a procedure for evaluating key
factors in internal operations, acquisitions, and takeovers / Jerry
W. Anderson, Jr. and John B. Camealy.
        p.   cm.
    Includes index.
    ISBN 0–89930–535–0 (alk. paper)
    1. Organizational effectiveness—Evaluation.   I. Camealy, John B.
II. Title.
HD58.9.A54   1991
658.4′013—dc20   90–47592

British Library Cataloguing in Publication Data is available.

Library of Congress Catalog Card Number: 90–47592
ISBN: 0–89930–535–0

First published in 1991

Quorum Books, 88 Post Road West, Westport, CT 06881
An imprint of Greenwood Publishing Group, Inc.

Printed in the United States of America

The paper used in this book complies with the
Permanent Paper Standard issued by the National
Information Standards Organization (Z39.48–1984).

10 9 8 7 6 5 4 3 2 1

Copyright Acknowledgment

Chapter 12 is reprinted from *Business Horizons* 29, no. 4 (July/August 1986): 22–27. Copyright 1986 by the Foundation for the School of Business at Indiana University. Used with
permission.

Contents

Figures and Tables

FIGURES

TABLES

Preface

Organizations rarely operate at their optimum level of efficiency and capability. Much of the stated justification for the wave of takeovers and mergers experienced in recent years has been a need to rescue shareholders from the ineffective leadership skills of incumbent management. Seldom is an organization as ineffective as corporate raiders would have us believe; rarely is the quality of management as excellent as current leadership might wish. The truth lies somewhere between these two positions.

For those desiring to find where their organization stands in terms of the key functions of management, and for those interested in following a proven method for overall enhancement of operations, this book offers a system for problem-finding analysis applicable over the broad spectrum of the total organization. A comprehensive and tested procedure for complete and total analysis is covered in detail. Basically, the corporate operational analysis procedure is a comprehensive problem-finding process in which tests are applied to a broad spectrum of functions, structures, strategies, goals, and procedures. Whether the organization is a commercial firm, a public or private nonprofit entity, or a municipal, state, or federal institution, it cannot long exist while facing inefficient, ineffective internal operations. The purpose of this book is to open avenues of thoughtful, questioning analysis that will provide answers leading to effective change.

An added advantage to be gained from applying this system of analysis to the functions of any organization is that this process will serve to enhance employee confidence and motivation, which is the end result of developing a correct strategy, a correct structure, and the correct systems.

Not until a suspicious tumor in the body is subjected to analysis can its status as a benign or malignant substance be made known. In like manner, it is not possible to assess the positive or negative aspects of strategy, systems, and procedures without first subjecting them to a rigorous analytical process. Chapters 2 through 13 provide such an analysis of the key management functions of planning, organizing, directing, and controlling, which are sequentially overlayed on the following functions:

corporate planning and strategic formulation and implementation

research and development

engineering

manufacturing

marketing

logistics

finance/accounting

management information systems (MIS)

organization structure and human resources

organizational interface, takeovers, mergers, and acquisitions

social responsibility

multinational operations

Part I is a concise introduction to the concept of corporate operational analysis, as defined through use of the procedure modeled in this book. The importance of use of this procedure in evaluating key factors in the areas of internal operation, acquisitions, and takeovers is discussed in depth.

Part II, which contains the aforementioned chapters, details the breadth of special considerations to be covered in the analysis of both internal functional areas and external areas of assessment. Problem-finding tests are applied to a broad spectrum of functions, structures, strategies, goals, and procedures. Each chapter reviews thoroughly a specific management function or process. At the conclusion of each chapter an example of the application of the procedure as a tool for identifying important areas of strength and weakness is given in an outline format. These tables are designed to focus the general concept of operational analysis in a specific, identifiable area. Each reader should find one or more in which he or she is knowledgeable and skilled.

Part III discusses application and use of the procedure. Chapter 14 covers the analysis procedure in depth. In Chapter 15 a case study of a complex corporation engaged in world trade presents an opportunity for application of the procedure for analysis, problem finding, and evaluation. Chapter 16 provides an actual case situation and the application of the procedure to the various issues raised within the analysis. Chapter 16 should answer any questions the reader has accumulated while reading prior chapters.

Part IV presents the conclusions and recommendations of the authors from years of testing and application of the analysis procedure in classrooms and consultations. The chapter details the more conceptual recommendations for future use of this tool as a creative, productive, decision enhancing system.

We wish to thank our students who had the confidence in their professors to apply this model within their own organizations. We also wish to thank those major U.S. companies, both large and small, and their executives who have used this procedure and have helped us with its development. Their data and feedback have proven invaluable in helping perfect this procedure. Also, without the excellent assistance, cooperation, and understanding of several people who were deeply involved in this work, it might not have been completed. We want to give our deepest and appreciative thanks to Margaret Maybury who reviewed the manuscript several times before its completion; Anne Marie Wilson who helped format and structure much of the initial graphic work; and to Tom Gannon, for his confidence in us and for his help and sincere understanding while preparing the manuscript. Ultimately the support of our wives—Joan, with her solid spiritual support, and Lois, with her grace and speed at the computer keyboard—provided the environment necessary to see this project through to completion.

I

Introduction to Corporate Operational Analysis

1

The Importance of Corporate Operational Analysis

Success in the development of business strategy leading to clearly defined policies, procedures, and standards is rightfully a hallmark of the respected and admired executive of the 1990s. Few actions demand greater skill or insight from a business or political leader than these. There is general agreement that the basic, high priority objective in strategic thinking is to pinpoint the *single* critical issue faced by an organization.[1] Emphasis upon the singular is intentional. Too often multiple factors of varied importance compete for attention and dilute the quality and ultimate effectiveness of strategy.

THE CHALLENGE

In the typical broad and uncharted triangle of interrelationships between organization functions, resources, and operating plans, asking the "right" questions is often a more demanding task than the ultimate drafting of a feasible strategic solution. Observers of U.S. management actions in both Japan and the European Economic Community (EEC) tend to attribute our successful problem-solving actions to luck as much as to skill. This viewpoint strikes at the heart of what is termed *strategic credibility*. While an organization may enjoy a solid reputation of overall management, its credibility for insight into technical mastery leading to great strategies does have both internal and external payoffs.[2]

As critical as the role of visionary skill may be, there remains a need for orderly and systematic examination. Such examination provides necessary structure to both problem area focus and the demanding task of prioritizing assets in the solution of problems and attainment of objectives. As shortages in people, material and financial assets, and time become apparent, structural changes may be required, which create stress in the total organizational system. The relative impact of such stress upon an organization and its culture requires determination to carry through the changes. This in turn raises more basic questions regarding the needs and expanded problems facing the organization—questions that may be related to survival of the organization itself. In far too many instances, weeks and possibly months go by and key resources are allocated to suboptimal priorities before the question is asked that should have been addressed at the beginning: "What is the real problem facing this organization?" To answer this question and to properly formulate the necessary strategy, structure, and policy to deal with core problem areas, one encounters a critical need for solid tools of analysis and a system for proper, effective application of the analysis to the problem.

Peter F. Drucker, in his classic discussion *The Effective Executive*, takes the position that people first approach the decision process with an opinion, not with a rigorous search for facts.[3] If a search for facts is initiated, it will often be for facts that simply fit the conclusions already reached. It is recognition of this most prevalent tendency to focus upon an opinion—often related to an area of functional specialization—that fueled development of the corporate operational analysis procedure, which is the cornerstone of this book.

This effective management tool for identification and solving of key strategic impact problems has been developed, tested, and applied broadly with great success. Field and case study analysis and application have been supervised by the authors over an eight-year period. Concept application has evolved into a three-phase corporate operational analysis procedure. The framework of this procedure is discussed in detail in Chapter 15 and detailed in Figure 15.1.

BASIC AREAS OF INTERNAL AND EXTERNAL ASSESSMENT

It is important in following the pattern of analysis of this future-oriented corporate operational analysis procedure to remember the basic objective: that is, development of a diagnostic approach that tries to find basic causal actions or factors, not symptoms. This requires a thorough and total macro- and microdiagnostic analysis and evaluation of all internal and external factors of the company's entire operating environment as well as prescriptive corrective actions.

Internal analysis of an organization is a basic requirement in the study and evaluation of its management strategy and policy. For such analysis to be truly effective, formulation, implementation, and the interrelationship of strategy and policy must be considered. The breadth and depth of understanding that the evaluation of an organization reveals to an analyst becomes the foundation for all future decisions, recommendations, and corrective actions. For many students of management, internal analysis and evaluation become the appraisal of simulated situations based upon case studies or their involvement in business games. For the business manager or consultant, analysis and evaluation are focused upon actual operating firms. Each form of assessment (real life, cases, and games) offers some advantages in terms of individual skill development. Cases and games provide a variety not always available in real-world analysis, but the intense realization of decision impact and the ability to probe beyond the written word is missing in these techniques.

Evaluation of internal resources of an organization is intended to reveal what the company has accomplished in the past, its current operating capacity, and its future potential—all in relationship to its resource profile.

In performing internal analysis, the analyst should assemble and evaluate all available information pertinent to the organization. Included in such a resource package are facts, opinions, observations, and general statements. Sources of such data are company documents, discussions with employees, and knowledgeable sources external to the firm. It is from this type of internal analysis that a useful profile is developed to show basic strengths and weaknesses of the company. From such profiles, judgments can be made about the organization and its divisions. Such information helps establish the foundation upon which to generate corrective actions.

Although the internal analysis reveals to a great extent the past, present, and, to some extent, future state and actions of the company, it does not permit a complete company analysis and evaluation. Complete analysis and evaluation of the corporate situation requires that factors external to the corporation also be seriously weighed in the evaluation. Only by combining both the internal and external analysis and evaluation of the company can a complete assessment be made to determine what the company is capable of accomplishing with its existing resources in the competitive external environment in which it operates.

To help understand this complex and comprehensive analysis and to establish a valuable profile of the entire company, an analyst must:

1. examine all the parts of the company as individual functions and decision-making areas:
   a. corporate planning and strategy (Chapter 2)
   b. research and development (Chapter 3)
   c. engineering (Chapter 4)

    d. manufacturing (Chapter 5)

    e. marketing (Chapter 6)

    f. logistics (Chapter 7)

    g. finance/accounting (Chapter 8)

    h. management information systems (Chapter 9)

    i. organization structure and human resources management (Chapter 10)

    j. organization interface, takeovers, mergers, and acquisitions (Chapter 11)

    k. social responsibility (Chapter 12)

    l. multinational business (Chapter 13)

2. examine and understand the interrelationships between all the parts of the company

3. determine and understand how the parts operate in conjunction with one another

With careful gathering of this information and an adequate examination and digestion of the findings, a set of conclusions can be drawn. If these conclusions are properly made, the strengths and weaknesses within the various departments, between the departments, and within the company as a whole will be illustrated. This picture will present a comprehensive analysis of the company's internal organization and operation.

A company, however, does not exist only in its own little world. There are all forms of external factors that also influence the operation and success of the company. Some of these factors include:

1. competition (domestic and foreign)

2. local, state, national, and multinational customs and laws

3. taxes

4. inflation rates

5. interest rates

6. international currency exchange rates

7. economic environment

8. money availability

9. political stability of foreign countries

Information on many of the external areas is often difficult to find, or time does not permit the in-depth search that is needed to properly uncover, analyze, and evaluate the data. For a thorough company analysis, however, it is imperative that as many of these factors as possible be taken into account and combined with the results of the internal evaluation.

By combining the results of both the internal and external findings, a

Figure 1.1
Relationship Between Internal and External Environmental Analysis and Final Strategy Selection and Implementation

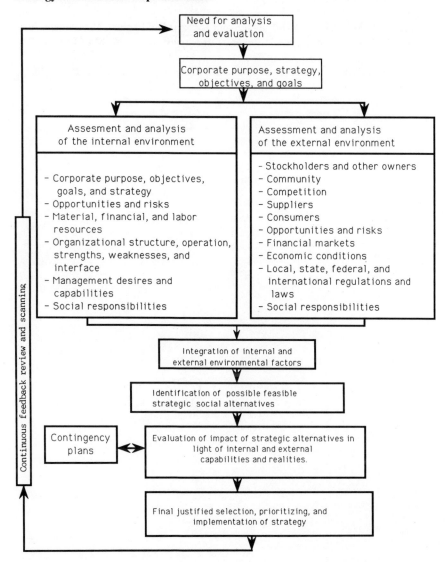

complete understanding of the company's strengths, weaknesses, and problems can be observed so that constructive positive action can be taken. Figure 1.1 shows how the internal and external area analyses fit together to provide a comprehensive understanding of the company in its total environment.

NOTES

1. Kenichi Ohmae, *The Mind of the Strategist* (New York: McGraw-Hill, 1982): 17.

2. Ibid., 4. See also John Diffenbach and Richard B. Higgins, "Strategic Credibility Can Make a Difference," *Business Horizons* 30, no. 3 (May-June 1987): 13.

3. Peter F. Drucker, *The Effective Executive* (New York: Harper & Row, 1967): 144–145.

II
Functional Area Review

2

Corporate Planning and Strategy Formulation and Implementation

The prime purpose of planning is to determine future opportunities and formulate and implement strategy to exploit these opportunities. The most effective plans will not only show how to exploit the opportunities but will also include information that will remove obstacles on the basis of an objective understanding of the strengths and weaknesses of the company and its external environment.

Planning is vital to every organization's survival because it is a continuous process that, if done properly, will show the company how to adapt to its ever-changing internal and external environment. Most companies do some type of long-range, intermediate-range, and short-range planning; however, in many companies planning is poorly conceptualized and executed and has very little impact on day-to-day decisions throughout the company. For planning to be successful, it must be participated in and supported by all levels of management and must supply the criteria for making organizational decisions and commitments. It is the "road map" by which all decisions and commitments can be made and evaluated.

To organize and maintain an effective planning process is complex and difficult, and to develop effective plans requires hard work at all levels of management. If done properly, it can be extremely rewarding to the company.

A CONCEPTUAL MODEL FOR CORPORATE PLANNING
AND STRATEGY FORMULATION AND IMPLEMENTATION

By definition, a conceptual model is one that presents a general idea or outline defining something. To provide a basic understanding of the planning process, this chapter will present and discuss a conceptual model of the broad structure of an effective and efficient planning process. This model, depicted in Figure 2.1, is flexible and adaptable to almost any size or type of organization.

Initial examination shows that all parts of the model are interrelated, and no one part of the model can be considered without considering all other parts. For best results, utilizing the model requires interaction and a scanning process among all parts of the model once work has started; this process should continue as long as the company exists.

Even though it is fully understood that planning and strategy formulation and implementation are an integrated process, for ease of presentation and understanding, major concepts and sections of the model will be discussed separately. Then it will be shown how they are related to one another and why the entire process must work as a continuously changing integrated whole.

CORPORATE STRATEGY

Corporate strategy must articulate many things other than just financial objectives; it must involve economic, personal, and social purposes as well. It must lay out the pattern of company purposes, missions, objectives, and goals, all of which will define the area or areas of business in which the company will participate as well as what kind of a company it will be. The major policies for achieving these purposes, objectives, and goals must then be established.

Corporate strategy arises from a perception and understanding of its present and future market opportunities, available resources, strengths and weaknesses, and personal desires and aspirations of top management. These must then all be reconciled with what is legal, ethical, and moral and how deeply management wants the company to become involved in philanthropic endeavors.

The concept of strategy has many attributes that are important and beneficial to management. Strategy:

• provides the board of directors with specific evidence that the company's management has a process by which it can consider, evaluate, develop, and choose from various alternatives available to the company.

• furnishes the board with a guide of what matters should be presented to it and a reference point upon which to make decisions.

Figure 2.1
A Conceptual Model for Corporate Planning and Strategy Formulation and Implementation

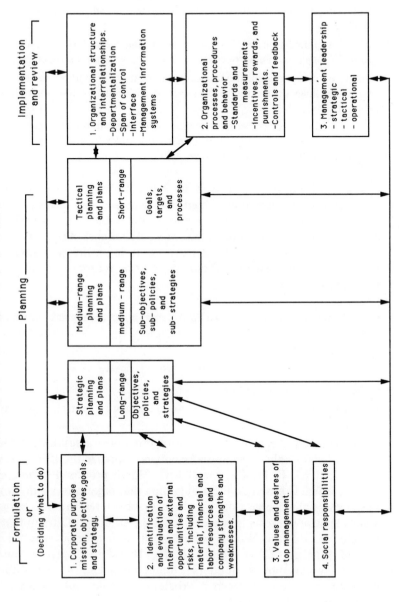

- helps in the stimulation, identification, and development of basic missions, long-range objectives, and short-range goals.
- is of significant help and value in corporate long-range, intermediate-range, and short-range planning because it helps the managers to see new opportunities and then permits them to apply their imagination and innovative skills to exploiting them.
- provides a foundation and "road map" for management throughout the company to make major and minor decisions conforming with top management desires.
- helps coordinate organizational needs and changes in staffing, facilities, materials, and finances and forces managers at all levels to make commitments to these needs.
- can, if well conceived, permit managers at all levels to measure both the quantitative and qualitative attributes in managers under their authority, as well as serve as a guide for improving their abilities.

The concept of strategy also has its shortcomings. Comprehensive strategy requires complex, tough, high-risk decisions and commitments to a direction of operation. Some people do not want to make these tough decisions and commitments, so they present a number of reasons for either not developing a strategy or at least "watering it down." Some of the problems of comprehensive strategy cited as reasons for not adopting such a strategy are:

- It does not give the answers to all managerial problems anyway, so why bother with it?
- It is too difficult and time consuming.
- It is too costly; money can be better spent elsewhere.
- There are more important tasks that have to be accomplished at this time.
- Environmental events are too complex and cannot be controlled anyway.

Unfortunately there is still much of this antistrategy and "muddling through" philosophy, which was heavily promoted in the 1960s, prevalent today. In 1963, R. M. Cyert and J. G. March proposed their coalition theory, which is based on the assumption that organizations do not have purposes—only people do; their theory substitutes internal bargaining among special interests in place of company strategy.[1] Later in that same decade, H. Edward Wrapp published his antistrategic article entitled "Good Managers Don't Make Policy Decisions."[2] This "muddling through" philosophy is, of course, totally debunked by successful companies such as Hewlett-Packard, Procter & Gamble, and General Electric who have an extremely effective strategy in place.

According to Richard F. Vancil there are three levels of strategy making.[3] The three levels of management included in the process are corporate managers, the business (or division) managers, and the activity managers (who include the line managers and functional area managers). Around this concept Vancil has constructed his three-cycle system for strategic planning in diversified companies.[4] In cycle one, corporate objectives are developed by top management and sent down to division managers, who add divisional objectives, goals, and resource requirements. It is then returned to corporate management for review and changes. In cycle two, corporate management returns the modified data to divisional management and asks for divisional plans consistent with corporate objectives and goals. Divisional management generates its objectives and goals and sends the entire process down to the activity managers for their input. The activity managers then return the data to the divisional managers who in turn review it, modify it where necessary, and forward it back to corporate management for their review. The path of the third cycle is the same as that of the second cycle except that discussion and activity goals are firmed up, and budgets are generated and returned to corporate management for review and approval.

The two terms *objectives* and *goals* are used in the discussion of strategy, terms whose meanings are often confused and require clarification. Most scholars of planning and strategy define objectives as being long range, timeless, broad in nature, and general in terms; goals, on the other hand, are short range, time phased, fairly specific with respect to results, and more internally focused. These definitions are not exclusive to business objectives and goals but apply to other areas as well. For instance, in sports, the long-term objective of the game is to win; the team that wins is the one that has scored the most short-term goals during the period of the game.

STRATEGY FORMULATION

Strategy formulation is the process of defining and understanding the business the company is in or wants to be in. It is a process whereby the company determines where it wishes to go, how it plans to get there, what decisions it must make, and when and by whom these decisions must be made. The net outcome of this process is that the company does the right thing at the right time by profitably producing and distributing goods and/or services for which there is a demand or a need in the external market.

The principal subactivities of strategy formulation are shown in Figure 2.1. They include the initial phase of development of the basic corporate strategy, discussed in the previous section. Also, the formulation section of the figure identifies the company opportunities and risks to the feasible strategic alternatives. As part of this operation and before any choice can be made, the available resources and company strengths and weaknesses must be taken into account. This second phase of the formulation process will ascertain the possible paths the company might take.

The next step in the formulation process is to take into consideration the values and desires of top management; this brings into the picture the important factors relative to what top management wants to do and emphasizes which of the many alternatives are preferred by top management. Since higher-level management actively participates in the process of developing the company strategy, their continued enthusiastic support in the final decision process can only help ensure continued support and, hopefully, success for their favored projects.

The final consideration in the chain of strategy formulation is in the area of social responsibility. This falls into the categories of what should be done and, in some cases, what must be done. It takes into consideration the legal, ethical/moral, and philanthropic areas that the company must evaluate when making its strategy decisions. Social responsibility and its implications on overall corporate strategy are covered in considerable detail in Chapter 12.

The pattern of interrelations among all parts of the overall concept of corporate planning and strategy formulation and implementation is now starting to display itself. The ability to identify, develop, and present the different components of strategy formulation is no simple task. An even more awesome task is the reconciliation of the implications posed by the sometimes conflicting directions indicated by all of this information, which requires careful, thoughtful consideration and decisions.

STRATEGY IMPLEMENTATION

Implementation provides the means by which the formulated strategy is put into action. It involves all levels of management in the mobilization of the company's resources and in the moving of the organization toward the accomplishment of its mission. For purposes of discussion of implementation, the process has been broken down into three major subactivities as shown on the righthand side of Figure 2.1. As can be seen, most of these activities are administrative in scope. First, an organizational structure that is appropriate to the efficient operation of the required tasks determined during the formulation process must be installed. This must be made effective in operations by management information systems (see Chapter 9), which will support and enhance coordination, interface, and control between all functional groups as well as in the areas of financial and resource allocation. Second, the organizational process, procedures, and behavior must be implemented through a system of standards, measurements, incentives, rewards, punishments, controls, and feedback. This must all be aimed toward the type of organizational behavior and performance desired for optimum organizational performance. Third is the role of management leadership in making firm decisions for the accomplishment of the corporate strategy.

THE PLANNING PROCESS

In most large companies the planning process is concerned with three main levels and time frames. First is the strategic planning phase, which is long term and looks five years or more into the future. The second level is intermediate-range planning and considers plans for three to five years into the future. The third level of planning is the tactical phase of the operation, is short term in nature, and usually covers only the next one to three years operations.

Strategic Planning

Strategic planning is the process of determining the objectives, missions, policies, and strategies that will control the pattern of acquisition, use, and distribution for corporate operations. Objectives are usually long range, but they may be short range, and if they have not been developed or determined elsewhere, they also include the missions or purposes of the strategy. The missions cover the line or lines of business that the company will pursue. Policies are broad guides to action. Strategies define the means to deploy resources.

Strategic planning includes every type of activity that is of concern to the corporation. Included in this list of activities are: profits, pricing, organization, capital utilization, production, marketing, finance, human resources, research and development, sales, management information systems, public relations, advertising, technological capabilities, legal matters, contract matters, product improvement, training, political activities, and so on.

The intricacies and details of the strategic plan are not always written but are stored in the minds of the chief executive officers. Company security is one reason for this; another reason is that some ambiguity may deter internal conflict or help executives avoid making a difficult final decision.

Medium-range Planning

Medium-range planning results in detailed, coordinated, and comprehensive plans for selected functions of business in order to deploy resources in a manner that will achieve the corporate objectives by following the policies and strategies developed and established in the strategic planning process. In this part of the process there is a special effort made to bring together all of the parts of the total operation.

As a company grows it may develop a number of product lines, services, and markets. To promote coordination and meshing of these units and to gain better control over the diverse business lines or units, divisions with similar business interests may be gathered into what are commonly called strategic business units (SBUs). Strategically each SBU is autonomous from other SBUs; however, it is coordinated with several corporate objectives and policy through the corporate strategic planning process.

A good example of the SBU concept in action is General Electric. In 1968, GE was a widely diversified company; it was decentralized into ten groups, forty-six divisions, and over 190 departments. Today GE is divided into about a dozen major SBUs and is first or second in each of the SBU product line areas.[5]

Basically, the characteristics of SBUs are:

- They establish their own profitability and accountability channels.

- They have customers and markets that are separate and distinct from every other SBU within the corporation.

- Each SBU should be oriented to its external market environment and have direct control over the operation, resources, and other key factors necessary for its success.

SBUs can be a tremendous success, and have been at GE, in increasing sales and profits and in helping the company perform in accordance with its strategic plans. Some shortcomings, however, include requirements for an additional layer of management, role conflict, and conflict over control and use of corporate resources.

Tactical Planning

Short-range tactical plans involve the setting of goals and the establishment of targets and processes for the deployment of resources within the functional areas of the company. Each of the functional areas must develop a set of feasible action programs that are compatible with the divisional strategy, which in turn is compatible with corporate objectives and strategy. These functional area strategies usually cover a one-year period and involve the selection, action sequencing, and budgeting of the goals of each of the functional areas of marketing, finance, engineering, research and development, production, and so on.

Great care must be taken to integrate the goals, actions, and strategy of all the functional areas in order to assure proper interface between all functional areas and to make certain that the company moves in the desired direction.

CONCLUSION

Corporate planning and strategy formulation and implementation are complex tasks, which are constantly going back and forth from formulation to planning to implementation and back again. This is a process that is constantly building upon itself and, hopefully, improving itself. Just as the human body cannot function at peak performance without the brain, heart, muscles, and all other functional organs operating in harmonious integration with one another, neither can corporate planning and strategy formulation and implementation produce optimum results without the harmonious integrated operation of all of its parts.

COMPANY EVALUATION

Corporate planning and strategy formulation and implementation is a continuing process within a company and should improve each year. Table 2.1 can help conduct a preliminary evaluation of a company in this area.

NOTES

1. R. M. Cyert and J. G. March, *A Behavioral Theory of the Firm* (Englewood Cliffs, NJ: Prentice-Hall, 1963).

2. H. Edward Wrapp, "Good Managers Don't Make Policy Decisions," *Harvard Business Review* 45, no. 5 (September-October 1967): 91–99.

3. Richard F. Vancil, "Strategy Formulation in Complex Organizations," *Sloan Management Review* 17, no. 2 (Winter 1976): 1–18.

4. Richard F. Vancil and Peter Lorange, "Strategic Planning in Diversified Companies," *Harvard Business Review* 53, no. 1 (January-February 1975): 81–90.

5. Stratford P. Sherman, "The Mind of Jack Welch," *Fortune* 119, no. 7 (March 27, 1989): 39–50.

Table 2.1
Typical Strengths and Weaknesses in Corporate Planning and Strategy Formulation and Implementation

	Strengths	Weaknesses
PLANNING	Top management participates in and is committed to a strong planning effort.	Planning is done on a departmental basis only with no strong support or commitment from top management.
	Corporate mission statements, objectives, and goals are clearly delineated by top management.	No clearcut mission statements, objectives, or goals exist within the company.
	Both internal and external environmental factors are taken into consideration.	Little or no consideration is given to internal or external environmental factors.
	Long-range, intermediate-range, and short-range plans are generated in all areas.	Only short-range plans or budgets are generated on a departmental basis.
	Detailed strategies, policies, and procedures are generated and implemented.	Few or limited strategies, policies, and procedures exist or are contemplated.
	Detailed plans and budgets are generated and reviewed for acceptance or rejection on all programs.	Few or limited plans or budgets are generated or reviewed outside of the program area.
	The company, through a planning review committee, is committed to planning for leadership in its field.	No planning or budget review committee exists within the company.
ORGANIZING	The planning review committee works with the president and division managers and reports directly to the president.	No planning or budget review committee exists. Plans and budgets are reviewed, if at all, at the manager or director level only.
	Planning strategy is a corporate or company wide integrated operation.	Planning strategy, if it exists, involves only the product group concerned with the product.
	The planning committee only advises the president and the division managers and reviews, recommends and helps formulate plans and strategy but does not direct them or implement them.	No planning or buget committee exists. Program managers and directors formulate and recommend planning strategy tactics and policy.
	Line vice presidents, directors, and managers	Program managers and directors implement and direct their own planning strategies, tactics, and

	implement and direct planning strategy, tactics, and policy.	policy.
DIRECTING	Planning and strategy formulation, implementation, and directing is undertaken by company or division vice presidents.	Implementing and directing planning strategy, if it exists, is initiated at the director or manager level.
	MIS is used to help implement and direct planning strategy.	No MIS is involved in planning, implementation, and directing.
	Excellent interface, integration, and coordination exist between planning and all other company functional areas.	Inadequate interface integration and coordination exists between planning and other company functional areas.
CONTROLLING	Strategy, tactics, budgets, policies, and procedures are constantly reviewed at all management levels to make certain that all programs are proceeding as planned.	Only periodic reviews are made of program progress to see if they are on schedule and within budget.
	MIS is used to track and provide feedback on the status of all programs.	At best, only limited use is made of MIS within the company as a control mechanism.
	Both quantitative and qualitative standards are used as guidelines to evaluate and control program progress and performance.	Only "seat of the pants" guidelines are used to evaluate program progress and performance.

21

3

Research and Development

The importance of an organization's research and development (R&D) function varies with the nature and size of the organization. In some cases it is of minor or no importance to the organization, while in other cases it is of major importance. R&D can be broadly interpreted to be technical or product oriented, market oriented, organizational research oriented, and human resources development oriented; thus, almost every existing organization is involved in some phase or area of R&D. For the purpose of discussion in this chapter, the term *research and development* will be oriented toward technical development of products.

Research and development may be defined as the application of human intelligence in a systematic manner to a problem whose solution is not immediately available. It is a company resource that must not be wasted but must be directed to solving problems in an efficient and effective manner. To be effective, technical R&D must contribute to the profitability of the company by providing new products or services, improved products or services, or new applications or markets for existing products or services.

The approaches taken by various companies to R&D are from the simple to the complex and vary budgetwise from less than 1 percent of sales for some long-established companies in the businesses of steel, home furnishings, paper products, oil, gas, and coal to well over 15 percent for many high technology companies. In 1988, total industry spending on R&D reached $59.4 billion (up 11 percent from 1987) and averaged 3.4 percent of sales.[1] In 1988, the top 10 industrial U.S. spenders on R&D

(General Motors, IBM, Ford Motor, AT&T, DuPont, Digital Equipment, General Electric, Eastman Kodak, Hewlett-Packard, and United Technologies) spent a total of $21.58 billion or approximately 40 percent of the R&D spending by the top 100 companies.[2]

Successful R&D programs are targeted programs. However, accurate targeting requires good information systems (internal and external to the company) and good interface between R&D, marketing, engineering, manufacturing, and other functional areas within the company as well as assessment of customer and market needs and desires external to the company. All of this collective information, along with economic evaluations, is necessary for optimum R&D targeting and project selection as a part of the company's overall strategic plan.

Regardless of where the R&D function is positioned within the company organizational structure, it is a key part of the strategic planning system where the input of money is expected to result in an output of profitable products. As with most other systems, this requires a monitoring and feedback system to constantly follow the progress and results of the R&D programs so that money can be diverted from less successful programs and channeled into programs with greater potential. To accomplish this task successfully, the many complexities and unique problems associated with R&D need to be thoroughly understood.

UNIQUE PROBLEMS AND CONFLICTING DEMANDS

The range of managerial planning problems in the area of R&D are extensive and sometimes complex. On one end of the spectrum, they include monumental problems, such as plans for advanced state-of-the-art techniques and products for U.S. government contracts to match or surpass potential technical developments of a foreign nation in the area of military weapons and space projects, or how to compete with the Asiatic and European countries in high technology, automobiles, machine tools, and other manufactured goods. At the other end of the spectrum are the R&D planning problems of the small business, which feels that it needs to increase or improve its R&D position in order to improve its competitive position.

A few areas that must be considered in establishing technical R&D programs are:

—top management involvement

—strategy, including goals, objectives, priorities, and factors influencing strategy and decisions

—types and levels of R&D

—structure, complexity, and location

—internal versus external

—R&D expenditures and ratios

—working relationships and involvement with other departments

—project classification

—offensive versus defensive

—leader versus follower

—government versus commercial

—research versus development

—project selection and protection

—innovation and creativity

—sources of ideas

—market type and share

—product lifecycle

—honors, patents, and copyrights

—nondisclosure and security

—project control and support

—project prioritizing

—scheduling

—budgeting

—project start, readjustment, and completion or termination

—external environment and influences

This list in no way exhausts all the areas to be considered in establishing and operating an R&D department; on the other hand it is not as complex as it might at first appear. It is possible to group the items into five major categories and briefly discuss them under these major groupings:

- *Corporate involvement* concerns itself with establishing strategy, objectives, and goals for R&D; how and with whom R&D will work; and how much will be spent on what projects.
- *Project classification* examines the types of R&D in which the company might become engaged.
- *Project selection and protection* examines the factors involved in and used in the selection and protection of R&D programs.
- *Project control and support* reviews some concepts of R&D scheduling, prioritizing, and budgeting.
- *External environment* looks at how some of the factors external to the company impact and influence decisions made on internal R&D decisions.

Corporate Involvement

Without a continuous stream of new or updated products or services, a company's growth strategies may be limited. In today's world of rapid technological advances and increasing competition, the pressure of a shorter development timecycle and a shorter product lifecycle is forcing companies to develop new and improved innovative products and services at increasing rates in order to stay competitive. Companies must take care, however, that their R&D projects are not overrushed so as to be inadequate or performed without proper planning just for the sake of saying that the company is performing R&D; either of these two approaches can, and probably will, result in disaster.

Research and development programs are undertaken for three major reasons:

—to generate new scientific knowledge and concepts that can be used to assist in developing and producing profitable new products or services and fighting off competition.

—to develop and produce new products or services for growth and profit.

—to develop and produce profitable modifications and improvements on existing products or with existing services.

Top Management Involvement. In order for R&D to be successful, the development and implementation of its policies and funding must be strongly supported by top management and be totally consistent with and based upon overall long-range corporate strategy, objectives, and goals. The corporate strategy, objectives, and goals must, therefore, be communicated to all levels involved. Anything less than total company commitment at all involved levels can and often does result in failure of the strategy.

Another basic and important reason for top management involvement in R&D is that executives are often freer to think of various alternatives. Also, their lack of scientific or technical training in specific areas makes it less likely that technical constraints will inhibit their thinking. Finally, most top managers have intuitive skills, developed and honed by years of hard experience, which can be extremely valuable to the R&D effort.

Strategy, Objectives, and Goals. Realistic long-range strategy, objectives, and goals must be established by top management with a full understanding of the company finances, technological capabilities, and other internal and external factors. Some of these other factors include the short- and long-range position desired in the industry, maintaining or improving market share, a lead or follow technological position, quality position desired, and new or expanded markets for existing products and technology. Because of increased emphasis on social responsibility, top management's R&D planning strategy must also factor a larger share of the R&D budget into such areas as environmental matters, health, safety, energy considerations, and other environmental concerns.

The chief executive officer must make certain that the R&D objectives and goals are in line with corporate objectives and goals, which must also be understood and followed by all groups within the company.

Types and Levels of R&D. Technical R&D as practiced by most companies is either in the area of basic research, applied research, product development, product application, or a combination of these approaches. Although many companies would like to be involved in all levels of R&D, the large expense involved precludes all but the most successful companies from the capability of full-depth R&D. An examination of the four levels of R&D will show why it is not possible for every company to involve itself in all of the categories.

—*Basic research* starts with attempting to understand the universe, how it is organized, and how it operates. Based on this understanding, new items, devices, techniques, concepts, and methods are derived. Examples of basic research include initial work on transistors, lasers, holography, DNA, and many other concepts. Basic research is extremely time consuming and, as a result, is also expensive.

—*Applied research* involves the separation and/or identification of specific potentials or applications for devices and concepts developed in basic research.

—*Product development* involves using new techniques or combining and using both new and old developments from basic and applied research to form a potential end product, which could eventually move into production if it is proven to be effective, economical, and acceptable; that is, the "do-ability" of the product has been established and major future profit potentials are forseeable.

—*Product application* is moving the product into mass production or finding new uses and applications for existing methods, products, and services.

Structure, Complexity, and Location. The level of R&D involvement that a company will follow must be determined by top management. Structure, complexity, and location are all involved in this decision process.

Although there are various levels of R&D complexity, it will suffice for general understanding to categorize them into three major levels. The least complex level is practiced by a large number of companies, both large and small. This can be classified as simple innovation and involves such minor things as the redesign of a product to make it more appealing, less expensive to manufacture, or more efficient. It also may be as simple as replacing steel or aluminum components with plastic in automobiles, where less weight quite often means better gas mileage, ultimately resulting in more sales of the cars.

The second level of complexity is usually located in the industrial world in companies that use intensive new product R&D to advance the state of the art and the frontiers of technology in their fields of business. Minnesota Mining and Manufacturing (3M) is a company that fits well into both the first and second levels of R&D complexity. At 3M, researchers spend 15 percent of their time on projects that will pay off only far down the road and pump out new products (either totally new or variations on existing products) at the rate of approximately 200 a year.[3]

At the top level of R&D complexity can be found some of the large aerospace companies where R&D planning and success can be a major factor in determining the viability and long-range success of the company. In these companies, much of the R&D is involved in identifying and working on programs for the distant future (five to twenty years ahead) in the areas of strategic military and space missions and then identifying and assembling the technologies that will be needed for their success. In most instances, this level of R&D requires the movement of large amounts of technology into the company from outside sources as well as undertaking the responsibility for new inventions.

The structure and location of R&D varies from company to company. In small companies it is not uncommon for a single R&D group to be responsible for all of the R&D activities. In large companies, each division may have its own R&D function. In some large companies there may also be a central R&D group in addition to the divisional R&D groups. It is not uncommon for a centralized R&D group to work on both existing products and new products and later turn the R&D outputs over to the divisional levels at an appropriate time in the development cycle. All companies, regardless of size, also from time to time make use of outside research sources such as specialty houses and universities.

Internal versus External. Most companies do R&D internally or within the company. There are times, however, when special expertise is needed or the company is not large enough to perform all of the R&D it might wish to in specific areas. In these situations the company quite often resorts to the use of outside assistance.

There are advantages and disadvantages to both types of R&D. R&D done internally can be tightly monitored and controlled; new products or changes to old products can be worked on without competitors knowing what is going on. Also, funds can be swiftly moved from one program to another if and when needed. On the negative side of internal R&D is the possible lack of technical skills and knowledge and the availability of funds to perform the in-depth R&D needed to develop a new product adequately.

Both large and small companies resort to the use of outside R&D facilities. Universities are a major source of very specialized R&D, particularly in the areas of technology and medicine. Universities are also used for lower levels of research; it is not uncommon for a company to fund the dissertation research of talented masters and Ph.D. level students who are working in specialized areas. This form of research is often quite inexpensive and occasionally results in innovative development. The Tappan Company not only used this type of R&D but also used the services of engineers from Ford during periods of Ford's slack times. This gave Tappan the services of highly trained engineers at low costs and covered the base cost of these engineers so that Ford could afford to retain the engineers on the payroll and not have to go through a fire-hire-retrain cycle each time work became slack and then picked up again. The disadvantage to Tappan was that these engineers were on immediate recall by Ford when needed; this could leave a new Tappan research program in limbo for an extended period of time. Tappan also used research funds from the American Gas Association to help in new product research. This gave Tappan badly needed funds from outside the company. However, since the money came from an association to which most appliance manufacturers belonged, any ideas or products that Tappan developed with these funds also had to be made available to all other members of the association.

The decision whether to perform R&D internally or externally is not always an easy decision to make. It should be known, however, that such options do exist and, if properly evaluated, can maximize usage of R&D monies and hopefully lead to new and improved products.

R&D Expenditures and Ratios. There is no simple way to determine the amount of money that should be spent on R&D. There are, however, a number of established standards that may be helpful in this area:

—Establish R&D expenditures as some percentage of sales.

—Set R&D expenditures at levels equal to competitors.

—Use the industry average.

—Determine the cost of R&D projects needed to meet certain objectives, and use this as a guide to establish levels.

—Take a historical average of past expenditures, and increase R&D by a percentage equal to projected or desired internal growth.

Using the R&D expenditures as a percentage of sales, drug companies and computer software and services companies have spent the most money on R&D, with many of them spending 20 to 25 percent of sales on R&D; at the other extreme, almost all oil, gas, and coal companies have spent less than 1 percent of sales on R&D.[4]

Total projected R&D expenditures of U.S. industry, government, university, and other nonprofit research centers for 1989 was $141.75 billion. For 1990 the projected R&D expenditure was $149.7 billion, with the federal government spending $69.2 billion, industry spending $73.95 billion, and universities and nonprofit centers spending $6.55 billion.[5] Industrial R&D spending trends continue to show both European and Japanese companies increasing R&D expenditures at a greater rate than U.S. companies; both Japanese and European companies were projected to increase 1990 expenditures over 1989 expenditures by more than 12 percent, while the U.S. expenditure increase was projected at less than 8 percent.[6]

After a company determines how much it plans to spend on R&D, it must then determine the portion of this money to be used for the various levels of R&D: central versus divisional R&D, and internal R&D versus R&D purchased from outside sources.

Working Relationships with Other Departments and Other Companies and Agencies. Top management must be certain that there is proper and adequate interface and working relations between R&D, marketing, engineering, sales, manufacturing, finance, and other key departments of the company. It is essential to know that manufacturing has sufficient capacity to make the product, can make it in a timely manner, and can produce a cost-effective product. If new facilities or equipment are needed, both time and cost need to be factored into the end price.

The sales force must be examined to see if it is adequate; if new training is required; what effect, if any, the new product might have on the morale of the salesforce; and if a restructure or reduction of the salesforce is required.

Engineering must determine if and how the product can be designed to be safe, reliable, efficient, producible, and reproducible at a price that will be competitive with other similar products on the market.

Marketing quite often provides the greatest input in identifying the critical areas of consideration. They must identify such factors as market attractiveness of each product and product line, relative market share expected, product competition, business strategy, expected sales growth, forecasted product growth and lifecycle, and recommended investment strategy.

The finance department must examine the recommended investment strategy with respect to overall company financial strategy and other departmental financial strategies. All departments involved must be included in the decision-making process from its inception if a smooth, efficient, cost-effective program and product or service is to result. Only top management involvement in all areas can insure that this will happen.

Positive internal departmental interface may not by itself be sufficient for a company to stay competitive against encrouchment by large foreign competitors. Many foreign countries permit companies within their country to pool R&D and other resources. Companies in the United States may have to do the same thing. In 1983 President Reagan formed the

President's Commission on Industrial Competitiveness under the chairmanship of John A. Young of Hewlett-Packard. The commission's work became the basis for the 1984 law permitting joint R&D by competing companies.[7] Some companies have taken advantage of this opportunity to pool R&D activities, but not many.

Project Classification

The previous section discussed the four major areas or types of R&D. We now turn to the different aspects of emphasis placed on the R&D project.

Offensive versus Defensive R&D. A question all companies must answer is whether or not they will practice offensive or defensive R&D or both. In offensive R&D, the prime interest is to penetrate a new market as quickly and effectively as possible, replace an existing product, or satisfy some customer need. The emphasis is "first-to-market" with a product approach. Defensive R&D is quite often used to lengthen a product's lifecycle or to protect existing products from competitors. In most instances it concentrates on minor changes in style or improvements in operation or safety of existing products in order to protect the product line and profits.

Leader versus Follower. In determining how much money and effort to put into R&D, one of the questions that the company must ask is whether they want to be a product leader or a follower. A product leader approach is similar to the offensive approach in that the company prides itself on being "first to market" with a product. To fill this role a company must spend large amounts of money on R&D and then hope to reap large profits in the early stages of selling in order to recover its earlier large expenses.

Being a follower entails being second or later into the market with a product. Some companies choose to be followers while many have no choice since they do not have the funds to compete with giants like Procter & Gamble or General Electric. In theory, being a follower permits a company to profit by the leader's errors, requires smaller expenditures of R&D funds, and permits improvements on the product. On the negative side, if patents have been obtained by the leader, then it may delay or inhibit a follower from entering into the market. Also, extra funds may have to be expended on the marketing and sales operations in order to penetrate the market leader's territory. Being a follower does not necessarily mean success. Bic Pen was first on the market with a low-cost, quality ball-point pen and still holds first place in this product area. Bic, however, has always been a follower in its other product areas such as cigarette lighters and razors; however, through effective mass marketing and distribution they have also become number one in sales in these areas as well.

Government versus Commercial. Some companies attempt to achieve a fifty-fifty balance between government and commercial R&D and business while other companies try to avoid government business altogether because of the political and extensive red-tape nature of the business. Both types of business have their advantages and disadvantages. Government R&D is quite often paid for by the government on a progress payment (or pay-as-you-go) basis; however, in order to obtain a contract, variable amounts of company money must be expended in preparing and submitting a competitive proposal. Some companies submit proposal costs to perform the R&D at no profit or even at a loss to the company on the basis that the R&D contract will, if successful, result in a substantial lucrative production contract and supply technology spinoffs that can be used in commercial applications. Sometimes special expensive facilities and equipment, which the government may or may not pay for, are required to fulfill government R&D contracts. On the other hand, commercial (or industrial) R&D may also require special facilities and equipment that will have to be paid for by the company performing the R&D. In most government contracts, the government owns all ideas and patents generated on the program and can and often does make the data available to competitors. If an industrial company does its own R&D, it owns the ideas and patents.

These are only a few of the many advantages and disadvantages of government versus commercial R&D. It is an area that must be evaluated carefully when establishing total company strategy.

Research versus Development. Although the term *research and development* is almost always used as a single entity, there are some differences in the complexity and depth of performance of the two parts in such areas as structure, resources, specifications, scheduling, and engineering changes.

—Structure. Research is often conducted in a loose or campus-like work environment. Development of the product often requires more supervision and structured organization.

—Resources. Generally, not always, development work requires more extensive resources than research does.

—Specifications. Research quite often operates with minimum or weak specifications, thus permitting the researchers a fair amount of latitude in their creativity. Development specifications are more rigid in scope because the people involved are supposed to reduce available alternatives to one simple prospect for future implementation.

—Scheduling. Most researchers prefer a loose schedule; it is difficult to regiment creativity of productive thoughts and ideas. Development is usually on a tighter schedule and is sequential in nature with a prescribed time allocated to each sequence.

—Engineering changes. During the research stage, since nothing is firm, any changes in engineering drawings or specifications may have only minimal cost impact. During development, when firm drawings and specifications are being generated, any changes can become costly.

Project Selection and Protection

Any company that has an R&D department produces several ideas, thoughts, and prospective products or services. This by itself is not sufficient to make the company successful. It must now determine and select the most promising products or services, produce them, market them, and protect them from competition.

Innovation and Creativity. Innovation and creativity are two components of R&D that are essential to its success. It is basically the ability to develop and implement new and better solutions within existing environmental constraints. Some of these constraints involve changes in customer needs, available technology, government policy, social responsibility, competitive behavior, and available funds.

Booz, Allen & Hamilton, Inc., in a study of several hundred companies, describe the new product evolution, through its stages of creativity and innovation, as going through six steps from the idea stage to the commercialization stage: exploration, screening, business analysis, development, testing, and commercialization.[8] On the average, one successful new product resulted from sixty initial ideas. This same study also shows the cumulative expenditure of funds versus time through these various steps; development and commercialization consume the most cumulative time and costs in successfully bringing a product to market.[9]

Sources of Ideas. Many successful companies with a reputation for introducing a continuing line of new products into the marketplace have R&D teams that generate and develop their ideas in a relatively unstructured atmosphere. This, however, is not the only source of possible ideas. Some other sources that produce ideas for companies include customers, suppliers, competitors, private inventors, trade fairs, technology fairs, technical journals, trade journals, government agencies, and government-funded programs. Companies may also license, purchase, or share technologies.

Honors, Patents, and Copyrights. Paying good salaries, honoring top R&D ideas, and awarding patents and copyrights are only a few ways to help develop and protect new ideas and products. Happy, well-rewarded people tend to stay with the same company and continue to produce new ideas. Good salaries and honors bestowed upon good R&D personnel help protect company ideas by keeping the employee loyal to and employed at his or her present company. Patents and copyrights legally protect the company products and services for a specified period of time but at the same time may place additional costs upon the company to prepare and process the necessary paperwork and also provide information to competitors.

Nondisclosure and Other Security Agreements. Almost every company today must employ the services of some outside source during the development and marketing stages of a new product. It is essential to protect the proprietary nature of the new product or service during this time period; this protection can be accomplished through the signing of a properly executed and signed agreement between the parties involved.

Top management must develop a policy on how to handle the transfer of sensitive and proprietory information between cooperating parties. This is often accomplished through nondisclosure, secrecy, or confidential agreements.

Market Type and Share. These two terms are directly related to one another in that each company must first determine in which markets it wants to participate and then what share of this market it wishes to capture. These are not always easy decisions to make. General Electric choses to participate in a number of different markets, and if it does not become number one or number two in a particular market, it withdraws. Not all companies can have or achieve such lofty goals.

Product Lifecycle. The expected lifecycle of a product or service has a direct impact upon how much R&D money its company is willing to risk on it. Short lifecycle products are high-risk endeavors and may return inadequate money to make their development and release worthwhile. Long lifecycle products tend to produce adequate funds to cover the cost of R&D for the initial product and sufficient money for the development of additional products.

Some companies make a compromise, choosing a low-risk approach of development by extending the lifecycle of existing products and services through modifications or by releasing different forms of the existing product or service.

Project Control and Support

No matter how unique, innovative, and practical an R&D project might be, if it does not have adequate control and support it is likely to fail. The concept and techniques for controlling and supporting R&D programs must be initiated and included as part of the corporate strategic plan and adhered to throughout the entire project timecycle. Project prioritizing, scheduling, budgeting, and monitoring of the project from its initiation through its termination are but a few of the useful techniques for helping out in this area.

Project Prioritizing. Prioritizing R&D projects is not a simple task. Quite often the R&D project manager has one set of priorities in mind for each project, whereas the other departments or divisions may have a different set of priorities for their areas of responsibility. Short-range and long-range priorities may become entangled between departments and divisions. Where common facilities, equipment, or labor may be required, if they are not properly allocated and budgeted, costly conflicts and delays can be encountered; functional managers may try to supply needed resources from two or more conflicting priority lists.

Poor communication and the "free-spirit" type of operation utilized by some organizations during the early phase of R&D programs do not enhance the prioritizing situation. Also, priorities set at the divisional level might not be adequately passed on to the department level, or vice versa.

In spite of inherent problems in prioritizing R&D programs, it must be done. If all divisions are involved in both the corporation's strategic and tactical planning from the inception of the R&D projects, and if all departments are involved in its divisional strategic and tactical planning cycle, their most potential prioritizing problems should be eliminated or at least minimized.

Scheduling. All R&D projects must be scheduled into the corporation's strategic plan. Each year all new and continuing projects must be scheduled. Only by scheduling all previously evaluated and prioritized R&D programs into a master schedule of all proposed projects will the necessary information be made available to permit a review by top management for purposes of a final commitment of funding. Master scheduling, along with funding requirements, now becomes an iterative process with top management as they make a final determination of which programs will survive and which will be terminated.

The master schedule should focus on two main types of R&D programs. The first type of program involves projects with relatively certain timing and cost; most of these programs are in areas where similar types of work have been previously undertaken. The second type of program involves projects with some uncertainty with respect to timing and cost; most of these programs are in new or untried areas of R&D. Determining the schedule and cost for the first type of programs can be enhanced through the use of critical path method (CPM) techniques. Scheduling and costing for the second type of programs can be accomplished with problem evaluation and review techniques (PERT); this will determine the probability level of success for each project in both the time and cost areas.

Budgeting. R&D budgeting is no easier a task than scheduling and is integrated with scheduling. Developing an effective budget from an ineffective budget can present a challenge. To help resolve this problem, methods for budgeting programs range from the chief executive's personal ideas to fairly formal procedures. Formal procedures include requirements for facilities and services, personnel, capital equipment, and documentation. Also needed in the formal budgeting process are answers to such questions as: From where will the funds come? To whom should the costs be allocated? Who are the funding decision makers? When, how, and by whom will the project be carried out (solved by using time, cost, and activity CPM or PERT charts)?

Top management must make the final decision on the budget because only by full support and commitment from this level will the necessary funding be allocated in a consistent manner.

Project Start, Readjustment, and Completion or Termination. To be cost and time effective all projects must be periodically reviewed to make certain they are on schedule and within budget. Shortly after the start of the program, some readjustment may be needed in the schedule or budget of the program. Prior to permitting any readjustment in the program, an evaluation must determine the complete impact of this readjustment on the program itself, other programs in progress, and the corporation. Usually there is some flexibility in both the budgets and schedules of most programs to permit some readjustments.

Each program must be given a designated startup date and completion date as well as a dollar amount allocation. Some companies will not start producing a profit by the end of the second year. Others, particularly those involved in government R&D, may be looking at payoff times five to twenty years in the future. Some companies indulge in both types of programs.

No matter what time schedule and funding is allocated to the program, it must be monitored closely to see that it does not deviate outside of prescribed boundaries. If either scheduling or funding exceeds permitted variances and cannot get within prescribed boundaries or cannot be readjusted, the program should be terminated. Also, if prescribed technology is not forthcoming from the R&D project and there is no prospect of this occurring, then the project should be immediately terminated and the funds given to a more promising candidate.

External Environment and Influences

The external environment in which R&D programs must participate are not necessarily friendly and at times can be very unfriendly. Some of the areas of consideration of which any company must be aware include, but are not limited to:

—Current business and political factors. These include: competition from other businesses; local, state, national, and international laws and regulations; ethical and moral constraints; pressure from stockholders; pressure from unions and specialty groups; and other factors of inflation, trade policies, and economic conditions.
—Market stability and need for change. In a stable market or a time of low economic activity, a major new innovation may be required to move a large

number of people to purchase a new product; thus time, cost, and the extent of product improvement can have a large impact on whether or not the R&D effort will be successful. If the buying public can live with a less sophisticated, lower cost product in slow economic times, then new approaches may be required to move the new product.

—Already existing similar or identical items. Prior to initiating any serious research project, all technical and patent literature should be reviewed in order to avoid wasting time and money on reinventing something and then being subject to a patent infringement suit upon its completion and release of the product or service to the public.

—Position in the market. Being first in the market has the advantages of establishing the product name and concept and demanding a higher price. If this can be accomplished then attempts should be made to maintain this position of leadership. If market entry is at a lower position, then, as Bic has consistently done, attempts should be made to move up in position.

COMPANY EVALUATION

Now that a brief discussion has been concluded on the functional area of R&D, it is desirable to examine how well a company under consideration is doing in this area. Table 3.1 permits a preliminary evaluation in this area.

NOTES

1. "R&D in 1988," *Business Week,* no. 3110 (June 16, 1989): 178–232.
2. "Big Companies Are Big R&D Spenders," *Research and Development* 31, no. 8 (August 1989): 17.
3. Sarah Smith, "America's Most Admired Corporations," *Fortune* 121, no. 3 (January 29, 1990): 58.
4. "R&D in 1988," p. 196.
5. Tim Studt, "There's No Joy in This Year's $150 Billion for R&D," *Research and Development* 32, no. 1 (January 1990): 41.
6. Ibid., p. 42.
7. Robert Cassidy, "John Young of Hewlett-Packard Named Executive of the Year," *Research and Development* 31, no. 7 (July 1989): 61–66.
8. Booz, Allen & Hamilton, Inc., *Management of New Products* (Booz, Allen & Hamilton, Inc., 1984), p. 180.
9. Ibid., p. 181.

Table 3.1
Typical Strengths and Weaknesses in Planning, Organizing, Directing, and Controlling Research and Development

	Strengths	Weaknesses
PLANNING	Top management is committed to a strong R&D effort.	No strong commitment exists within the company for a programmed R&D effort.
	R&D effort follows a year-to-year logical chronological effort.	R&D is accomplished in a haphazard manner on a "pet project" concept.
	Detailed plans and budgets are generated and reviewed for acceptance or rejection on all proposed and in-process R&D projects.	The company is content to be a follower.
	The company is committed to creativity, innovation, and leadership in its field.	No provisions are made for balanced approach of money, people, and machines.
	A balanced approach of money, personnel, and machines is taken.	
ORGANIZING	R&D reports directly to the president.	R&D reports to a department manager.
	R&D is organized along existing product lines.	Each department conducts its own R&D as it thinks best.
	The company does all of its own R&D in central location or at divisional level.	No balanced approach taken to allocation of money, people, and equipment.
	A balanced approach of money, people, and equipment taken to R&D.	
DIRECTING	A VP reporting directly to the president heads up R&D.	Department managers direct R&D.
	A MIS system is used to track and coordinate projects.	Inadequate interface exists between R&D projects within R&D.
	Excellent interface exists between R&D and all other company functional areas.	Inadequate interface exists between R&D and other company functional areas.

38

Excellent interface exists between corporate R&D and divisional R&D.

CONTROLLING	
The Company does all of its own R&D.	The company uses outside agencies for R&D.
Basic R&D is conducted within each division.	Department managers control R&D.
A VP reporting directly to the president heads up R&D.	R&D funding is established as a fixed percentage of sales.
R&D funding is flexible to continue necessary R&D in lean sales years.	A large portion of R&D contingent on outside funding.
Budgets and schedules exist for each project.	R&D projects are not coordinated.
MIS systems are used to track and coordinate projects.	Inadequate or no budgets or schedules exist to control projects.

4

Engineering

The flow of information relevant to new products, processes, and services emanates from customers, marketing, R&D, manufacturing, engineering, and other sources. The information collected from these sources supplies the basic ideas and fuel for initial R&D and product and service innovation and modification. Engineering takes over from R&D at the product development and application level and in rare instances as early as the applied research level.

Although considered and operated as a separate functional area in most companies, engineering cannot and does not operate separately from the other functional areas. It must work closely with marketing to develop products and services that are competitive in design and price; in many instances engineering even goes into the field with marketing to research or sell new product ideas. It must work closely with manufacturing to ensure high-quality production and packaging of the product in a manner that will meet or beat competitors' products and services. Engineering must be aware of what R&D is developing, and it must also make R&D aware of innovations that, if developed, will make an existing product even more competitive. Cooperation and close working relationships with all other functional areas is also necessary but perhaps not quite as critical as the close relationships that must exist among engineering, R&D, marketing, and manufacturing.

UNIQUE PROBLEMS AND CONFLICTING DEMANDS

As in R&D, the range of managerial planning and strategy problems in engineering are extensive and sometimes complex. Much of what is discussed in Chapter 3 on R&D is also directly applicable to engineering, and some of what is discussed in this chapter on engineering is also applicable to R&D. This interrelationship can and does exist in a number of companies because of the way that technical R&D and engineering are defined and because in some companies there is much overlap between the two groups. In some instances, the same personnel may at times work in either R&D or engineering; some technical people like to and are permitted to start a project in R&D, follow it through engineering development and testing and then work with manufacturing to move the project through production.

This chapter will not repeat discussions of those areas similar to R&D but will examine a number of new areas of concern that are more engineering department oriented. The areas to be discussed include:

- the basic job of engineering
- the personnel necessary to perform engineering programs
- engineering task selection
- engineering task responsibility
- engineering task justification
- engineering support facilities
- engineering motivation
- engineering quality strategy

The Basic Job of Engineering

Engineering is concerned with the design, development, fabrication, testing, improvement, and installation of integrated systems of personnel, materials, and capital equipment. It involves all levels of management and employees and works toward reducing the cost of manufacturing, distributing, and selling a product or service.

With a new product, the steps in the engineering product cycle that travel the route from inception to completion usually start with the product's basic design and proceed through product development, breadboard or brassboard development, prototype fabrication, laboratory testing, environmental tests, transfer to manufacturing, field tests, and service support.

The initial idea for the basic design of a product quite often comes out of R&D; however, this is not always the case. The ideas and concepts can also come from marketing, customers, manufacturing, engineering itself, or any other source.

Regardless of where the idea or concept originates, it is the engineering department's job to develop it into a workable, saleable product, process, or service. Design and development are closely related and go hand in hand as the product evolves. The product is first designed on paper with drawings, computations, and specifications, which are then submitted to suppliers or to small model shops for fabrication of the development model components.

As the various components become available, they are assembled into subassemblies and what is commonly referred to as a breadboard or brass-board model. If the end product is a complex product composed of several subassemblies, these subassemblies are first assembled and tested in the laboratory to determine the adequacy of the design. This process may be repeated several times before an acceptable workable unit is available. The subassemblies are then married together into more complex systems and tested and modified until all subassemblies work together as an acceptable workable system.

After satisfactory completion of fabrication and laboratory testing of the brassboard model, updated and new drawings and specifications are generated for the purchase of parts and components for fabrication of an engineering or prototype model of the product. This is the predecessor model to the model that will eventually go into production. This model is fabricated and tested in engineering with the intention of producing a quality product at a competitive price. As the prototype model is fabricated and tested, drawings, specifications, and processes are updated to reflect the latest configuration. Marketing and manufacturing are kept abreast of progress and consulted in areas where product improvement from a technological, cost, and saleability standpoint can be incorporated.

Once the prototype model has been fabricated, it must undergo a series of tests to ensure that it is indeed a viable system. Extensive laboratory tests must be conducted to test for product quality and reliability. These tests are conducted under normal laboratory conditions and under simulated field operational conditions; these later tests are sometimes referred to as environmental tests. Environmental tests can range from simply testing a normal household product under conditions of complex temperature extremes, humidity, vibration, electronic interference, and so on to tests for systems that operate under variable or extreme environments.

Once the engineering prototype model has been fabricated and satisfactorily tested, the basic design is ready to be transferred to manufacturing. Unfortunately it is not always a simple transfer process. Engineering drawings and specifications may have to again be modified or changed for mass production. For example, if only a small quantity of units is to be made, it may be less expensive to machine-cut a base plate out of a solid piece of metal in the machine shop; on the other hand, in mass production, it is probably much less expensive to make this same base plate from a casting. All drawings and specifications must be modified to reflect this change and any other changes that take place when a product goes into mass production. Engineering will continue to work with manufacturing during the production preparation period and after production is in full operation.

Engineering's work on a product is not complete when the product is in full production. Many production problems can be eliminated by engineering product modification or improvement. Special groups of engineers must also work in the field with marketing to service and accurately assess product problems in the field. Field problems and customer feedback on desired changes or improvements often result in a better, more saleable product.

The Personnel Necessary to Perform Engineering Programs

The engineering department is made up of a large variety of engineering disciplines. Depending on the size of the engineering department, it may only include one or two types of engineers (electrical and mechanical, for instance) in a small operation, or it may employ several types of engineers, scientists, and specialists (electrical, mechanical, optical, chemical, aeronautical, etc.) in larger concerns. As in the medical profession, each of these major classifications of engineers may be broken down even further to specializations within the discipline. Some of these people may work only in R&D or in any separate area of engineering; in smaller companies some of these people may work in multiple areas at different times. In certain instances, an engineering specialist needed on an engineering program is not available within the company; it is not uncommon in these cases to hire an outside specialist from a consulting firm.

An engineering department cannot and does not function with only engineers and scientists. It also employs technicians, laboratory helpers, drafting personnel, and administrative personnel. The technicians, laboratory helpers, and drafting personnel help the engineer throughout the entire design, development, fabrication, and test process; they do much of the fabrication and testing of the product throughout its entire lifecycle. The administrative personnel connected with large engineering groups may include representatives from marketing, finance, contracts, and manufacturing. These people monitor the progress of engineering programs and supply necessary assistance; they also act as an interface between engineering and their respective functional departments.

Engineering Task Selection

Without going into too much detail, engineering is charged with performing a number of tasks. These tasks include, but are not limited to: designing, developing, and testing new products for new and existing business; helping produce new business; reducing cost to manufacture a product; reducing cost to the user; increasing reliability and maintainability; improving sales appeal; training and development of new engineers; standardization of materials, procedures, and processes; minimizing high cost labor content; and appraising the product for possible other uses and applications.

As part of this task selection, care must be exercised to ensure that someone's "pet project" does not repeatedly get funded if it does not have recognizable future potential. This can be controlled, as should all other programs, by placing time and financial limits for productive results on all programs. These time and cost criteria should be examined and evaluated at prescribed time intervals. Only those programs continuing to show promise should be continued.

Engineering Task Responsibility

The responsibility for deciding who will perform what tasks and on which products engineering will work varies from company to company. In some large companies, the corporate headquarters, division headquarters, or a committee makes such decisions. In small and medium sized companies it may be the company president, the R&D department, the engineering director, the marketing department, or even individual people within the engineering department. Regardless of who makes the decision on what programs to pursue, these programs must be carefully monitored and controlled if maximum utilization of people, funds, facilities, and equipment is to be achieved.

Engineering Task Justification

No program or task should be undertaken without adequate examination, review, and justification. This justification process should, as a minimum, include: a literature survey; a patent and copyright survey; a legal investigation; a company competence survey; a sales potential survey; compatibility with manufacturing capacity; an ability to economically and competitively manufacture, distribute, and sell the product; and an executive review and evaluation.

A literature survey, a patent and copyright survey, and a legal survey are usually conducted by and it conjunction with engineering prior to becoming deeply involved in a new product. The literature survey is conducted to see what other researchers, engineers, and companies have done in the same or similar areas in order to profit by their findings and minimize potential problem areas. The patent, copyright, and legal surveys must be conducted to make certain there will be no copyright or patent infringements or legal problems when the product is marketed.

The company competitive survey must be conducted to determine whether or not the company either has or can obtain the necessary people, equipment, facilities, and money to economically and profitably develop, manufacture, and market the end product.

The sales potential survey must be undertaken in order to determine whether or not the demand exists or can be created to sell the product at a price that makes it worthwhile to produce the product.

As an extension of the competence survey, the product under development must be examined to ascertain that it is compatible with manufacturing capabilities and capacities; if not, a determination must be made of what is required both physically and costwise to bring the plant up to the required operating level. An expansion of this survey can determine the ability of the company to economically and competitively manufacture, distribute, and sell the product.

Based on the information obtained from these studies, an executive review committee will be in a better position to determine whether or not to proceed with the engineering phase of the program.

Engineering Support Facilities

Engineering cannot perform its function without help from numerous other technical support groups. A few of the support groups on whom engineering must depend include analytical testing laboratories, model shops, photographic facilities, glass blowing facilities, optical testing laboratories, chemical testing laboratories, storage, test equipment calibration and accuracy verification operations, environmental testing facilities, MIS, and many other specialized facilities.

Most individual programs, except in some very large companies, do not need and cannot afford the full-time use of these specialized facilities. By having them as specialized support groups the cost of their operation can be allocated over several engineering programs on an "as needed" or "as used" basis. This requires integrated planning between the various engineering programs and the different specialized support groups.

Engineering Motivation

The products that come out of engineering are only as good as the engineers that design and develop them. They must be competent engineers who are challenged and motivated. In engineering departments, this motivation is achieved by having challenging projects, paying adequate compensation, having excellent facilities and equipment, having freedom to participate in discussions and decision making, excellent leadership, and a prestigious engineering department recognized both within and outside the company for their innovative quality products.

Engineering Quality Strategy

Product quality must be a fundamental part of company strategy. Concern for quality is not a new concept; however, more and more companies are refocusing their competitive approach in this area from attempting to inspect and test the quality of the equipment after it is built to designing and building quality into the equipment.

The system of quality assurance used by many firms in the United States today takes place in manufacturing, and the way it is conducted translates into poor quality. The predominant form of both incoming supplier control and intermediate and outgoing manufacturing control is by inspection. Incoming inspection is performed on raw materials and components from suppliers; outgoing inspection is performed on finished goods. This technique is not the best approach to prevent defects. It is, rather, an after-the-fact discovery of defects. Quality cannot be inspected into a product. Quality must be designed and built into the product through a process control system that prevents the defects from occurring in the first place. Sampling incoming material or the outgoing product is not necessary if both processes are stabilized and under control.[1]

New studies have shown that product quality has a direct effect on both market share and profit margins. A study of 2,000 business units, conducted by the Strategic Planning Institute of Cambridge, Massachusetts, showed that improving product quality was a good way to increase market share. The study further pointed out that companies with high quality and high market share typically had profit margins five times greater than companies at the opposite extreme.[2] This is a concept that Professor W. Edwards Deming, famous for his work in statistical quality control (SQC), has been preaching for years and the Japanese have accepted wholeheartedly.

In spite of the findings that quality pays off, there are still those who are not convinced that quality deserves serious consideration in corporate strategy. Many American managers still believe that high quality costs too much and reduces productivity. Using a two-cent resistor as an example, Hewlett-Packard shows the fault with not building quality products.

If you catch the resistor before it is used and throw it away, you lose 2¢. If you don't catch it until it has been soldered into a computer component, it may cost

Table 4.1
Typical Strengths and Weaknesses in Planning, Organizing, Directing, and Controlling Engineering

	Strengths	Weaknesses
PLANNING	Top management is committed to a strong engineering effort.	No strong commitment exists within the company for a programmed engineering effort.
	Detailed plans and budgets are generated and reviewed for acceptance or rejection on all proposed and in-process engineering projects.	Engineering is accomplished in a haphazard way or on a "pet project" concept.
	The company is committed to creativity, innovation, and leadership in its field.	The company is content to be a follower.
	All engineering plans are coordinated and consistent with company strategy and objectives.	Engineering planning is done on a short-term, day-to-day basis as needed or not at all.
	There is close coordination with R&D, marketing, and manufacturing.	There is no coordination with R&D, marketing, or manufacturing.
	A balanced approach of money, personnel, and machines is taken.	No provisions are made for a balanced approach of money, personnel, and machines.
ORGANIZING	Engineering reports directly to the president through a vice-president.	Engineering reports to a department manager.
	Engineering is organized along existing product lines.	Each department conducts its own engineering programs as it thinks best.
	Engineering is organized in such a manner as to be able to rapidly adjust to needed changes.	Engineering is organized in a manner which does not permit rapid response to needed changes.
	Adequate prestige, innovation, and motivation exists within engineering to attract and hold high-caliber personnel.	No provisions exist within engineering to attract or hold high-caliber personnel.
DIRECTING	Vice-president reporting directly to the president heads up engineering.	Department managers direct engineering.
	MIS systems are used to track, coordinate, and direct projects within engineering.	No coordination of projects within engineering exists.
		Inadequate interface exists between engineering and

Excellent interface exists between engineering and all other company functional areas.	other company functional areas.

CONTROLLING	
Company performs and directs all of its own engineering.	Company uses numerous loosely coordinated outside agencies for engineering.
Vice-president reporting directly to the president heads up engineering.	Department managers control engineering.
Engineering is conducted in a controlled manner within each division.	Engineering is conducted at several locations that are independent of one another.
Adequate funding is available to permit flexibility in engineering programs when needed.	Engineering funding is set as a fixed percentage of sales.
Budgets and schedules exist for each project.	Inadequate or no budgets exist to control projects.
MIS systems are used to track and coordinate all projects within engineering and with other departments.	Engineering projects are not coordinated.

$10 to repair the part. If you don't catch the component until it is in a computer user's hands, the repair cost will amount to hundreds of dollars and may exceed the manufacturing costs.[3]

Those companies who are getting on the quality and good service bandwagon are showing above-average sales and return on equity.[4]

COMPANY EVALUATION

Evaluating the strengths and weaknesses of engineering in the four critical areas of planning, organizing, directing, and controlling complements the evaluation performed on R&D. It will show how well engineering is performing as a separate entity as well as how well it is integrated with R&D and also marketing and manufacturing. Table 4.1 facilitates such an evaluation.

NOTES

1. "Making Service a Potent Marketing Tool," *Business Week,* no. 2846 (June 11, 1984): 194.
2. "Quality: The U.S. Drives to Catch Up," *Business Week,* no. 2763 (November 1, 1982): 66–67.
3. Jeremy Main, "The Battle for Quality Begins," *Fortune* 102, no. 13 (December 29, 1980): 28–43.
4. "King Customer," *Business Week,* no. 3149 (March 12, 1990): 88–94.

5

Manufacturing

Manufacturing (sometimes referred to as production) involves the conversion of raw materials into components, subassemblies, assemblies, or complete products through a series of steps defined by drawings, procedures, and processes. It includes such major functions as planning and scheduling, engineering, determination of resource requirements and sometimes procurement of these resources, fabrication and assembly, quality assurance, product testing and demonstration, and installation and checkout.

In more aggressive and forward-looking companies, manufacturing becomes involved in product strategy and decisions early in the planning stages. It works closely with marketing, R&D, and engineering to make certain that a high-quality, competitively priced, attractive, and usable product is manufactured. Gone are the days when marketing would come up with an idea or need for a product, talk it over with R&D and engineering, have engineering develop it, turn it over to manufacturing to produce, and then sell it. By involving manufacturing in early discussions, it may be possible to produce the same product quicker and less expensively. Manufacturing must also be deeply involved in the quality-determining process. Engineering must *design* quality into the product; however, it is manufacturing that must *build* the quality into the product. It is therefore imperative that manufacturing interface well with all closely related functional departments.

UNIQUE PROBLEMS AND CONFLICTING DEMANDS

In many areas, the once all-powerful American corporation no longer holds the predominant position either at home or in the world market. Foreign corporations in western Europe (and soon possibly in eastern Europe also) and the Pacific Rim area have continually increased their market share in both the multinational market and the United States. A few possible causes for this shift include:

1. a deterioration of the American work ethic, coupled with the adversarial role of labor and management, has resulted in debilitating strikes, higher wages, inflexible work rules, and costly fringe benefits not compensated for or justified by increased productivity.

2. increased government interference through increased taxes, rules, regulations, and other controls, which have considerably increased the cost of goods produced.

3. a massive influx of new people into the workforce. These people have a higher level of education than workers in the past and are more questioning of and resistant to past and existing values, often feeling that the traditional values of the past are not adequate for today's rapidly changing dynamic society and workplace.

4. that the perceived and/or actual rights of the stakeholders and business are more often in conflict today than in the past. Thus, there is pressure from stakeholders and others to emphasize short-run return on investment (ROI), which may not be the best way to improve overall long-term ROI and survival for the company. However, failure to produce positive continuous short-run ROI could result in a stakeholder revolt, a drop in stock prices, replacement of some top management, or a takeover from the outside.

5. high and ever-increasing capital costs driving up prices due to high interest rates and moderate to high inflation rates.

6. some companies, such as those in the steel industry, hampered by old plants and environmental restrictions.

7. the increased number of choices available to people to relocate, change careers, and choose where and for whom to work, thereby driving labor costs up for qualified workers.

8. lower labor costs and high productivity rates in countries in competition with the United States, making it difficult for this country to stay competitive in the world market.

9. refusal by most companies to design and build quality into their equipment and services in order to meet and beat competition.

10. supply interruptions, increasing prices, and poor supply networks resulting in inefficiencies and higher costs.

11. the unwillingness of many companies' top management to wholeheartedly commit themselves or their company's resources to available new and im-

proved manufacturing concepts and methods. This attitude is still held by top executives and their companies because:

a. many top managers still live in the past and are either unaware of or do not understand many of the new techniques of high-technology factories;

b. high-technology factories are highly to completely automated;

c. many top managers do not have a totally objective overview of the present situation and do not care to know how the automated factory operates;

d. budget and finance techniques may be on the conservative and cautious side and may not permit risky or long-term automated capital expenditure programs;

e. there is so much information available that it makes the entire issue confusing, especially if management does not know upon whom it can rely or trust; and

f. top management may not understand the full need for or consequence of not investing in automated equipment if it is to remain competitive.

These problems are real and complex but are not reason to panic or give up. Manufacturing decisions are usually tradeoff types and are made and incorporated over a period of time. These are strategy decisions that must be made based on a large number of variables. Robert H. Hayes and Steven C. Wheelwright have classified the strategic variables into eight categories.[1] These categories are:

- Capacity: amount, timing, and type.
- Facilities: size, location, and specialization.
- Technology: equipment, automation, and linkages.
- Vertical integration: direction, extent, and balance.
- Workforce: skill level, wage policies, and employment security.
- Quality: defect prevention, monitoring, and intervention.
- Production planning/materials control: sourcing policies, centralization, and decision rules.
- Organization: structure, control/reward system, and role of staff groups.

To better understand some of these issues, a brief examination of the key issues is required.

FEDERAL LEGISLATION

Federal legislation has been passed in a number of areas requiring businesses and other organizations to meet with and fulfill certain costly social responsibilities. Although manufacturing is not the only part of the business enterprise responsible for meeting this legislation, it is deeply involved in complying with all aspects of it. Legislation has been enacted in the areas of human resources, environmental protection, consumer protection, minority business, labor unions, and many other areas. All of this legislation, although in many instances necessary, has been costly to industry.

Human Resources Legislation

Human resources legislation has been passed by the federal government primarily to protect workers from unfair and variable employment practices by businesses and various cities and states. Much of this legislation covers many of the areas where unions had been seeking protection for many years. This legislation includes such laws as the Civil Rights Act, Equal Pay Act, Voting Rights Act, Age Discrimination in Employment Act, Privacy Act, Equal Employment Act, and many more. A number of these laws and regulations have been amended, added to, or modified in some way in later years. One example is Title VII, Civil Rights Act of 1964. In 1980 the Equal Employment Opportunity Commission (EEOC), in its role of monitoring compliance with federal law, issued a variety of interpretive guidelines. In 1980, the EEOC published in the *Federal Register* guidelines directed toward sexual discrimination and harassment. This is listed as Section 1604.11 of the guidelines.[2]

Environmental Protection Legislation

As businesses have grown and expanded throughout the country, the amount of environmental pollution has increased in the areas of the atmosphere, water, noise, and chemical waste. The key piece of legislation in environmental protection was the National Environmental Policy Act of 1969. It committed the government to preserving the country's ecology and established a White House Council on Environmental Quality that advises the president on environmental issues. Two agencies are involved in setting standards on pollution. Where it involves the environment, the primary responsibility falls on the shoulders of the Environmental Protection Agency (EPA); where the health, safety, and welfare of workers are involved, the government looks to standards authorized by the Occupational Safety and Health Act. In overlapping areas, it is not uncommon for the two agencies to disagree on what levels of pollution are safe.

The Clean Air Act was passed in December 1963, and the Clean Water Restoration Act was passed in November 1966, but at the time of their inception, they were of limited effectiveness. This situation changed dramatically, however, in the late 1960s with the active ecology movement, the creation of the Council on Environment Quality (CEQ) and the EPA, and the passage of the National Environmental Policy Act of 1969. The purpose of the CEQ is to consider policy on new environmental legislation and programs. The EPA was given the responsibility of administering and enforcing a wide range of environmental protection programs. These programs include air and water pollution control; solid waste management; and the control of noise, pesticides, and radiation.

The EPA's activities focus on its power and ability to establish and enforce standards in all the above areas. With its regulatory authority over these forms of pollution, the agency has available several avenues of enforcement when it observes a violation of the established standards, including seeking voluntary compliance, court action, fines, and even prison sentences.

The power of the EPA to enforce standards and its pressure on business to abide by the standards have resulted in much controversy between the EPA, business, and environmentalists. Businesses say the EPA is moving too fast; environmentalists say that the EPA is not tough enough and moves too slowly; and the EPA tells business that compliance with its standards is essential and it tells environmentalists that changes cannot be made overnight. Each group has valid arguments to support its position.

Employee safety and health in the workplace are of paramount importance, which is why the Occupational Safety and Health Act of 1970 was passed. The purpose of the act is "to assure as far as possible every working man and woman in the nation has safe and healthful working conditions and to preserve our human resources." It covers every business, regardless of size, that affects interstate commerce. Under present-day rulings, almost every business affects interstate commerce. Only federal, state, and local government workers are exempt because the government cannot readily proceed against itself in the event of violations.

This same act established three government agencies to administer and enforce the act: (1) the Occupational Safety and Health Administration (OSHA), to establish and enforce the necessary safety and health standards; (2) the Occupational Safety and Health Review Commission (OSHRC), to rule on the appropriateness of OSHA's enforcement of the act whenever OSHA's actions are contested by employers, employees, or unions; and (3) the National Institute for Occupational Safety and Health (NIOSH), to conduct research on the causes and prevention of occupational health, safety, injury, and illness in order to recommend new standards to the secretary of labor and to develop associated educational programs.

Detailed standards covering most environmental hazards have been issued by OSHA. They cover such areas as material handling and storage; compressed gas; power tools; and toxic substances such as asbestos, cotton dust, lead, coal dust, and carbon monoxide. While most standards are helpful and important there are also a number of nuisance rules as well. Almost 1,000 of those were abolished as a result of complaints and in compliance with a directive from President Carter.[3]

OSHA inspectors administer health and safety standards primarily by priority level because of the limited number of agency inspectors. First priority inspection is assigned to workplaces where there is imminent danger to worker health and safety; second priority inspection is reserved to looking into employee complaints where safety and health standards have been violated. Special inspection attention is applied to hazardous types of business, such as production of meat and meat products, lumber and wood products, and roofing and sheet metal. Finally, random inspections of OSHA health and safety standards compliance are conducted on all sizes of workplaces that do not fall into one of the preceding categories.

Every employee can expect workplace safety and healthy working conditions. If these conditions do not exist, then OSHA is the agency that will look into the situation and rectify any deviation from acceptable standards. Fines are mandatory where serious violations are found. First-time willful offenses can be assessed a civil penalty of up to $10,000 for each violation; there is a $1,000-per-day penalty for each day it is not corrected beyond the OSHA-designated deadline date. If the first willful offense results in the death of a worker, a criminal penalty of $10,000 and six months in jail can be mandated. A second such conviction can mean a $20,000 fine and a one-year jail term. Employers can appeal citations, proposed penalties, and corrections they have been ordered to make. OSHA must prove the case when an employer appeals. If a state has a program at least as effective as the federal program, then the Occupational Safety and Health Act permits the state to develop and administer such a program.

The value and effectiveness of OSHA continues to be debated; however, in 1982, there were 530,000 fewer occupational injuries and illnesses than in 1980, and 4.7 million fewer people lost workdays in the United States. In 1983, serious injuries dropped another 8 percent, and deaths in the workplace dropped 6 percent.[4]

Consumer Protection Legislation

Consumer protection has always been a point of concern with the public. Some of the enacted laws protect both the consumer and business. According to Robert H. Malott, during the last thirty years the focus of product liability law has switched from emphasis on the conduct of the manufacturer and the marketer to the conditions of the product. This has resulted in a variety of interpretations of the law in different states. He feels that this is confusing to both the consumer and the manufacturer and should be corrected. He recommends four standards that, if enacted by the federal government, could establish uniform interpretation of the law in all states.[5] Some key pieces of legislation in this area include the

Federal Trade Commission Act, Fair Packaging and Labeling Act, Consumer Credit Protection Act, Child Protection and Toy Safety Act, Truth-in-Lending Act, Fair Credit Reporting Act, Consumer Protection Safety Act, and Privacy Act.

The Federal Trade Commission (FTC) has broad and sweeping powers and is the federal government's law enforcement arm in handling product information in advertising, packaging and labeling, deceptive practices, consumer credit, warranties, and other related areas. The FTC was established under the Federal Trade Commission Act (1914) and now has the responsibility of policing and enforcing all aspects of the consumer-oriented legislation listed above, as well as ones not listed.

The FTC is also responsible for seeing that the customer obtains the proper information in order to make a safe and wise choice of purchase. Customers assumably know what they want (not always the case) and can get all the information they need (again, not always true) to obtain their greatest satisfaction. When either or both of these situations are not fulfilled, the FTC and many consumers feel that the FTC must step in and rectify the situation. In many instances it does this and either by persuasion, court action, or through newly recommended legislation is able to force the businessman into doing what is desired by the consumer or required by law. As consumers have become more sophisticated and products more complex, the concept of what is good information has changed. It is also not clear to most people what the term *full disclosure* truly means. It is apparent, then, that much dialogue is needed among business, government, and consumers in order to determine what fair and appropriate actions should be taken. Those manufacturers that do not take responsibility for their products' problems either face legal action, boycott, or other actions by the consumer.

According to Nancy Harvey Steorts there are ten regulatory trends that will affect the future product safety regulatory environment:

1. Increased concern by company executives for product safety.

2. Increasing cooperation between business, regulators, and consumers on reaching product safety goals.

3. Increasing compliance by business in meeting safety regulations in order to reduce the involvement of lawyers and expenses from litigation.

4. More sharing of product hazard information between business and regulators.

5. Continued improvement in product safety from food and drug manufacturers.

6. Increased customer education by business and regulators.

7. Increased emphasis on product safety attributes through marketing endeavors.

8. Increased participation by retailers in product safety.

9. Greater international cooperation in the promotion of product safety.

10. Greater involvement of both business and the consumer in establishing safety priorities and regulations.[6]

Minority Business Legislation

For years, many companies have extended concerted efforts to hire members from minority groups as well as the physically and mentally handicapped. Much of the emphasis has been concentrated on hiring the hardcore unemployed such as black native American ghetto youths and any other group that might have difficulty obtaining jobs. In recent years, increased emphasis has been placed on hiring the physically handicapped with the passage of the Vocational Rehabilitation Act of 1973. This act addresses discrimination against handicapped people by anyone working on government contracts. A Department of Labor survey conducted several years after enactment of this law revealed that 91 percent of 300 companies surveyed were in violation of the act. Some other recent legislation in this area includes Title 41 Federal Procurement Regulation, Public Works Employment Act, Railroad Revitalization and Regulatory Reform Act, and others.

Labor Legislation

Labor legislation and interpretations were made primarily by the judiciary prior to the 1930s with increasing labor legislation occurring after the 1930s. Prior to 1930, big business held the upper hand over the unions; by the mid–1930s the power had swung over to the unions with the passage of the Norris-Laguardia Act of 1932 and the Wagner Act of 1935. The power swung back more to the center with the passage of the Taft-Hartley Act in 1947 and the Landrum-Griffin Act of 1959. With this legislation in place, many of the detailed areas of workers' concern were covered by all of the various pieces of legislation.

Union membership continued to grow rapidly during the 1930s and early 1940s in a period when the presidential administration was sympathetic to labor, and labor was winning court battles for its causes. However, by 1945 union membership momentum had slowed down and membership leveled off at close to 25 percent of the civilian workforce, where it plateaued until close to 1965; it continued to slowly decline in the late 1970s and early 1980s.

Union membership today is slightly below 20 percent of the workforce, and a continued decrease is projected. This recent decline in union membership can be attributed primarily to several causes, including changing times, changing characteristics of the workforce, the changing legal environment, the unions themselves, and increased cooperation between labor and management.

Structural changes within the American economy itself have been significant since the end of World War II. Manufacturing, construction, and mining—the industries that have traditionally been unionized—have declined somewhat in importance in relationship to the emerging and rapidly growing areas of finance, service, and high technology. These newer areas of business have been more resistant to unionization.

The changing face of the labor force also has been a major contributor to the decline of unionization. Women and young workers, who are less apt to belong to unions, now make up a major part of the labor force. Also increasing in numbers are professional and white collar workers. By 1980, 40 million of the workers in the United States had completed four years of high school with almost an equal number having completed and graduated from college; these persons represent almost 75 percent of the labor force. As each of these two groups has increased, the proportion of the labor force belonging to unions has decreased.

The changing legal environment has also contributed to the reduction in unionization. Many of the things for which the unions fought in the past have been accomplished. In many instances, laws now exist and protect workers in areas where they were once unprotected (i.e., right-to-know laws, equal pay act, sexual harassment laws, and so on). As general legal protection for the employee has grown, the need to affiliate through unions has decreased.

Organized labor itself is also a strong contributor to declining union membership. Unions have been slow to react to the changing social and economic conditions, and as a result many of their programs and goals fail to meet the needs of today's workers. Unions have also had problems discarding their somewhat negative image. The new union leaders are trying hard to change their image and update their causes and organizations.

Government deregulation and increased foreign competition during the 1980s have forced both labor and management to become more cooperative and work closer together to fight for a common cause—their business and their jobs—against a common enemy—foreign encroachment. In many instances unions have made previously unheard-of concessions and give-backs to management in order for labor to keep jobs and to be competitive with both domestic and foreign companies. Joint labor-management committees and groups, under numerous names and titles, have been formed to work cooperatively to solve and resolve both technical problems and management-labor problems.

Union membership, although still in a declining trend, remains a powerful force in this country. If it becomes necessary, or to their advantage, they still have the power to shut down large companies and large segments of the economy if they so desire. Unions may be relatively docile at the moment; however, they cannot be ignored and are still a force to be reckoned with by management. Revival of unions may not be as far off as some may think or hope. However, in recent years, union members have received smaller pay raises than nonunion members, and real wages of union members have fallen (wage raises have not kept up with inflation).[7]

FACILITIES

It is not uncommon in marketing to think and talk about product lifecycles. The same concept also applies to facilities or plants, which also have lifecycles. A facility lifecycle can generally be broken down into three stages: (1) the initial startup; (2) growth and maturity; and (3) obsolescence and deterioration. In order to minimize cost and maximize profits, rapid construction and plant startups are normally desirable. For the initial planning and startup stage, Roger Schmenner presents several critical areas that must be considered:

- The definition of the products to be manufactured and their desired output levels.
- The plant's capacity and technological capabilities.
- The specific process technology to be used, and the workflow pattern to be followed within the plant.
- The number of workers and the mix of their skills.
- The recruiting, training, and other human resource policies to be adopted in pursuit of the workforce goals.
- The production scheduling and control systems to be employed.
- The interrelationship between this facility and other facilities, as well as the suppliers, the distribution system, and ultimate customers.
- The overhead functions and support staff to be provided—both those contained within the facility and those "borrowed" from outside sources.
- A provision for the subsequent expansion and development of the facility and its human resources.
- The capabilities and tasks that will not be required of the plant (at least during early stages).
- The events that would cause a change in the basic plan for the facility.[8]

The second stage of growth and maturity concentrates on improving productivity, quality, materials control, personnel utilization, technology improvements, and overall plant operations and utilization.

Eventually plants reach the point of obsolescence and deterioration. Since this is known in advance, it must be included in the company's strategic planning process. Several warnings signs that indicate a plant is approaching this stage in its lifecycle are:

- Obsolescence reflected in technology deterring plant layout, poor materials handling, or problems with other physical aspects of the plant.
- Severe and unremitting sales declines.
- Substantial cost increases in labor, transportation, or raw materials.
- Militant union or other personnel problems.
- Needless duplication of operations of other plants.[9]

For many companies, and certainly their employees, one of the most difficult parts in closing a plant is what to do with the employees. Fortunately, many companies today are quite sympathetic to this problem and retrain the people for other jobs whenever practical; most of these programs are operated by individual firms. It is imperative, however, if these people are not to end up in the unemployment lines that the training be in meaningful work areas and not just handout jobs where the person is paid for something like summer work but actually gains very little useful work experience. Companies such as General Electric have set up retraining programs in areas where they have had to close down plants. They retrain the laid-off employees in new skills so that they have a better chance of being employed by other businesses in the area or elsewhere, or even starting up their own businesses. More companies are letting released professional people return for three to six months and use an office, a secretary, a telephone, and a copy machine to make resumes and try to locate a new position.

In 1983, the federal government passed the Federal Job Training Partnership Act (JTPA). This act replaces the inefficient Comprehensive Education and Training Act which lasted from 1973 to 1982. JTPA concentrates on training rather than other social goals. Under JTPA, employers and local governments negotiate the type of training that will be offered by the employers, based on their perception of the local job vacancies and requirements.

These are only a few of the different job training programs that are available to the employer and employee. As long as the job and the training are useful and productive to both the employer and employee, the community should benefit from it.

CAPACITY

Plant capacity determination and strategy are complex problems. They require either knowledge of or at least fairly reliable estimates in such areas as product demand, product lifecycle, product competition, possible changes in technology, and cost of construction and operation for the initial plant as well as incremental expansions.

Costs, advantages, and disadvantages can vary considerably in cases of overcapacity versus undercapacity and of incremental plant expansion versus building all at one time.

Unused capacity in a plant that is too large is expensive. However, the firm may benefit from lower total construction costs and faster response to an increase in demand. This latter advantage might also retain or increase market share and make customers happy by staying abreast or ahead of demand. On the other hand, if unused capacity is excessive or persists too long it could keep a company below its breakeven point.

Undercapacity, conversely, can be devastating if it is extensive or if it persists for any length of time. Market share and profits can be lost, possibly never to be recovered. Capacity may be added to a plant in increments, but it is usually more costly than initially building a larger, overcapacity plant. These added incremental costs may, however, be larger or smaller than the costs from an overcapacity, underutilized plant. This is a tradeoff situation that must be evaluated carefully. If product demand increases rapidly, incremental expansion may not be timely and market share and profits could be lost.

In today's market, as an industry begins to mature, the trend is in the direction of smaller multiple plant facilities. This tends to result in optimized plant size and operation, better control, minimum confusion and duplication of effect, easier disposal of the plant if required, and a non-dominant force in the community.

PERSONNEL

When locating a new plant or expanding facilities, several factors must be considered regarding personnel. These include such things as availability of the type of personnel needed, the population of the plant location and surrounding area, unionization in the area, existing community facilities, and community expectations.

Both population and skill levels of people in the surrounding plant area are critical. A plant may want to locate in a rural area of low skill population. This might initially keep labor rates down but incur additional costs in training programs. If the population of the general area is limited, after skills have been learned by the employees, they may demand higher wages, unionize or move on to higher paying jobs in the city. In the long run, low-population areas may also increase labor costs through an aging workforce and increased health care and other fringe benefits. If it is the dominant business in the area, the community may expect costly community involvement by the company.

A high-technology company may want to locate its plant close to cities or areas where such things are available as highly skilled specialty labor; universities for help in technical training and additional education; and a zoo, opera, arts, sports, and other cosmopolitan activities to help attract high-skilled labor from other cities into the area.

INVENTORY CONTROL

Inventory is the amount of resources or products kept in storage in order to insure flexibility in production operations, smooth out periods of excess capacity or unusual demands, or to achieve economies of scale through large quantity purchases. The basic objective of any good inventory control system is to control the inventory quantity in order to insure an efficient and effective operation.

Most organizations group inventories into three or four classifications: raw materials, materials in transit, work in progress, and finished goods. Raw-materials inventories are basic inventories drawn upon in the fabrication and assembly process of components or finished products. Materials-in-transit is an inventory classification that may or may not exist in a company; if raw materials have to be moved from one location to another, it may take hours or days, and this time must be accounted for in the inventory cycle. Work-in-process inventories are all goods in the process of being assembled into components or final products. Finished-goods inventories are goods completed but unsold.

There are many inventory control systems in operation that attempt to control inventory levels for an efficient and effective operation. Only a few of the more popular ones will be discussed here.

Economic Order Quantity

There are two major cost factors associated with this concept: the inventory ordering cost and the inventory carrying or holding costs. The more often inventory is ordered, the higher are the total ordering or paperwork processing costs. On the other hand, the larger the inventory level, the higher the storage and holding costs. This is a tradeoff situation in that inventory order costs increase the more times inventory is ordered (keeping storage and carrying costs to a minimum), while storage and carrying costs increase when the same amount of inventory is ordered less often in larger batches. The total of these two costs is minimized when the two costs are equal; that is, inventory costs are minimized when ordering costs equal carrying and storage costs.

The ABC Analysis

Some medium-sized and large-sized companies have several hundreds of thousands of inventory transactions each year. It may not be economical to apply a detailed inventory control system to all items carried in the inventory. The ABC system classifies the inventory into three levels, where A equals high-value items, B equals medium-value items, and C equals low-value items. In a typical situation, the A items represent 15 to 20 percent of the total items and 75 to 80 percent of the total inventory value, B items account for 20 to 25 percent of the total items and approximately 10 to 15 percent of the total inventory value, and C items account for about 60 to 65 percent of the total items and 5 to 10 percent of the inventory value.

An ABC inventory control analysis is primarily intended for end items that are characterized by a demand that is independent of other end items. It, therefore, does not apply to dependent demand items controlled under materials requirements planning (MRP), to be discussed later. Also, in this type of a system, factors other than strictly financial ones must be taken into consideration.

Perpetual Inventory System

In this system, whenever the inventory stock level falls to a predetermined reorder level or below, a buy order is triggered for a quantity purchase equal to the economic order quantity (EOQ). This system requires an inventory check, daily records, material issue and receiving slips, and a guarded or locked stockroom.

A two-bin inventory system is a simplified version of the perpetual inventory system in that it reduces paperwork; eliminates the need to maintain accurate records for each transaction; and is well suited for items of low value, consistent usage, and short lead time. The reorder point is determined by visual observation; when the inventory stock is depleted in one bin this triggers an order for more material, and manufacturing demands are filled from the second bin.

Periodic Inventory System

In this type of system, the inventory level is only checked periodically. This reduces checking costs and possibly reorder costs by either lumping several reorders together and ordering larger quantities at one time (discounts may be realized on larger orders). Danger of stock running out and increased cost from larger safety stocks may also occur with a periodic inventory system.

Materials Requirements Planning (MRP) Inventory System

In situations of dependent inventory demand, such as when dealing with in-process inventories of component parts, planned orders are based on an MRP schedule. This system operates by working backward from the scheduled completion dates of end products or major assemblies to determine the dates and quantities of the various materials and components that are to be ordered. Unless an MRP system is thoroughly planned before installation, however, the time, expense, and effort may be extensive.

The MRP takes the master production schedule for the end item and determines the gross quantities of the various materials needed by using product structure records (bills of materials); the gross quantities are then obtained by "blowing up" the end item product records into all of their lower level required parts. The next step in the process is to take a list of existing inventory, or an inventory status list, and compare it against the inventory requirement for gross parts quantity needed. By subtracting inventory on hand from the gross inventory needed, the net inventory quantities can be determined. As a final step, the time period when the part or material is needed is determined by time phasing backward the lead times for each item.

MRP is an excellent planning and inventory control tool that can minimize inventory investment and prevent shortages and overstock by predicting them before they occur. This type of system is particularly effective in electronic, automotive, and other assembly-oriented operations.

Chapter 7, "Logistics," gives a more detailed and comprehensive discussion of both MRP and JIT, discussed below.

Just-in-time delivery

The Japanese have very effectively used the *kanban* or just-in-time (JIT) delivery of parts and materials. This approach of inventory control embraces the concept of minimizing storage and carrying costs and maintaining almost no inventories; this is usually accomplished by ordering parts and materials only in small lots for delivery no earlier than necessary for use.

The Japanese word *kanban* means the piece of paper that accompanies an order, such as the slip with a bin of parts for a camera factory.[10] When a worker takes the parts from a new bin, the *kanban* is expedited back to the supplier and serves as the purchase order for new material.

Although relatively simple in concept, there are several ingredients needed for its efficient and effective usage. These include:

• relatively short transit times from the supplier's plants to the customer's plants. Less than one day is the preferred time.

• a dependable and controllable transportation system.

• receipt of only top-quality parts and materials from the supplier.

• a limited number of dependable and cooperative suppliers. This usually requires long-term commitments on behalf of both the supplier and the purchaser.
• dependable and efficient receiving and distribution of materials.
• a commitment from top management to make the system work.

Integrated MRP, Bar Coding, and Kanban Form System

To help combat intensifying global competition, Raymond Louis proposes combining the best features of MRP, bar coding, and *kanban*.[11] He states:

The unique features of this system are automated MRP adjustment to the kanban lot size which interfaces with the bar code file, a sample part on the container allowing a quick visual check and the quantity marker on the inside of the container allowing a quick visual check on the count.[12]

By using this system, Louis feels that a company can significantly reduce both time and costs and improve efficiencies.

QUALITY

Product quality is essential if a company is to remain competitive. As discussed in Chapter 4, "Engineering," poor quality can also be extremely costly. A recent communications satellite, costing millions of dollars, was launched into an ineffective low-level orbiting path due to faulty wiring in one of the satellite's electrical cable harnesses.

Conventional quality assurance calls for inspection of incoming components, including inspection of each unit, sampling, go/no-go tests, physical dimensions, or cosmetic examination. This is followed by in-process inspection at critical points in the assembly process and final performance tests on the end product. This is an attempt to *test* quality into the product. By most of today's standards, this is not the way to go. Quality must be *designed* into the product by engineering and then *built* into the product by manufacturing. This means that quality must already exist in the basic parts that come into the plant; *kanban* cannot effectively operate if quality is not built into the just-in-time arrival of parts and material.

Quality circles and other quality-oriented groups have been established in many companies to come up with ideas and initiate programs to improve product quality, with the ideal goal being "zero defects." Quality must be practiced at all levels and in all areas. This is aptly expressed by E. S. Woolard, chairman and CEO of E. I. DuPont:

To compete and win, we must redouble our efforts—not only in the quality of our goods and services, but in the quality of our thinking, in the quality of our response to customers, in the quality of our decision-making, in the quality of everything we do.[13]

PRODUCTIVITY

Total productivity can be defined as the ratio of total output to the sum of all input factors (capital, facilities, materials, people, etc.). Total productivity then measures the joint impact of all inputs in producing the output. Increased productivity simply means increasing output with a level equivalent to previous inputs.

From 1973 to 1979, U.S. manufacturing productivity increased an average 1.4 percent per year, while Japan's rose by 5.5 percent, West Germany by 4.3 percent, Canada by 2.1 percent, and Italy by 3.3 percent. U.S. productivity continued to lag in the early 1980s, but in 1986 it increased to 3.7 percent with an additional gain of 3.3 percent in 1987. In 1986 Japan's productivity rate increased by only 2.8 percent, so the United States once again gained the initiative.[14] In 1988 America's productivity gain was 2.7 percent, while in 1989 it rose by 2.8 percent.[15] However, if the U.S. productivity rate continues growing at its historic average rate of 2.3 percent, Japan, Germany, and France could surpass the United States in productivity in less than a generation.[16]

An examination of the productivity issue might help explain why it is such a vital issue. To continue living, a person must have an adequate income. Since most people obtain this income by working, they must produce a product that is competitive in both quality and price. This can be accomplished by continuously improving quality and productivity at a rate greater than that of the competition. If properly administered, this can be accomplished with increased income and profits to the employer, improved real wages and benefits to the employee, increased employment levels, and relatively stable prices and inflation rates.

Figure 5.1 shows what productivity improvements are all about. Prior to explaining how the chart works, a few terms must be explained: N is the level of labor employment; W/P is the real wage of the employee, with W representing the take-home pay and benefits and P representing the price that must be paid by the employee for goods and services. If W increases relative to P or P decreases relative to W, then employee real wage or purchasing power will increase. MPL is the productivity of labor (the amount of output per a given unit of input), while MPL_1 is the increased level of productivity (the increased amount of output with the original equivalent unit of input). S or L is the supply of labor (N) available and willing to work at a given real wage (W/P).

Putting the plan into operation and increasing productivity is beneficial to everyone. At time zero (present), the level of labor employment is N_0 and the employee's real wage is W_0/P_0. This is point A on the figure.

Figure 5.1
The Effect of Increasing the Marginal Rate of Productivity of Labor on Employment and Real Wages

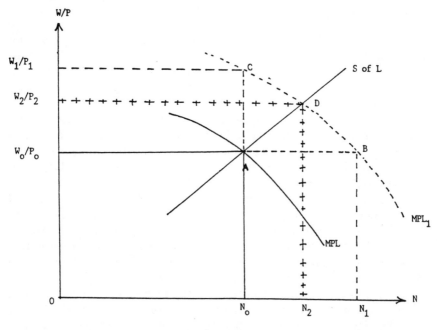

LEVEL OF LABOR EMPLOYMENT

Increasing worker productivity from MPL to MPL_1 can have several favorable outputs. If real wages W_0/P_0 are kept constant, then the business can hire more people to level N_1 without having to increase employee wages W_0 or product price P_0; this is point B on the chart. This has often been a goal of unions in an attempt to increase membership; it would, however, give all gains to labor, in the form of increased employment, and none to management. If labor is held constant at N_0, then real wages can be increased to W_1/P_1, as depicted by point C on the chart. This does not increase employment, but it does permit an increase in real wages. The key here is that real wage W_1/P_1 is higher than real wage W_0/P_0, which means that the spread has increased between take-home pay W and prices P charged or paid for items; a person can now improve his or her standard of living because he or she has more purchasing power. P_1 can be higher, the same as, or lower than P_0, and W_1/P_1 will still increase as long as P_1 does not increase as much as W_1. At point C, then, the employee is better off because of increased real wages, the business is better off because it can hold prices fairly stable, and society will be better off because of low inflation. An even more desirable point on the chart, brought about by the increase in productivity, is point D. At this point all of the advantages listed for point C exist but the ability to hire more people to level N_2 also exists. Under this condition, labor, management, and society as a whole all benefit because both the company and the employees can make more money and more people can be employed. If productivity rates can be kept abreast or ahead of inflation, then even the customer will come out ahead because prices can be held stable or increased only a small amount while both management and labor also improve their positions. This is the best of all worlds. It does, however, require absolute trust, cooperation, dedication, and restraint among labor, management, and government. There are some steps being made in this direction through the changing nature of work and the workplace.

PRODUCTIVITY IMPROVEMENT TECHNIQUES

There are many ways to improve productivity. Only a few of the better known ones, however, will be briefly discussed here. The four main groups to be discussed are: (1) employee-based techniques; (2) employer-initiated techniques; (3) technology-based techniques; and (4) quantitative mathematical techniques.

Employee-based Productivity Improvement Techniques

Employee-based techniques can be broken down further into three major subgroups: (1) individual financial incentives, (2) group financial incentives, and (3) worker participation techniques.

There are and have been numerous individual financial incentive programs in use for a long time. Some of these include piecework, standard hours, measured days, and bonuses. In piecework, the employee is paid a specified amount for each unit produced, and pay is directly proportional to the number of units produced; in most cases a minimum daily rate is guaranteed. In the standard hour plan, standard hours per piece replace dollars per piece. The incentive is not as high in this system as in the piecework system, but it minimizes the problems of possible poor quality (due to haste) in the piecework system. The measured daywork (MDW) plan is similar to the standard hour plan except that the base rate in any hour or day is based on the previous hour or day's work as a calculated percentage of the previous rate. The incentive is to always outperform the standard rate; as in the piecework case, a minimum daily rate is guaranteed. A bonus system is quite often based on a guaranteed wage for a given output with additional compensation awarded for each preestablished incremental increase beyond the base output quantity.

There are a large number of group financial incentive plans, five of which will be briefly discussed here. These plans are the Scanlon plan, the Kaiser plan, the tonnage plan, profit sharing, and improshare.

Under the Scanlon plan, developed by a trade union official, the workers are paid a certain percentage (usually 75 percent) of the labor cost savings. The labor cost savings are newly calculated each month by first computing the sales value of production at the selling price, computing the allowable labor cost, compiling the actual labor cost, and then subtracting the actual labor cost from the allowable labor cost. The difference is the labor savings. Commonly 75 percent of this money is given to the employees in the form of a cash bonus, with 25 percent set aside in an employee bonus reserve fund. At the end of the year, if the reserve fund is positive, the remainder goes to the employees; if the reserve fund is zero or negative the deficiency is wiped clean. This has been a very popular plan, but problems occur when automation or labor-saving capital equipment installations are made.

The Kaiser plan was first presented in 1962, giving the employees a 32.5 percent share in the savings from increased productivity over the base-year cost of labor plus material. The 32.5 percent share was guaranteed to the employees even if the company did not make a profit. This plan did not have the wide following or popularity that the Scanlon plan enjoyed.

The tonnage plan is used by some foundries and steel companies. Using historical data, a standard number of tons of material produced per year is established as a base level. The entire workforce shares in the percent increase above this base level in succeeding periods. For instance, if output tonnage increases by 15 percent, the employees receive a 15 percent bonus.

Profit sharing plans may vary from company to company; however, they all encourage everyone in the company to endeavor to increase company profits. Profits are usually distributed to employees either in direct cash on a prescribed periodic basis, on a deferred plan where the profits are invested for the employee and paid upon retirement, or a combination of these two plans.

The improshare group incentive plan was developed by Mitchell Fein and is used by many companies. Similarly to methods of productivity improvement, this plan assumes that both workers and management are interested in raising productivity because they both benefit from this increase, no matter what the source of gains is or how much either party contributes to the gain.

Employer-initiated Techniques

As in the other productivity improvement techniques already discussed, there are numerous employer-initiated (or employer-enhanced) productivity improvement techniques, such as fringe benefits, management by objectives, job enlargement, job rotation, job enrichment, autonomous work groups, quality circles, flexible working hours, compressed work weeks, job sharing, and working at home.

Although fringe benefits cost the company considerable amounts of money, they are considered necessary to obtain, retain, and motivate the employee to greater productivity. Fringe benefits offered by many companies include relocation expenses and free air fare for a family and employees, subsidies for purchasing or renting a home, free use of a company car and other amenities, free education, medical insurance, entertainment expenses, sick leave, paid vacations, disability insurance, child care, and many others. Some companies offer what is termed a "market basket" of fringe benefits. In these cases the employee is permitted to choose a given amount from a large assortment of fringe benefits.

Another combined motivation and behavior process that has enjoyed relative popularity for several years is a concept known as management by objectives (MBO). Peter S. Drucker was one of the early proponents of this concept,[17] and G. S. Odiorne has popularized it.[18] Basically it brings both management and workers together to discuss and jointly establish the company's goals and objectives and how they are to be measured. There are four to six major steps in the process. In January 1979, Mark L. McConkie reviewed and compared forty different articles on the concepts of MBO and listed their similarities and differences.[19] If four major steps are followed, the supervisor and worker will meet and (1) establish the goals and objectives in terms of specific measurable results; (2) develop action plans including costs, labor, and time to perform the tasks; (3) conduct periodic reviews and modify the plan as needed; and (4) evaluate and appraise the plan at the end of program or at the end of the year, whichever comes first.

Many other changes have been made by management since the 1930s in an attempt to increase worker motivation and productivity. Prior to the 1930s and through much of World War II, production was based on the assembly line where each person on the line did one frustrating and monotonous task day after day. This was referred to as *job simplification*. To help relieve some of this boredom, the production process moved to *job enlargement*; this was still a horizontal assembly line process, but now one person performed several operations that were previously assigned to several people. Another similar system is *job rotation*, where a person is periodically shifted from one job to another.

The next step taken toward expanding employee responsibility was *job enrichment*. This concept increases both the breadth and depth of a job. In addition to normal assembly line work it involves some planning and evaluating duties that were formerly performed by supervisors. It not only gives employees horizontal assembly line responsibilities but also offers them vertical expansion to take over some previously supervisory duties. Cost, technological constraints, and union opposition can cause some problems in initiating job enrichment.

Beyond job enrichment are *autonomous work groups*. These are self-managed work teams responsible for the accomplishment of specifically defined performance requirements on an entire assembly project. This creates the atmosphere of a workshop, which allows for decentralization and delegation. Volvo has used this concept to build its automobiles. The benefits reported from such a concept are improved worker attitudes, improved quality of output, lower absenteeism and turnover, ease of covering absent workers, and reduced number of supervisory personnel. Some disadvantages of implementing this concept are possibly higher costs, reduced production rates, increased space requirements, and the need for radically new plant designs.

One attempt to take advantage of the positive aspects and minimize the negative aspects found in autonomous work groups is the creation of *quality circles*. A recent study concludes that quality circles have distinct advantages, but they are also designed with certain inherent factors that often lead to self-destruction.[20]

Other working concepts that attempt to accommodate the social desires of both the employees and the employer include *flexible work hours*, where all people in the organization work a specific set of core hours but can normally adjust their starting and quitting times; *compressed work weeks*, where employees may work four ten-hour days instead of five eight-hour days; *job sharing*, where two or more people fill the same job but, for example, one may work mornings on Mondays and Wednesdays while the other person works in the afternoon or the other days of the week when the other person is not working; and *working at home* either by picking up work at a central location and doing it at home for redelivery back to the central location or by the use of computer terminals in the home. All of these concepts give both the employee and the employer more flexibility and help meet the social needs of both parties as well as improving productivity.

Technology Techniques

A few of the many popular present-day techniques for improving productivity include computer-aided design (CAD), computer-aided manufacturing (CAM), computer-integrated manufacturing (CIM), computer graphics, flexible manufacturing systems (FMS), robotics, and laser technology.

Computer-aided Design (CAD). CAD is the design of products, processes, and systems with the aid of a computer. Initially CAD was used for the design of components, subassemblies, and assemblies in companies oriented toward manufacturing, especially where three-dimensional geo-metrics were involved. Today CAD is used for productivity improvement in almost every conceivable area from the design of the simplest com-ponent to the most complex machine.

Computer-aided Manufacturing (CAM). CAM employs computers to assist in the design and control of manufacturing processes. It replaces much of the previously used manual design and control. Good software design is essential to efficient and flexible operation.

Computer-integrated Manufacturing (CIM). CAD and CAM have been integrated to form the CIM system in which computers assist everywhere from marketing to product shipment. It includes several functions such as product design, manufacturing process planning, production operations management, vendor control, materials and parts storage and retrieval, finished product storage and retrieval, shipping, and manufacturing proper.

This is not a simple concept or a simple installation. It is costly and requires extensive time to install and employ. Both technological feasi-bility and economic realities of a completely installed CIM system will hinder total operational adaptability of this concept, at least for the pres-ent, by any but the largest of companies and government facilities.

Computer Graphics. Computer graphics is closely related to both CAD and CAM. Computer graphics involves the use of a computer to generate graphic displays of objects on a cathode ray display in either two- or three-dimensional formats. The displayed image and data can then be stored for future reference or be transferred to paper or other processes if desired. Software to perform the desired operations is again a critical item. The prime advantages of computer graphics include: the ease with which objects can be created, modified, and stored; the ability to rotate three-dimensional objects to study all aspects of the situation; and the virtual elimination of the need for costly storage of drawings, specifica-tions, processes, and so on.

Flexible Manufacturing Systems (FMS). FMS is a self-contained group-ing of machinery—robots, machine tools, computers, and so on—that are able to perform all of the operations necessary for the manufacture of a number of different parts that have similar processing requirements. The operations of FMS, including the transport of material from one machine to another, are performed primarily by computer control with little, or preferably no, human intervention. Processing and sequencing of parts, as well as variations in parts, can be handled by the machinery as directed by the controlling computers.

FMS is not for everyone. Implementation and operation require pro-ficiency in machine tools, automated materials handling systems, high-level computer controls, and a complete understanding of how the dif-ferent automation systems interact under a variety of situations.

Robotics. Industrial robots consist of three basic parts: a manipulator, which has several axes of motion incorporated into it; a power supply; and a control system, which sequences and coordinates the operations. In most instances the industrial robot is a general-purpose automation system.

Robots can either stand alone in units or, in many cases, are integrated with other devices and machines. Robots have the advantage of being able to work twenty-four hours a day, save on salaries and fringe benefits, perform boring and dangerous tasks, help overcome personnel problems, and can be integrated with CAD and CAM.

Laser Technology. The laser generates a higher energy beam of coherent light that can be accurately focused where desired. Laser technology has many applications. Initially it was used to cut metals, drill holes, weld, and do other simple technical tests. Today it is also used in clothing manufacture, surgery, communications in conjunction with fiber optics, and where precise measurements are required in machine tools and surveying (its energy travels at the speed of light, and thus distances can be accurately measured).

There is a tremendous savings potential associated with lasers, even though initial costs may be high. Their precision, accuracy, and ability to work with robotics and flexible manufacturing systems dramatically increases their possible applications.

Quantitative Mathematical Techniques

Many mathematical techniques can be employed to improve productivity. Breakeven analysis can be used when trying to determine the quantity of a product that must be fabricated and sold before all fixed and variable costs are covered. Linear programming can be used to determine the best mix of products to use to maximize profits under various boundary constraints. Transportation models are a special form of linear programming for determining where to locate plants and warehouses relative to supplies and customers, the best product mix, and many other cost-minimizing factors. Gantt charts, PERT, and CPM can be used to plan timing and cost step by step for almost any operation, from the simplest to the most complex. Trend line (least squares) analysis and forecasting techniques can be used to project future sales, profits, or any other number of things. Queuing theory can be used to solve any waiting-line type of problem such as tool rooms. It is normally used to determine the number of service personnel or workstations needed to minimize customer waiting time and service costs economically and efficiently. Markov analysis is best applied to brand-switching problems where simple observational analysis in terms of net gain or loss of customers is not adequate for intelligent decision making. Markov analysis also helps determine in more detail the rate of gains and losses from competitors. Decision tree analysis techniques are used in making business decisions by laying out decision points in a tree format where each branch shows alternative courses of action, chance events, probabilities, and net cash flow or payoffs. The choice route or alternative is arrived at by a comparison of the composite payoff, or combined value, of the events and probabilities in each case.

These are only a few of the many quantitative techniques available to assist the manufacturing manager or any other functional area manager minimize costs and maximize profits. All of these techniques are now available in software programs so that the present-day manager has only to load the basic data into the program to receive results. This convenience does not, however, excuse the manager from understanding and properly interpreting the resultant computer output.

COMPANY EVALUATION

Table 5.1 can help evaluate manufacturing in the four critical areas of planning, organizing, directing, and controlling. It shows how well manufacturing is doing as a separate functional area as well as how well it is performing in conjunction with R&D, engineering, marketing, MIS, and other critical functional areas.

Table 5.1
Typical Strengths and Weaknesses in Planning, Organizing, Directing, and Controlling Manufacturing

	Strengths	Weaknesses
PLANNING	Top management is committed to a strong manufacturing effort.	No strong commitment exists within the company for an integrated manufacturing effort.
	All manufacturing plans are consistent with company strategy and goals.	Manufacturing planning is inadequate in many areas.
	Detailed long, intermediate, and short-range manufacturing plans are generated and reviewed for acceptance or rejection on all proposed and in-process work.	Manufacturing planning is haphazard or nonexistent. Manufacturing planning is not coordinated with other functional areas.
	All manufacturing planning schedules are coordinated for proper interface with R&D, engineering, marketing, MIS, purchasing, and other critical functional areas.	Machines and facilities are changed or updated only when they wear out or become inadequate.
	Latest up-to-date mix of people, machines, and facilities is planned for.	Overtime in existing plans or inadequate production levels exists when product demand increases.
	Multiple manufacturing locations are planned for well ahead of need.	
ORGANIZING	Manufacturing reports directly to the president through a vice president.	Manufacturing operations reports to a plant manager.
	Manufacturing is organized in a manner to respond quickly to increases in product demand or change.	Manufacturing requires long time periods to respond to increased product demand or changes.
	Manufacturing is organized to make the most efficient use of people, machines, and facilities.	Antiquated equipment and facilities prevent efficient use of people, machines, and facilities.
	Manufacturing is organized to apply all the latest concepts of inventory control, quality assurance, technology improvements, and quantitative analysis techniques.	Manufacturing still uses basic concepts developed for past periods of time. Neither improved quality nor productivity are of major concern to manufacturing.
	Manufacturing is organized to continuously improve quality and productivity.	

76

DIRECTING	A competent vice president reporting directly to the president heads up manufacturing.	The manufacturing operation is headed up by a managerial level person.
	MIS systems are used to track, coordinate, and direct projects within manufacturing.	No constant tracking or coordination of projects exists within manufacturing.
	Excellent coordination and interface exist between manufacturing and all other company functional areas.	Inadequate coordination and interface exist between manufacturing and other company functional areas.
CONTROLLING	Manufacturing operations are integrated with those of other operating departments through MIS.	Manufacturing operates primarily as a separate entity with little coordinated effort with other company departments.
	Manufacturing efforts are monitored and coordinated from a central location.	Various manufacturing programs are independent of one another and are not coordinated by a central source.
	Budgets and schedules exist for each manufacturing effort.	Inadequate or no budgets or schedules exist to control manufacturing programs.
	Equipment, facilities, processes, and procedures are constantly reviewed and updated to minimize costs and maximize profits.	Equipment, facilities, processes, and procedures are only changed or updated when absolutely required. A "don't change it if it works" attitude persists.

NOTES

1. Robert H. Hayes and Steven C. Wheelwright, *Restoring Our Competitive Edge* (New York: John Wiley & Sons, 1984), p. 31.

2. *Federal Register* 45, no. 72 (1980): 25024.

3. "Gobbledygook Out," *Miami Herald*, December 6, 1977, p. A–17.

4. "OSHA Chief Leaves Agency in Limbo," *NFIB Mandate* (April-May 1984): 6.

5. Robert H. Malott, "Let's Restore Balance to Product Liability Law," *Harvard Business Review* 61, no. 3 (1983): 66–74.

6. Nancy Harvey Steorts, "New Direction in Product Safety Regulations," *Directors & Boards* 8, no. 4 (1984): 28–32.

7. Vivian Brownstein, "Here Comes the Pay Packet Price Push," *Fortune* 117, no. 6 (March 14, 1988): 73–76.

8. Roger Schmenner, *Making Business Location Decisions* (Englewood Cliffs, NJ: Prentice-Hall, 1982), p. 28.

9. Roger Schmenner, "Every Factory Has a Life Cycle," *Harvard Business Review* 61, no. 2 (March-April 1983): 128.

10. Urban C. Sehner, "The Nuts and Bolts of Japan's Factories," *Wall Street Journal*, March 31, 1981, p. 20.

11. Raymond Louis, "MRP, Bar Coding, Kanban Form System," *The Cincinnati Purchaser* (March-April 1990): 21.

12. Ibid.

13. "The Race to Qualify Improvement," *Fortune* 107, no. 7, Special Advertising Report.

14. "America's Blue Collars Get Down to Business," *U.S. News & World Report* 194, no. 8 (February 29, 1988): 52–53.

15. "'89 Productivity Rise Slows; Hourly Labor Costs Increase," *The Cincinnati Enquirer*, February 6, 1990, p. C–6.

16. "Economic Outlook: Taking the Long View of America's Decline," *U.S. News & World Report* 108, no. 1 (January 8, 1990): 58.

17. Peter S. Drucker, *The Practice of Management* (New York: Harper & Row, 1954); "What Results Should You Expect? A User's Guide to MBO," *Public Administration Review* 36, no. 1 (1976): 12.

18. G. S. Odiorne, *Management by Objectives: A System of Management Leadership* (New York: Pitman Publishing, 1965); "Management by Objectives and the Phenomenon of Goals Displacement," *Human Resources Management* 13, no. 1 (1974): 2–7.

19. Mark L. McConkie, "A Clarification of the Goal Setting and Appraisal Process in MBO," *The Academy of Management Review* 4, no. 1 (1979): 29–40.

20. E. E. Lawler, III, and Susan A. Morhman, "Quality Circles after the Fad," *Harvard Business Review* 63, no. 1 (1985): 64–71.

6

Marketing

Marketing involves the activities necessary and incidental for bringing about exchange relationships. It identifies and segments the markets to be served; further, it selects, distributes, and prices the products and services to be exchanged.

Marketing performs this exchange function with two flows of action and utilities. The first flow creates utility of form through the process of production, which in turn creates utility of both place and time through the process of distribution. The second flow of action is in the opposite direction in the form of cash and orders from customers. Marketing attempts to match these two flows in a manner that will maximize customer satisfaction and maximize company profits. In order to accomplish this exchange effectively and efficiently, the marketing manager must consider many things: market research, new product development, product pricing, branding, packaging, displays, promotion, advertising, personal selling, sales organization, distribution channels, physical distribution, marketing field organization, marketing administration, and industry and consumer relations. This complex combination of responsibilities is no simple matter to control. This chapter discusses some of the unique problems and conflicting demands that the marketing department is confronted with in responding to some of these tasks.

UNIQUE PROBLEMS AND CONFLICTING DEMANDS

The unique problems and conflicting demands fall into seven major areas:

- Identifying the market
- Product evolution and lifecycle
- Alternative market strategies
- Product line policies and strategies
- Pricing policies and strategies
- Promotion policies and strategies
- Distribution policies and strategies

Identifying the Market

The market or markets to be entered must be compatible with the company's mission statement, strategies, and objectives. Precisely defining the prospective market or markets requires careful scrutiny and analysis of the supply and demand interchange function of products and services. Determining the stage of product evolution and lifecycle currently taking place within the industries participating in the total market, along with company and marketplace opportunities and threats, will establish how attractive the marketplace is for companies already in the market and those considering entering the market.

A few of the factors that must be considered before entering a market are:

the number of buyers and sellers in the market and their relative size;

the demand for the product;

market leadership;

ease of entry and exit;

manufacturing costs and number of value-added points in the chain from maker to user;

extent of vertical integration of self and competition;

expected product evolution and lifecycle;

geographic boundaries and limitations; and

expected profits.

Once this information has been gathered together, its relative importance must be analyzed and evaluated in terms of opportunities, threats, and risks. Then, based on the evaluation of this information, an intelligent decision can be made on whether or not to enter the market with a particular product.

Michael E. Porter developed a technique called strategic group mapping, which can be used in identifying the market.[1] The first step in this process is to identify the strategic group of rival companies that employ competitively similar market approaches, that is, using identical marketing strategies. If all companies within a given industry group use identical marketing strategies then the industry would be classified as one strategic group. If, however, each company within the industry uses a different marketing strategy, then each company within the industry would comprise a separate strategic group. A map of strategic groups can be presented on a chart containing a vertical and horizontal axis. Each axis is identified with a different important market characteristic selected from several characteristics. The relative positions of the companies within the strategic group are then plotted on the chart. For example, one chart plots vertical integration (horizontal axis) against specialization (vertical axis) for a hypothetical strategic group. Another chart might use type of merchandise as the horizontal axis and level of quality of brand image as the vertical axis.

Other techniques exist for identifying the market, but these two examples suffice to show the importance of this early step in any marketing endeavor.

Product Evolution and Lifecycle

Several similar models depict product evolution and lifecycle at different levels of complexity. John A. Pearce II and Richard B. Robinson, Jr., use a four-stage model of product introduction, growth, maturity, and decline.[2] George A. Steiner uses a similar model but adds a fifth stage, saturation, between Pearce and Robinson's stages of maturity and decline.[3] Charles W. Hofer, Edwin A. Murray, Jr., Ram Charan, and Robert A. Pitts use a more extensive seven-stage model depicting product development, growth, shakeout, maturity, saturation, decline, and petrification.[4]

Regardless of which model is used, they all show similarly shaped growth and decline curves for sales and profits. Sales start out slowly in the development or introduction stage, increase quite rapidly up to midway through the saturation stage, and decline dramatically after that point. Profits, on the other hand, are small or even negative during the initial development or introduction stage and then increase moderately through the growth stage, level off or decline slightly through the maturity and into the early parts of the saturation stage, and then decline dramatically after that point.

All companies and industries do not always precisely follow the lifecycle sequences described above. However, it is generally agreed that the described lifecycle characteristics are reasonable presentations of how products behave in the marketplace and that all products follow some variations of the lifecycle theory. A more difficult task is determining the duration of each phase of the lifecycle. However, all products do go through such a cycle, and companies must be prepared with new, updated, or modified products for the market before the existing product reaches its saturation point and starts declining in sales and profits.

Alternative Market Strategies

At different times in the history of a company, its vulnerability to competition varies. To remain as invulnerable as possible a company must always have a dynamic view of the marketing operation. This requires the generation of alternative marketing strategies for consideration and final selection. A company must, therefore, examine its current state of affairs and how it might be changed to improve the total exchange process. In terms of market position, the market strategy (or strategies) should aim to maintain or improve the performance of the company in the niche it presently occupies, to even abandon its position, to improve or enlarge its position, or to accomplish a movement and profitable transition into a new area of operation. Regardless of which strategy is considered, each stage of a product's lifecycle may require a special strategy.

Product Line Policies and Strategies

Once the market is identified and defined, product line policies and strategies must be established. This requires close coordination and integration with planning, R&D, engineering, and manufacturing.

A major early product line policy and strategy decision that must be made is whether or not to concentrate on a single product or on several products. Closely allied to this decision is how much variation or how many models should exist within a product line. Normally, the operation is more cost efficient if fewer product lines or model variations are available. This may, however, leave the manufacturer more vulnerable to competition and consumer demands. Several product-oriented strategies can be considered in trying to solve this dilemma.

Product Differentiation. Product differentiation is based on technical superiority, quality, customer service and support, or a combination of any or all of these. The theory behind product differentiation is that the good will derived from the nonprice-competitive factor will be more palatable and lasting than that based on price appeal; and competitors may find it more difficult to overcome factors not related to price than to compete with or meet price changes.

Nonprice competition may take many different forms, such as packaging, performance, advertising, quality, or service. This complicates the consumer's decision of which product to purchase. The purchaser may prefer a lower price over a combination of extra features and services; however, the seller essentially makes the decision for the purchaser when nonprice factors, quite often accompanied by higher prices, are forced upon the customer. If handled properly, this can result in higher profits for the company.

Vertical Integration. A company can choose whether to use middlemen or to own and control the complete line of distribution from raw materials to the sale of the final product. Vertical integration can move either forward or backward. Forward vertical integration occurs when a company moves forward in the value-added chain, and backward vertical integration occurs when the company moves backward in the value-added chain. Total or full vertical integration occurs when the company owns and controls the complete line of distribution. Some oil companies are fully integrated in that they own and control the entire operation from oil wells to service stations.

The theoretical advantage of being fully integrated is that the company has complete control of the distribution process from start to finish and can thus increase its profits by eliminating the middleman. In good economic times this is quite often the case; however, when the economy is tight, the company may be caught with a considerable amount of fixed costs in buildings, equipment, and materials that must be paid for even though money coming in from end-product sales drops dramatically. In this situation, a company could be hurt considerably by being fully vertically integrated. Some companies hedge against this latter situation by becoming fully vertically integrated but still purchase and sell a certain percentage of their merchandise through middlemen. This procedure permits them to drop some or all of their middlemen in poor economic times and, thus, make them take the brunt of the cost of the bad economic situation.

Market Segmentation. From a strategic standpoint, market segmentation follows the concept of divide and conquer, and its implementation takes many forms. It is based on a distinction among the prospective customers who make up the market. It differs from product differentiation in that the latter is concerned with the supply side, whereas market segmentation is concerned with the differences among customers on the demand side.

Almost all companies segment their markets to some extent. Segmentation groups customers into categories whose constituents behave alike or have similar desires or needs. The strategy of market segmentation requires a continuous scanning for differences in constituents, geographic regions, or other differentiating factors throughout the entire market and then exploiting these differences. In theory, market segmentation can dramatically increase sales and, ultimately, total profits.

The opposite of market segmentation is market aggregation. This concept tends to lump together into one mass market many groups of buyers who might be only marginally differentiated. Market aggregation takes into account the concerns of production costs, warehousing, transportation, and distribution. For example, long production runs, due to fewer models, are more economical than short runs. Also inventory costs, warehousing, and distribution costs decrease with fewer models, and promotional funds can be used more efficiently and economically.

Any company desiring to use the market segmentation concept must carefully weigh all factors and decide whether a submarket is worth cultivating.

Pricing Policies and Strategies

The price decision is affected and influenced by all factors comprising the competitive structure of the industry; this includes both the internal strengths, weaknesses, and resources of the company and the external environment in which the firm operates.

Price involves much more than just the amount of money the customer pays for the purchased good. Price involves the quality of the product, the form of money that will be used, the time and place at which the transaction will take place, the credit terms and/or discounts that apply to the transaction, the delivery terms, guarantees and warranties, service, and other factors. The buyer and the seller must consider the "total package" because the "true" price of the purchased item changes whenever any of the associated parts of the package change.

Pricing falls into two major categories: market pricing and administered or business-controlled pricing. Market pricing exists when the seller does not have control over the price of his or her goods in the marketplace. This situation is akin to pure competition in economic theory where price is determined solely by the free play of the forces of supply and demand. The seller either accepts the price determined by the free market mechanism or refuses to sell. This situation rarely occurs. Administered or business-controlled prices are established by business firms at their own discretion. The seller establishes the price, and the buyer purchases the items at this price or does without it. The situation is not that clearcut since buyers do have some influence on selling price if large numbers of them refuse to buy the merchandise.

Pricing policy is established in order to achieve a number of goals, such as to attain a target rate of return; to meet, follow, or beat competition; to maintain or improve the company's share of the market; to stabilize price and margins; to survive; to improve short- and long-run profitability; and to combat product differentiation.

Prices set by companies can be determined and established in several ways. If product demand is known with a relative amount of certainty, then pricing can be established to maximize unit volume, total revenue, and profits. The other major approach to establishing price is on the basis of cost, which is not always accurately known. Some of the more popular cost approaches include breakeven pricing, variable-cost pricing, peak-load pricing, rate-of-return pricing, and mark-up pricing. Mark-up pricing is the simplest because it requires only the marking up of the price of the goods by a fixed percentage of the goods' base cost. Breakeven pricing helps determine what price and volume of production will cover total cost. Variable-cost pricing uses variable costs to determine the product price rather than total cost. Peak-load pricing is used by companies, such as telephone companies, when there are only so many goods or services available at a certain time. Rate-of-return pricing is based on achieving a targeted rate of return. The biggest problem of all of these techniques is that they have to be based on some demand level that is never known with any great certainty.

One of the major purposes of pricing policy is obviously to achieve an advantage over a competitor. When a company is a low-cost producer, it can use pricing strategy most effectively when it produces a standardized product (such as a ball-point pen), purchasers have common needs and requirements, demand is relatively price elastic, and product differentiation is difficult.

Pricing policy and strategy is an area that requires careful study and planning. It is not a simple decision made by the marketing department but involves all internal departments of the company as well as consideration of all external environmental factors.

Promotion Policies and Strategies

Promotion serves the consumer by presenting a flow of information from the business to the marketplace. It usually discloses information on the company's products, services, prices, distributors, sellers, and other key information. The communication presented to the customer is persuasive in nature because the company is attempting to influence the buying behavior of the customer in a direction favorable to its product. The direction and mix of promotion employed by a company depends on the type of product, the product's stage in the lifecycle, the composition of the markets, the competition, available financial resources, and the audience to be attracted. Some of the elements involved in the marketing mix of promotion include personal selling, advertising, packaging, pricing (discussed earlier), branding, sales promotions, displays, and publicity.

Salespersons, retail clerks, manufacturing representatives, and brokers are common avenues of personal selling. Personal selling has the advantage of direct one-on-one contact with the customer, two-way communication, and special emphasis on the customer's particular need or desire for the product. On the negative side, it can be an expensive form of promotion.

Advertising is any paid form of nonpersonal communication about the product to the customer. It can be transmitted to the public in oral, written, or visual form or a combination of any of these forms. The prime purpose of advertising is most easily explained by the AIDA concept of marketing: the first step is to get the customer's *A*ttention; the second step is to gain the customer's *I*nterest; the third step is to invoke the customer's *D*esire for the product; and the final step is to get the customer to take *A*ction and purchase the item.

Packaging is a lasting, ever-present form of visual and written advertising. Its purpose is the same as advertising's, but it also serves as an attention-getter and reminder of the positive aspects of a "good" product. In many instances (especially in self-service stores), packaging must replace the living salesperson as a vital link between the manufacturer and the consumer. It tells the purchaser what the manufacturer thinks of the product and of the customer. A well-designed package conveys the message that the manufacturer truly cares about the customer and the product.

Product branding is usually classified as private (distributor's brand) or manufacturer's (national brand). A private brand is a product sponsored or owned by a company whose normal business is distributing that product line under the company brand name. A manufacturer's brand is sponsored or owned by a company whose normal business is producing the given product line. A firm may decide to be a private brand company, a manufacturer's brand company, or a mixed brand company. Deciding the category of brand policy to promote is not always easy. For certain types of products, one brand policy may be superior to another, but this may reverse over a period of time. A mixed brand policy enables the company to shift emphasis from one brand policy to the other as situations change.

Sales promotions of a product usually supplement personal selling and regular advertising and are short in duration and noncontinuous. Dealer promotions are designed to improve dealer participation and cooperation as well as to attract customers' attention. Initial costs for such endeavors may be high, but increased product name exposure and future resultant sales usually justify such expense.

Displays are similar in nature and intent to sales promotions and may in some instances, be used simultaneously with promotions or as follow-ups to remind consumers of the product's availability.

Publicity of a product can be achieved through seminars, newspaper articles, sponsored events, or through the use of any number of techniques that display the product in a favorable manner.

Distribution Policies and Strategies

To move raw materials, agricultural goods, processed goods, or manufactured items from the area where they are mined, grown, or fabricated to the point of their ultimate use and consumption involves the functions of buying, selling, storage, transportation, standardization and grading, risk taking, information gathering and dispersing, and financing. All of this is known as marketing or the marketing system. The goods and services involved in these functions must travel along a distribution path or channel to get from one place to another. Distribution channels differ in length and route depending on many factors such as the country's economic development, literacy, communication facilities, transportation availability, cultural homogeneity or fragmentation, available credit, government intervention or support, and so on.

Three definitions will help define what is involved in the process of distribution and service:

1. *Channels of distribution.* Some people define wholesaling as just the portion of marketing that handles the goods between the producer (manufacturer or farmer) and the retailer , not taking into account the fact that the manufacturer, farmer, or retailer may be doing his or her own wholesaling. A more common view is that wholesaling extends all the way from raw materials and basic farm products to and through retail of those materials. For purposes of this book, channels of distribution cover wholesale distribution from beginning to end and are defined as the paths taken by any economic good or service in traveling from its point of inception to its ultimate point of consumption. For clarity and ease of discussion, the point of inception for both agricultural goods and manufactured goods is defined as the producer and the point of ultimate consumption is defined as the consumer.

2. *Stages of economic development.* Every country goes through several stages of economic development from infancy to maturity and sometimes even regresses a little under certain circumstances. It is also possible for one section of a country to be in one stage of economic development while other sections are in other stages. Turkey, Italy, India, and many countries of Africa are good examples of this. A country can be in one of four stages of economic development:

- Subsistence level: This is a level where people have only sufficient food and clothing to barely exist. This level of existence is found in certain areas of Africa, India, Egypt, Turkey, and Central America.

- Subsistence level with some excess: This is a level where people have enough food and/or manufactured goods to supply their own needs plus some excess with which to trade. This level can be found in almost any country, including parts of the United States, but is more prevalent in large portions of Africa, India, Central America, Egypt, and Turkey.

- Production-oriented economy: This is a level where the country has a considerable amount of industrialization, people have moved into large cities, the percentage of money spent on food is decreasing, export and import trade is increasing, and GNP (gross national product) per capita is increasing steadily. Many emerging countries fit into this category.

- Highly industrialized and highly market-oriented economy: This is the level of a mature country that is highly industrialized, highly educated, has good communication and transportation systems, and is interested in economical and expeditious movement of economic goods and services throughout the entire market. Examples of countries in this category are Germany, Japan, and the United States.

3. *Stages of market development.* Interestingly enough, the stages of market development improve along with the improvement in economic development of the country. Which comes first is a question that can be debated at length but will be ignored here because it is not critical to the subject under discussion. Any country, or a section of a country, can be placed into one of six stages of market development. These stages are:

- Peasant market: This is a simple marketplace with easy entry and exit. It is the type of market that carries fresh fruits, vegetables, and simple manufactured goods. There are variable prices, haggling, and some barter, and in many instances it is run by women. This type of market is prevalent in parts of Africa and India.

- Public markets and market rings: Public markets are usually stationary, but market rings are groups of specialty stores that may, in most instances, move from one area to another. Quite often they will be at the same location on the same day of each week. Both types of markets exist mostly in areas of higher population density and carry many different types of goods above the bare necessity level. These types of markets are still prevalent in parts of Africa, India, and Egypt.

- Small wholesalers and small retailers: These are quite often run by a single entrepreneur or are family affairs, and usually have short distribution channels. These small wholesalers and retailers are very prevalent in Italy, Turkey, Egypt, Japan, parts of Germany and in many other countries throughout the world.

- A combination of small wholesalers and retailers and an increasing number of larger wholesalers and retailers: As a country develops and matures, the size of both the wholesalers and retailers will in general increase, and the length of the channels of distribution will increase. Countries in this classification are Finland, Italy, parts of India, and parts of Turkey.

- Highly developed integrated market: This is the situation in mature countries and quite often results in a return to shorter channels of distribution as some of the unnecessary channels are either eliminated, bypassed, or combined. This type of marketing endeavor is typical of parts of Germany, Italy, the Netherlands, Austria, Japan, and the United States.

• Government-controlled markets: This is the case where the government dictates the major portion of the marketing policy, as in the U.S.S.R. and Communist China.

There are many variations in the channels of distribution throughout the world. Channels of distribution can exist at a subsistence level, where all agricultural goods and manufactured goods are consumed by the producer. It has a channel length of zero and is located at the subsistence level of economic development. This type of economic development exists in Africa, Egypt, India, Turkey, and Central America.

One of the shortest true channels of distribution (directly from the producer to the consumer) exists in both very primitive and very advanced societies. As a country emerges in its economic development to the subsistence level with some excess, the excess is sold directly to another consumer, probably either in the peasant market or the public market. When a country reaches the highly industrialized level of economic development and the highly developed and integrated level of market development, a number of the larger manufacturing firms bypass the general wholesaler and sell directly to a large consumer.

The channels of distribution that are probably most often thought of as being standard are those typical of the automobile industry, some appliance manufacturers, and producers of many goods purchased at food markets and local department and general stores. These channels of distribution exist in all countries and are indicative of a production-oriented country (or section of a country) where there are small and intermediate-size wholesalers and retailers.

The import and export trade is always important to an expanding and growing company. Various channels of distribution that imports and exports go through are found in Japan, the Netherlands, Israel, Africa, Central America, Finland, Egypt, England, and other places.

Auctions also influence the channel of distribution in such areas as the Netherlands, Africa, and Israel. The auction predominates in the area of agricultural goods. In places like Africa, India, and Central America, the processor is very important, and in India and Africa the producer is protected from the processor through the cooperative.

Geography plays a part in determining channels of distribution. Japan has some unique distribution problems because of the length of its land, its high central hills and mountains, its many small manufacturers and retailers, and its existence as an island.

Government-controlled countries have different and specialized channels for agricultural goods versus manufactured goods. In all cases, they are presently directed and controlled, to a great extent, by the central government.

There are numerous factors that contribute to variations in the channels of distribution in the market structure. Some of these factors are more important than others. However, for purposes of this discussion, no priority will be given to any of the major contributors to channel variations.

Providing that all of the various income factors of a country have been taken into consideration, *per capita GNP* can be one of the most meaningful factors for comparing the economic development of one country to another. It appears that in the larger, more developed countries, production of capital goods and consumer durable goods reach an important level and start contributing considerably to the per capita GNP.

Literacy rate is another contributor to variability of distribution and is related to per capita GNP. Those countries that rate very low on per capita GNP also rate extremely low on the literacy level; the literacy level in these countries runs from 5 percent or less in parts of tropical Africa to a high of 50 percent in the People's Republic of China. Conversely, those countries with higher per capita GNP show literacy levels of 80 percent and above. A low literacy level, of course, makes communications and advertising much more difficult; to convey a message by symbols is more difficult than by words and pictures. The less aware people are of products, the less apt they are to buy them. Even in countries with restrictions on radio and television advertising, illiteracy further blocks or limits such an avenue to advertising, In low-literacy, low-GNP countries, where demand is primarily for necessities or local luxuries, market expansion is slow and channels of distribution relatively stagnant.

The level of *communication* and forms of communication available are always important contributors to the variability of channels of distribution. As mentioned earlier, communication is difficult when people cannot read. For example, in many parts of Africa where the average literacy rate is less than 10 percent, most advertising is done with emphasis on symbols, especially trademarks. Market expansion is made difficult without adequate communications; channels of distribution are slow to press forward where profits are low or nonexistent.

Good *transportation facilities* in the form of roads, railroads, and navigable waterways are important for ease of movement of goods. Where transportation is poor, goods must be stored for further use in warehouses, inventory requirements must be anticipated, stocks of goods must be financed in advance, and goods may circulate mostly in a local market. Without a continuous flow of goods, wholesalers are limited in number and limit their risks by moving goods only short distances or moving only high-profit items. This limits channels of distribution and stifles market expansion. Data show that those countries with poor transportation facilities also rate low on per capita GNP and literacy, and those with good transportation facilities rate high on per capita GNP and literacy.

Another general trend is that the level of market activity through the channels of distribution increases as the number of *people employed in industry* increases. This ties in with earlier statements about per capita GNP improving as industrialization increases within a country. With more people involved in industry, more goods must be moved, purchased, exchanged, and shipped, and channels of distribution change to accommodate these changes efficiently and economically.

Another factor that helps indicate what stage of economic and market development a country is in is the *percentage of income spent on food*. More money is spent on industrial, recreational, and service goods in countries where a smaller percentage is spent on food. This in turn modifies the channels of distribution to accommodate the changing pattern of living.

Geographic considerations, such as climate, land topography, soil fertility, availability and location of water surfaces, and accessibility to mineral and other natural resources, strongly influence the ease or complexity of development of a country. As an example, parts of Africa have vast mineral resources (e.g., gold and diamonds in South Africa and copper in Angola) to help develop the countries, but much of its climate is excessively hot and humid, there are practically no naturally accessible inland river routes, and much of the land is mountainous or overgrown with thick jungle to block passages. Agriculture is poor in many regions, and population density is approximately twenty per square mile. These obstacles, along with cultural and communication problems, have made progress difficult. However, a few large foreign countries have large businesses in different parts of Africa (diamond mining, copper, uranium, etc.). As new areas are developed, the marketing conditions will change, and the channels of distribution will change to accommodate those changes.

Cultural homogeneity or fragmentation is another deterrent to economic and market growth if a country is composed of segmented educational levels, technological levels, age brackets, and cultural religious groups. Africa and India both have groups with vast educational differences, technological skill differences, and strong family and caste or tribal loyalties. These latter groups often keep businesses within the family and find it difficult to work with others. As these barriers break down, the marketing system and channels of distribution change.

Government intervention and support greatly impact distribution. Channels of distribution often change rapidly when governments get deeply involved. In Communist China free-trade channels of distribution were rapidly changed into government-molded channels of an extremely different nature where the Communist government took over. Channels were opened up somewhat in the mid- to late 1980s and were then closed down and heavily controlled by the government again in 1989. In the Soviet

Union, channels of distribution change as the government sees fit. Whenever the government either helps business to grow or takes control of it, the channels of distribution change.

Ready access to cash and credit is generally conducive to business and market expansion, depending on the strings attached to the credit. In parts of Africa, India, and Central America brokers and agents advance money and credit forward and backward but in many instances demand exorbitant fees, thus preventing rapid market expansion and independence. In the U.S.S.R. and China loans can be obtained but under very restrictive conditions from the state bank. Reasonable access to cash and credit helps promote improved economic and market growth. As growth takes place, the channels of distribution change.

As a country's *export and import trade* grows, it starts to specialize and have products in excess of those needed to support its own people. It then resorts to exporting and importing goods. This international market often has marked effects on the domestic marketing system and channels of distribution by encouraging producers to work in a moneyed economy and by whetting the appetite of the people for new and interesting foreign goods.

This list is by no means exhaustive, but it shows some of the more important contributors to distribution channel variations and changes.

Countries go through a definite economic and marketing growth pattern, and certain indicators exist in these countries to show the general trend of this growth. A note of caution is expressed at this point, however, that no single or even few indicators discussed earlier should be used even as a rough guide for determining the general location of a country in the overall spectrum of economic and marketing growth. As a minimum, several key indicators are required for examination prior to judging a country's growth.

Present channels of distribution within the world's marketing system vary from the very short in subsistence-level countries to the extremely complex in emerging and growing countries and back to the relatively short in the mature industrial countries. The complexities of the channels of distribution are part of the growth pattern of an emerging nation probing its way to maturity. Some features in the channels, such as cooperatives and auctions, help safeguard the producer. Other features, such as the agent and the money lender, make possible the existence of the producer and the wholesaler or retailer. The various channels of distribution are sometimes confusing but seem to be a normal evolutionary economic process that a country goes through. Although it is not safe to make too broad a set of generalizations, different sections within any given country or area may deviate considerably from the general level of economic and market development within the area as a whole.

Based on the material presented in this section, the following statements and conclusions can be drawn.

- A definite pattern of economic and marketing development can be noted in growing countries. Carefully chosen indicators can be examined to observe the progress of the country.
- With few exceptions, the growth and development of a country takes place at a relatively slow pace.
- Local government and national government interference can be extremely depressive to the natural expansion of the marketing system.
- Low literacy rates retard market expansion of a country due to difficulties in communication, advertising, breakdown of social barriers through education, and other matters. Progressive education systems with increased literacy can help eliminate many of these areas of market retardation and help overcome other problems such as transportation and geography.
- The growth (or change) pattern of the channels of distribution progresses from a short channel in a newly emerging country, to a complex network during the intermediate stages of growth, and back to shorter channels of distribution as the country reaches maturity. This seems to be the normal evolutionary process of growing countries.
- Most countries have several levels of economic and marketing development going on at the same time. This situation is more likely to exist if the country's literacy rate is low, the communication system is inadequate, the transportation system is poor, and the population is widely dispersed throughout the country.
- Too few countries have adequate facilities for extending low interest rate credit to producers and retailers. The result, in many instances, is exorbitant interest rates and repression by agents and money lenders. This leads to abuse and retards the growth of the country.
- Countries with mature marketing systems and channels of distribution have achieved this status with private and/or public capital and without undue government interference.
- When wholesalers become inefficient in performing the wholesaling function, then the manufacturers often step in and take over (at least temporarily), and the channels of distribution are again changed. It is not too much to expect the wholesale market to move all goods through the market.

COMPANY EVALUATION

Marketing quite often is the initiator of a new product as well as the end distributor of the product. This requires close cooperation and coordination with all other functional areas within the company. Table 6.1 helps evaluate how well marketing performs these tasks in the areas of planning, organizing, directing, and controlling.

Table 6.1
Typical Strengths and Weaknesses in Planning, Organizing, Directing, and Controlling Marketing

	Strengths	Weaknesses
PLANNING	Top management is committed to a strong marketing effort.	No strong commitment exists within the company for a programmed marketing effort.
	Detailed long range, intermediate range, and short range plans and budgets are generated and reviewed for acceptance or rejection on all proposed and in-process marketing projects.	Marketing is performed in a haphazard or on a day-to-day, as-it-happens basis.
	All marketing plans are consistent with company strategy and goals.	Marketing planning is based on whatever needs attention at the moment.
	Marketing creativity, innovation, and leadership are emphasized and encouraged by top management.	The company pays little attnetion to marketing personnel.
	Marketing closely coordinates all projects with engineering, R&D, manufacturing, finance, and MIS.	There is little or no coordination between marketing and other company functional groups.
	All elements of the marketing mix are given due consideration.	Little, if any, consideration is given to marketing mix.
	A balanced approach of money, personnel, and machines is taken.	No provisions are made for a balanced approach to the marketing effort.
	Domestic and multinational operations exist and are coordinated with one another.	No concerted effort is made to become involved in multinational marketing.
ORGANIZING	Marketing reports directly to the president through a vice president.	Marketing reports to a department manager.
	Marketing is organized along product lines.	Marketing is not organized in any clearcut manner.
	Marketing is organized to perform coordinated corporate wide sales administration, customer relations, marketing planning and research, distribution services, and advertising and sales promotions both domestically and multinationally.	Each product area conducts its sales and marketing efforts as it feels is appropriate. There is no coordinated or organized company wide marketing effort.
		No concerted effort is made to quickly respond to new market opportunities.

94

	(Strengths)	(Weaknesses)
	Marketing is able to respond quickly to almost any new marketing situation.	No provisions exist within marketing to attract or hold high caliber personnel.
	Adequate prestige, innovation, and motivation exists within marketing to attract and hold high caliber personnel.	
DIRECTING	Vice president reporting directly to the president heads up marketing.	Department managers direct marketing.
	MIS systems are used to track, coordinate, and direct projects within marketing.	No consistent coordination of projects exists within marketing.
	Excellent coordinated interface exists between marketing and all other company functional areas.	Inadequate interface exists between marketing and other company functional areas.
CONTROLLING	Company performs and directs all of its own marketing.	Company uses numerous loosely coordinated outside agencies for marketing.
	Vice president reporting directly to the president heads up marketing.	Department managers control marketing.
	Marketing efforts and control are coordinated from a central location.	Marketing efforts are conducted at several locations and are independent of one another.
	Adequate funding is available to permit flexibility in marketing programs where and when needed.	Marketing funds are set as a fixed percentage of sales.
	Budgets and schedules exist for each marketing effort.	Inadequate or no budgets or schedules exist to control programs.
	Marketing mix is constantly reviewed and updated to minimize costs and maximize profits.	Little or no attention or concern is placed on marketing mix.
	MIS systems are used to track and coordinate all programs within marketing and with all other departments and divisions both domestically and multinationally.	Marketing programs are not considered.

NOTES

1. Michael E. Porter, *Competitive Strategy* (New York: The Free Press, 1980), pp. 157–162.

2. John A. Pearce II and Richard B. Robinson, Jr., *Strategic Management*, 2d ed. (Homewood, IL: Richard D. Irwin, Inc., 1985), p. 194.

3. George A. Steiner, *Top Management Planning* (New York: Macmillan, 1969), p. 545.

4. Charles W. Hofer, Edwin A. Murray, Jr., Ram Charan, Robert A. Pitts, *Strategic Management* (St. Paul, MN: West Publishing Company, 1980), p. 231.

7

Logistics

World-class organizations today must provide an organizational structure supportive of their integrated logistics goals. Such an integrated system links global sales and procurement information with online assembly planning, inventory management including just-in-time supplier support and other key electronic data processing applications. Electronic data transfer and close technical cooperation is necessary to integrate suppliers with the firm. A key objective of such integration is total cost analysis (TCA) and total quality control (TQC). Both of these concepts require an integrated logistics management approach. Just-in-time manufacturing is a logical blending of quality costs and logistics total costs, which takes place both within each firm and within the set of firms comprising a distribution channel. The channel ideally becomes one entity, thereby minimizing total costs while achieving predetermined customer service objectives.

Effective logistics management is concerned first and foremost with the interface of two distinct flows through the organization: materials and information flows. Flow of materials involves the world of transportation, which is itself in the midst of adapting to tremendous economic changes and to the continuing effects of deregulation. The pressures toward change of management of the dynamics of the new logistics of inbound and outbound movements demand a degree of flexibility and professionalism only dreamed of in the not-too-distant past. By the year 2000 it may be commonplace for the area of logistical systems management to be the brain center of a successful corporation. Work in such centers will be of great strategic importance as operations are interfaced with new national contracts worked out between large carriers and central corporation management. Many, if not the majority, of these interfaces between physical distribution, manufacturing, and purchasing will depend upon sophisticated computer-based materials logistics management programs such as that which is under development at Michigan State University.[1] The most critical variances of such programs are those between customers and manufacturing. For manufacturing, at the interfaces between distribution and purchasing, the concepts of master schedule management, just-in-time scheduling, and flexibility are the key factors. Increased use of computer-based information is required to achieve ever more difficult and complex target objectives.

REMARRIAGE OF LOGISTICS FUNCTIONS

Within the structures of many contemporary organizations, the tendency is to keep employing past procedures that separate functions, such as marketing and purchasing, that could work more effectively if integrated. Segregation of functions within a corporation deprives untold numbers of U.S. firms of opportunities to exploit logistics in a manner which gives meaningful competitive advantage to those with sophisticated management concepts.[2] Where marketing, physical distribution, purchasing, and like functions are managed as separate entities, customer service is often the first area to suffer.

Nowhere in the marketing/service area can advanced computerization, automation, and modern quantitative techniques be used in a more extensive and profitable manner than in physical distribution. Critical decisions in terms of facility location, transportation, and inventory decisions are interdependent with significant tradeoffs between associated costs. Such decisions are not optimized in a nonintegrated environment.

Expanding upon the logic of mating functions under a logistics umbrella, both total cost analysis (TCA) and total quality control (TQC) require such integration of functions. Many logistics system decisions have a significant impact on the quality of the offered product. At the same time, decisions that are made in the marketing channel to ensure and preserve quality can and will impact logistics costs.[3] Such quality costs may be classified into three areas—prevention, appraisal, and failure expenses—from both internal and external sources.

Just-in-time (JIT) systems are based on a consumer-oriented philosophy that includes a natural merger of quality costs and logistical total costs. Optimal customer service is a critical payoff from enlightened system planning and flows from a study of the tradeoffs among customer service and the other channels of the physical distribution logistics system.

Just-in-time: The Objective and Reality

The focus upon just-in-time manufacturing is producing an imbalance in the ubiquitous debates about how to get materials to and work in process through the manufacturing facilities linked with the distribution channel. Basically, JIT is a statement of objectives. It highlights the vital importance of lead-time management in all aspects of the manufacturing process. Incremental reductions in lead times are viewed as indices of manufacturing improvement. To achieve such reductions, a JIT system should deliver to every operator in any conversion process whatever he or she needs just when it is needed. Money that would otherwise be tied up in inventory is saved. The costly sectors of materials storage and handling, work-in-process inventory, and buffer stock are significantly reduced or eliminated. Although the objectives of JIT are quite simple, the methods of attaining them with optimal effectiveness are more open to discussion and conflict.

JIT is a tool intended to manage lead times and eliminate waste. For decades the flaws in planning for materials requirements have forced manufacturers to tie up cash in more stock than needed and then face the frustration of salvaging outdated material for a fraction of listed value following discovery in a full annual inventory. In the early 1970s materials requirements planning (MRP) attempted to bring order to chaos through a fairly mechanistic system that views the entire manufacturing operation as discrete parts making up the whole. Demand is then projected, as well as the time and materials needed to meet such requirements.[4] A critical part of any MRP system is that lead times to manufacture a part, component, or assembled product must be determined and entered into the formula. MRP orders only the parts actually going into the items to be sold, not an economic order quantity. Calculations in MRP are directly related to end items to be shipped. It proceeds step by step through the bills of materials, releasing orders for parts and assemblies, according to a previously determined quantity and time. This planned process then repeats for each level of parts as they go into each component or assembled product. Acceptance of MRP in various manufacturing sectors has been significant, especially in areas requiring complex bills of materials, significant numbers of open orders, and high level needs for materials control among key members of the manufacturing/distribution channel. In reaction to the heavy demands of MRP systems for computer data and software support, management information system (MIS) departments have become heavily involved in the processes of manufacturing management. As would be expected, this level of data support is costly and becomes a heavy burden for smaller firms and productive systems. A key part of this cost burden is the expense of personnel training. A significant amount of time is required to indoctrinate hourly workers who often are not that familiar or eager to deal with the precise requirements of data input.

As MRP systems become established, the process of change and its intended benefits become institutionalized, orthodox, and highly resistant to change. The introduction of new methods to the manufacturing process may serve as a threat to a number of consultants, material control managers, vendors, and MIS personnel. Of the key elements in an MRP system, the inflexibility of lead times is, perhaps, the most fallible factor. In concept, a single lead-time number must serve the MRP system for all situations faced on the floor. To discharge this objective, the lead-time must be sufficiently high to cover all contingencies, including the worst case. If, even if the face of this procedure, an order arrives late, there is pressure to increase lead time as inserted into the system and, thus, insure that such delay does not occur again. With such focus on avoidance of delay, the incentive to reduce lead time and to complete work in less time on MRP's fixed standard is slim to none.

As with many manufacturing systems intended to enhance efficiency and productivity, bureaucracy enters the picture. Procedures become complex and centralized. Flexibility is reduced. As was found in the early movement for automation in warehousing, the tradeoffs between efficiency and flexibility must be seriously considered. Large open floors, easily moved and reconfigured storage bins, and numerous fork lifts are still the "weapons of choice" for many of the newest warehouse and redistribution system designers.

Kanban to the Rescue

The *kanban* method of posting circulating work orders is a JIT technique that overcomes the basic deficiencies of MRP.[5] The ability of *kanban* to communicate factors, such as current work commitments of a manufacturing cell, in an immediate and noncomplex manner can be a significant advantage. Information advantages of *kanban* provide an opportunity to consolidate batches and save on setups through advanced planning. The inevitable mix of changes and demand surges that require personnel changes or reassignments are easier to determine.

Kanban systems are subject to problems when faced with complex operations where variations are too large or too ingrained to be corrected with ease. Suppliers are most often faced with intransigent large users who are not at all hesitant to come down forcibly upon undisciplined actions by the supplier.

Effective *kanban* methods thrive under uniform flow conditions. *Kanban* is not, however, a solid system for planning, especially when it is implemented in an environment faced with significant variations in supply and demand. In such cases *kanban* is less effective than work-in-process methods when the object is operation without stockouts and when there is a heavy burden of work in process. Under such conditions extra containers or buffers must be introduced to cover variations and avoid back orders.

There is no magic formula in *kanban* systems, which reduce inventory levels in reaction to an internal rule or formula. The key variable in *kanban* is reaction. Changes in demand levels percolate slowly from each state of operations. When faced with a nearly 100 percent certainty of rising demand, there is no standard method to prepare for this change. Comments from U.S. assemblers working with Japanese suppliers using pull systems have noted that a three- to six-month reaction time is necessary to adjust to steep demand changes.[6] *Kanban* as a classic pull system can work well in the JIT environment that is not too demanding. It is a chain system that reacts to output changes in relationship to the capabilities of its weakest link.

JIT and the Complex Environment

Integration of logistics planning and JIT systems remains one of the most viable cost savings areas of production planning. Inventory positions related to materials coordination, materials planning, and procurement are best managed by MRP systems. Such systems, as discussed earlier, require an investment in data systems and MIS management that burden smaller producers. *Kanban* systems work well and are cost effective in terms of operation production processes with a steady demand, such as injection molding.

One solution to the problem of finding possible systems to meet the JIT objective is the selection of the best of both worlds, resulting in integrated hybrid systems. There are no commandments precluding the use of less expensive, noncomputerized pull methods where materials planning and coordination is not an issue. The problem in building a hybrid system is planning. Analysis of both the production process and the logistics system necessary for its support reveals interesting variations and applicable concepts. Starting with continuous-flow processes where materials planning on an ongoing basis is not required, JIT systems with *kanban*-type pull techniques work well. In more repetitive production environments with relatively stable yet varying schedules, combination systems integrating MRP calculations provide the push while pull methods still are effective on the shop floor.

Pull techniques cannot cope with the high-level demand and lead-time variability of variable systems necessary in job shop manufacturing. In the complex environment, JIT must encounter the problem of exceedingly complex materials flow. Scheduling sophistication and tracking systems can be enhanced to a position where JIT is maintained—at a cost. If the cost of reasonably sophisticated push methods is deemed too high, then consider the cost of excessive inventories and poor time performance. Effective integrated systems take time. *Kanban*, like many JIT techniques, has evolved over the years. JIT is an objective that may be obtained through a variety of methods. Integration of logistics-based and production-based concepts is one viable method. As sophistication in the use and collection of production data evolves, including bar coding and "smart cards," more input from those sources may be examined on the factory floors.

Evaluation of Supplier Quality

Availability of supplies in the JIT environment assumes a near perfect level of quality in arriving parts. JIT does not provide for 10 percent rejection. Buyers who must certify that suppliers are meeting JIT quality then need sensitive financial information to negotiate the price of these parts. Complete cost breakdowns on labor rates, material costs, selling and administrative expenses, and profit levels are needed and are not easily obtained. Here, as in many sectors, the logistics practitioner must enhance technical skills with significant sophistication in human resource management knowledge.

If procurement personnel are to attain confidential supplier information, there is a need for trust. To gain such trust, the buyer must essentially become an outside partner in the supplier's business. Factors such as lowered costs, product improvements, and, most critical, quality enhancement are priority objectives. This, of course, is far more demanding than simply searching for an alternate source of supply. An example of such commitment, in this case General Motors, begins when a potential supplier fills out a self-assessment form on the subjects of operating philosophy, business systems, research and development, and overhead costs. A team of three to four GM people visit the supplier's facilities for several days to focus upon the issues of: (1) organizational effectiveness and commitment; (2) planning systems and documentation; (3) cost awareness, monitoring, and reduction; (4) scheduling and delivery compliance; and (5) technology capabilities and R&D.[7] A conflict of interest between buyer and supplier arises when quality problems crop up. Manufacturing at this time may pressure a buyer to negotiate with a new supplier or apply a heavy hand to the current one. Since buyers carry a great deal of the responsibility for project relations, they need information and support from various echelons of GM management. How GM is perceived by suppliers in such crisis situations is critical to this factor of trust.

With U.S. manufacturing spending, on the average, 56 cents of each sales dollar on purchased production materials and with JIT assembly operations requiring perfect quality, supplier channels are under heavy stress in areas of both price and quality.[8] While these two factors represent a heavy load of objectives for both buyer and supplier, they are only a part of today's complex picture. Because markets are increasingly fragmented, manufacturing must be able to react to pressures for new product programs designed and delivered in minimum time. Time pressures call for suggestions in component design from suppliers of these parts. Thus, a partnership originally conceived as providing a desired component with design furnished by the manufacturer may now become a high pressure development program with design support provided mainly by the supplier. Now the issue of trust originally faced in the relationship has moved to a relationship of more complex dimensions. Moving toward such a partnership while keeping necessary control of price and quality is demanding of skills that for many in both logistics and manufacturing have not been well prepared. Not only must new skills be learned, but old patterns of behavior must be questioned.

In the world of expensive analysis of supplier capabilities and potential, where do old patterns of competitive award of contracts to multiple suppliers, for the safety of the manufacturer, stand the test of logic? The answer is that they no longer serve their intended purpose. Logic states that where capacity is adequate, manufacturers are better served by single-source suppliers. Marks and Spencer, the British department store chain noted for its quality, has maintained the single-source strategy for almost 100 years. At times this has resulted in stockouts and rare quality problems, but overall it has resulted in superb quality products at low prices to customers while still providing adequate profits for both the stores and suppliers. Commitment to producers who feel themselves part of the parent organization is a great insurance of constant quality, especially when information and support from the buying organization is continuously available. For high volume production such as automobiles or large home appliances, even a 1 percent defect rate will result in 10,000 defective parts per million delivers. In JIT systems there are no inventories of purchased goods awaiting inspection, in fact, there should be no inventories awaiting manufacture anywhere. Such systems objectively require defect levels of 100 or less per million—essentially zero defects. With such objectives, lowest bid cost seldom, if ever, meets objectives. Lowest overall cost, quality, and design considered is needed. Where deliveries are being made every two hours or less, multiple sources of supply create scheduling and integration problems that would not be effective either in cost or efficiency.

Price: What Is Fair?

As more suppliers enter into long-term single-source contracts for products, which they have in many cases designed, price negotiation enters new ground. The "level playing field" objective for price and production run has significantly changed. Can an arm's length negotiation take place with newly accepted partners? The answers for both parties are to a degree ambivalent. The presumption is that pressure is off suppliers to shave margins in order to close a contract. Even an acceptable initial contract does not preclude pressure within a few weeks to investigate establishment of production facilities in, say, Mexico to insure the lowest possible price and continued association. Since few items of such overall impact are kept confidential, it is not long before rumors may abound that pressure is on to move 50 to 60 percent of production out of the United States. For one client supplying a big three auto manufacturer, this exact scenario was a key factor in the loss of a UAW election. Unionization cost this firm flexibility, which was originally a key factor in their agreed-upon production price. In firms supplying big three and Japanese auto firms, while initial price negotiation reflects concern for a fair return, subsequent events reveal continued price pressure, especially from the U.S. firms. Unfortunately, large customers tend to be insensitive to the need for a supplier to make a fair return on investment. This position is amplified through incentives placed upon buyers to negotiate prices advantageous to the manufacturer.

One of the more difficult price issues involves long-run considerations such as investment in R&D, training, and equipment. If the supplier is forced by tightly negotiated prices to forego the investments in research, staff, and facilities that make it competitive and attractive in the first place, the manufacturer will in the end lose a key component in its total system. Cooperative partnerships need to consider the long-term consequences of their actions. Almost without exception all large firms espouse a recognition of the need for capable long-term suppliers. General Electric, Boeing, and Ford have strong recognition programs honoring top suppliers. It is in the dilution of these overall objectives, especially at lower staff levels, where insensitive actions occur. Focused monetary objectives assigned to divisions seldom provide for the long-term necessities of suppliers. Only enlightened understanding of buyers, who are often not in a position of great power, can serve the needs of suppliers. Upper-level management needs to understand these conflicts, avoid beating suppliers into submission, and avoid taking action detrimental to their organizational stability. Honda and other Japanese manufacturers have invested extensively in their supplier firms on both a monetary and managerial level, resulting in, essentially, a vertically integrated organization with an extended and deadly objective in terms of future market share. The thoughtful, enlightened management of suppliers is a necessity to remain competitively viable in today's market and to survive into the future.

COMPANY EVALUATION

Logistical planning concepts have truly come of age within the past decade. Such concepts were perfected by the military in the latter stages of World War II and embraced years ago by the Japanese especially in the areas of packaging and JIT delivery. American firms are still reacting with mixed signals to the application of these highly efficient methods of production, marketing, and distribution interface. Table 7.1 provides a guide to evaluation of this most important area.

NOTES

1. Bowerson, Carter, and Monczka, "Materials Logistics Management," *International Journal of Physical Distribution and Materials Management* II, no. 3 (1985): 27–35.

2. Richard Watson and Leyland Pitt, "Remarrying Marketing and Logistics with Information Systems Technology," *Industrial Management and Data Systems*, no. 1 (1989): 4–11.

3. James M. Kenderdrive and Paul D. Larson, "Quality and Logistics: A Framework for Strategic Integration," *International Journal of Physical Distribution and Materials Management* 18, no. 6 (1988): 5–10.

4. Jeffrey G. Miller and Linda G. Sprague, "Behind the Growth in Materials Requirements Planning," *Harvard Business Review* 53, no. 5 (September–October 1975): 83.

5. Vday Karmarkar, "Getting Control of Just-in-Time," *Harvard Business Review* 67, no. 5 (September–October 1989): 126.

6. Ibid., p. 127.

7. Marybeth Pallas, "GM's Evaluation Procedure," *Harvard Business Review* 67, no. 4 (July–August 1989): 130.

8. David N. Burt, "Managing Suppliers Up to Speed," *Harvard Business Review* 67, no. 4 (July–August 1989): 127.

Table 7.1
Typical Strengths and Weaknesses in Planning, Organizing, Directing, and Controlling Logistics

	Strengths	Weaknesses
PLANNING	Top management is committed to a strong, well-integrated logistics system -- in all aspects.	Inability to properly evaluate the strengths and weaknesses of various choices in systems available for production, distribution, inventory management, and integration.
	Detailed plans for effective interface of material and information flows according to a solidly maintained master schedule in place.	Lack of necessary levels of sophistication in the scheduling and tracking of selected systems.
	Upstream quality control is part of all planning activity.	Inability to equate the costs of sophisticated push methods of materials flow against the cost of excessive inventories or poor time performance.
	Integrated planning for facility locations and inventory levels/locations as needed for production and customer service is a priority.	Acceptance of planning levels for quality standards which were competitively unacceptable, i.e., failure to set near zero defect levels as the target figure.
	JIT delivery is viewed as a planning objective both internally and externally. Internal JIT is used as a tool to limit work-in-process inventories and buffer stocks and externally as a key competitive tool for gaining customer orders.	Failure to integrate logistics planning in its overall conceptual aspect with JIT systems--thus failing to realize some of the most viable cost savings in production planning.
	MRP, MRPII, and *kanban* systems are utilized where appropriate in the planning process. Key factors of needed degrees of flexibility, data support, complexity, and reaction time are factored into utilization decisions.	Failure to properly evaluate supplier quality. Along with this weakness is the loss of opportunity to work with potentially good suppliers who lack or are weak in easily correctable areas.
		Ambivalence or lack of thoughtful planning in the area of single-source, multiple-source suppliers. Such a lack of position has lead to excessive dependence upon multiple-source suppliers and failure to realize the benefits often realized from single-source strategies.
ORGANIZING	Distribution channels are designed for solid support of materials flow and handling while data systems are fully capable of reacting to the heavy demands of MRP and MRPII systems for computer data and software support.	The director of logistics systems reports to the V.P. of production. Conflicts between marketing and production are thus felt by not only the senior managers in logistics but well down the scalar levels into middle management.

Organized under a general staff level vice president, logistical systems reports directly to the executive vice president of the organization. Authority for the expenditure of operational funds and the hiring of personnel is fully in line with system responsibilities.

Staff support for logistical activities is preauthorized in a manner which encourages the minimum amount of delay in response to requests for service.

The subsystem environments are structured for maximum effectiveness in terms of their specific needs and operating goals, but the overall objective of effective interface is maintained.

Within the key structural areas of this organization, decisions relating to organization and location are made more to meet the needs and desires of specific functions such as distribution, manufacturing, sales, and inventory than customer service in the most rapid and economical manner.

Internal and external factors such as information processing, mechanistic, and organic organization variables are not reflected in the design of key functions. Evidence points to limited consideration of these broad issues in both design and practice.

Functional control rather than optimal interface constantly appears to have been a basic factor in design considerations.

Slow decision making results from design factors which give functional interests priority over system considerations. One basic cause of this problem is a design which allows excessive numbers of individual, autonomous units which should be grouped together under one authority.

DIRECTING

All senior executives, from the chief executive officer through operational vice presidents, agree upon the basic goals and objectives. The objective of logistical interface for maximum customer service is a key and critical part of these goals.

Reward systems encourage group interface objectives and discourage actions which benefit a subgroup to the detriment of the overall organization.

It is made clear that service and high office in areas of logistical operations is a direct route to senior positions within the organization.

Qualitative as well as quantitative measures of performance are used in the evaluation of personnel. Performance which meets these objectives is rewarded both in verbal and in monetary/position terms.

Team effectiveness and intergroup dynamics is effectively encouraged by senior executives. Positive actions in these important areas are

The most critical weakness in attaining strong interface relationships and operations exists in terms of the failure of senior management to communicate their objectives and desires in this area. Lacking strong direction, subordinates have become provincial and protective of their own areas of interest to the detriment of the overall organization.

A reward system which is basically quantitative in design and short-term in application further supports the above weakness in terms of communication. Actions contrary to logistical system objectives and, in fact, quite destructive are repeatedly rewarded under the poorly conceived guidelines.

Inadequate interface, even contrary to policy, is not identified and rectified in a prompt and effective manner.

Promotions appear to be the result of individual actions in the traditional marketing, production, and finance functional areas. Group interactions and system

Table 7.1 (Continued)

	Strengths	Weaknesses
	recognized and rewarded.	accomplishments are not recognized on a regular basis, allowing the perception that this is the quick and proper avenue to organizational esteem.
		Team building activities are not encouraged by upper management on a regular basis. Of great impact is the rare mention or reward of important group activity of overall benefit to the organization.
CONTROLLING	Controlling is viewed as secondary to motivation. Senior management takes care to fully consider logistical system objectives in the design and application of performance appraisals, compensation and benefit packages, and employee discipline systems.	Control is considered one of the most important management functions. Deviation from standards and policy is unacceptable and will not be condoned. Failure is to be punished.
	Financial and operational objectives are framed in medium and long-term numbers as well as short-term figures where necessary.	Standards, policy, and objectives are not well communicated, leaving many managers little option than to expand standards beyond those which would appear to be adequate to avoid condemnation themselves.
	The budgeting process recognizes the need to encourage as well as to restrict activity when necessary. Care is taken to reduce the number and volume of reports and data forwarded on a recurring basis.	Fear has replaced creativity as a primary motive of organization members. Excessive time for coordination of excessive and unnecessary inventories is common.
	Restrictions upon the expenditure of resources, especially money and time, are made as flexible as possible in line with the priority and difficulty of objectives.	The pressure to control cost has cost the organization in terms of customer service and goodwill. Proper warranty actions are delayed while approval for expenditures is obtained.
	Feedback is considered a key part of the control process. Employees are informed that failure is only unacceptable when no learning takes place as a result. A key and critical adjutant to learning is the communication of the reasons for failure.	Management by exception systems is difficult to frame and program due to the excessive number of areas of concern. Ability to prioritize and eliminate secondary areas reduces the ability to identify and concentrate upon critical areas.
		Budgets are restricted to less than necessary in most requests. The assumption is made that truly important items will be resubmitted with better justification. This is done, but with delay and cost penalties.

8

Finance/Accounting

The objective of the financial area of a company is to determine and choose the sources of funds and the allocation of these funds as efficiently as possible within the constraints of the strategic objectives of the company.

Both financial and accounting strategies are discussed in this chapter; therefore, a brief comment must be made on how their basic objectives differ. Accounting strategy emphasizes how to handle the company resources to maximize the return to the firm in the short run. In short, it emphasizes short-run return on investment and short-run profit maximization. This can be accomplished, to the long-term detriment to the company, through such tactics as holding off purchase of new equipment; purchasing inexpensive, low-quality equipment; performing maintenance only when needed; delaying payment of bills as long as possible; pushing customers to pay their bills early; eliminating fringe benefits to employees; cutting back on R&D; and numerous other money-saving tactics. If only this approach is taken, the company may show excellent returns in the short run but be heading for long-run disaster. Accounting strategies also tend to focus on returns devoid of risk assessment.

Finance strategies, on the other hand, take into consideration risk and the time value of money. The higher the anticipated risk, the higher the expected return. Early year returns have a higher percent value than those in later years. An additional responsibility of the finance operation is to monitor the firm's performance to make certain that it is consistent with the array of short-term and long-term company objectives.

Both short-run and long-run monetary operations are of primary importance and concern to the company. The remainder of this chapter, therefore, examines and briefly discusses some of the methods employed in financial decision making, monitoring, and control.

CAPITAL EXPENDITURE PLANNING, EVALUATION, AND CONTROL TOOLS AND PROCEDURES

Effective management of capital expenditures consists of two basic requirements. The first is an administrative program that supplies management with timely, efficient, and comprehensive information on various investment opportunities. The second is a combination of reliable tools and techniques that management can use for analyzing and evaluating the merits of various individual investment opportunities and ranking them in order of priority.

Capital expenditures are usually spread over a period of time and placed in one of two categories. *Capitalized* expenditures normally have their costs charged against a later time as the operation with which they are associated produces income against which the cost can be charged. Physical plants and operating equipment fall into this category. *Expensed* expenditures are normally charged as a current operating cost; such things as advertising, training, and daily expendable supplies are items that fall into this category.

Some of the tools and techniques for planning, evaluating, and controlling capital expenditures are the payback method, return on investment, time-adjusted rates of return, and risk analysis.

Payout or Payback Method

The payout or payback method simply measures the period of time it takes for income from the investment (before depreciation but after taxes) to be equal to the cost of the investment. The shorter the time period for payback, the more favorable the project. Although it has simplicity in its favor, the payback method has a major shortcoming in that it does not take into consideration the total profitability of the project when the equipment has a usable life expectancy in excess of the payback period. In spite of this shortcoming, this method is often used because it is conservative and emphasizes liquidity.

Return on Investment

Return on investment (ROI) derives the percentage yield of anticipated income from the money outlay on the investment. There are many different ways of calculating ROI, and many companies use it as a way to ask many key questions about the details of the calculations. It has an advantage over the payback technique in that it does take into account the income receipt over the entire life of the project. It is also a good measure of the efficiency of capital usage. It provides a standard against which decisions can be made and performance measured. It focuses on profits, and it can help control operations. This method takes the emphasis off of sales growth and sales volume and can be used as a goal for planning purposes. Finally, ROI can clarify the responsibility of decentralized management.

ROI also has many disadvantages, however. The procedure must be carefully evaluated to make certain that all factors entering into the final decision are properly weighted and evaluated. It usually does not take into consideration the time value of money. It is but one measure of many alternative investment techniques and may by itself produce incorrect decisions. Also, ROI places heavy emphasis on capital resources in measuring management performance.

Time-adjusted Rates of Return

When annual inflation rates were in the 1 to 3 percent region and interest rates were in the 3 to 5 percent region, many companies did not seriously consider the time value of money in their calculations of capital equipment. Today there are very few companies that do *not* consider it. There are two basic methods used in considering the value of income flow over time in relation to cost: the discounted cash flow technique and the present worth technique. In the discounted cash flow technique, a rate of return is selected that discounts the cash inflows so that they exactly equal the cost of the project; this rate of discount must be determined by trial and error. The present worth technique calculates the present worth of the future income stream from the investment; since money is worth more today than in the future, higher rates of discount will favor investments that give high early time returns.

The present worth method has an advantage over the discounted cash flow technique in that it reflects changes in the firms cost of capital. However, it also assumes that the discounting rate and the reinvestment rate are equal; this is not usually true in actual practice. Some people have difficulty understanding the discounted cash flow method and feel that its computations are often time consuming and can be misleading or misunderstood. Even though the two procedures differ in technique, they yield similar results.

Time-adjusted rate of return methods yield more precise capital expenditure evaluation results but are still shunned by some companies in preference of simpler methods. For instance, the simple payback method or ROI calculations, both with high liquidity preference, yield more acceptable results to many managers, with much simpler calculations.

Risk Analysis

Even though risk (or some level of uncertainty) exists with all the previous forms of calculations, they are in most cases treated as if the results are certain. They do not take into consideration probabilities concerning many aspects of the decision. For example, if two alternative discounted cash flow returns on investment proposals show that one will yield 15 percent and the other will yield 30 percent, the 30 percent one will be chosen—assuming all other things are equal. But what happens if all other things are not equal, which is the case in most situations? Assume for a moment that the 30 percent yield case has a 40 percent chance of achieving the 30 percent yield but also has a 10 percent chance that it could lose money; on the other hand, assume that the 15 percent yield case has no chance of losing money and an 80 percent chance of achieving the 15 percent. Under such conditions, high risk takers might still go with the 30 percent yield cases, and conservative investors would almost certainly go with the higher probability 15 percent yield case.

BUDGETS

Budgets are quantitative and financial in nature and serve as a pattern for and a control over future operations, as well as presenting a systematic plan for using labor, materials, and other resources.

Budgets may be long term or short term in nature. Regardless of the time period covered, they require managers to divert their attention to quantitatively formulate corporate objectives and goals; they coordinate operations; they provide a means, by establishing standards against which performance can be measured, whereby managers can discharge their responsibilities in controlling their performance; and they integrate the various functional elements in the development of plans and the execution of the plans.

Although many types of budgets exist, they can be classified into three major types: fixed budgets, variable budgets, and zero-based budgets. Fixed or static budgets are basically firm and remain that way for a specified period of time. Flexible budgets can be adjusted over time to accommodate relevant changes in the internal and/or external environment. Zero-based budgets require that each manager rejustify everything in the budget at the beginning of each year rather than letting the budget continuously run from year to year. In competing for limited financial resources, this places new programs and older programs on an equal footing at the beginning of each budget year.

For budgets to be effective, they must be made, reviewed, and supported at all levels of management in a superior-subordinate face-to-face relationship. This supplies a mix of helpful guidance from the top down and a development and execution of plans and budgets from the working level up.

MANAGEMENT CONTROL CENTERS

The basic concept around which management control centers are structured is *responsibility accounting*. The manager of each functional area within a company and the leader of each division of a multidivisional corporation have financial responsibility for their portions of the total operation. There are a number of different types of financially controlled management control centers designed to yield a measurement of how well each of these financially responsible entities are doing. A few of the better known ones include profit centers, cost centers, revenue centers, investment centers, and discretionary expense centers. Each type of center is designed with a specific objective in mind and has its own advantages and disadvantages.

Profit Centers

Although there are many types of profit centers, they all operate in a capacity similar to a minicompany within a larger company. The basic objective is to operate in a manner that brings together the right combination of costs and revenues that will result in the largest possible amount of bottom-line profit.

An advantage of profit centers is that they promote competition between the various company managers to do their best individually for the company. It also educates the managers to a greater understanding of what generating profit is all about.

On the disadvantage side is the aspect that the individual managers can become overzealous in promoting profits within their own departments or divisions at the expense of other departments or divisions and the company as an integrated whole. The company as a whole must be concerned about the total profit picture, whereas the profit center usually concerns itself only with profit in its prime area of concern. It may also have a tendency to isolate each department or division from other areas of the company, and those areas may not be aware of, or may ignore, certain problem areas elsewhere in the company.

The primary solution to developing fully aware, smoothly operating profit centers is through centralized control and decentralized responsibility.

Cost Centers

Cost centers emphasize responsibility accounting by keeping the overall costs as low as possible. The objective in this case is to maximize revenues by keeping the actual cost as low as possible by comparing the actual cost of production to the standard cost of production and keeping the variation between the two as small as possible.

There are several advantages to this concept. Since standard costs of time, labor, material, and so on are fairly well known, it is relatively easy to bid on new products. In most cases the end product costs are fairly closely known at all times and under all conditions. Also, there is an established goal cost to meet or preferably beat. Finally, if manufacturing cost or sales price corrections become necessary they are fairly quickly known and incorporated.

One of the major concerns of this concept is that if it is not handled properly, costs can be reduced by reducing product quality, which in turn can eventually result in reduced sales. A possible solution to this potential problem is constant surveillance to make certain reduced quality or other means are not being employed to reduce costs at the expense of sales and profits. Limited centralized control can also assist in this situation.

Revenue Centers

Revenue centers try to create as much revenue as possible while spending no more than budgeted expense amounts. Innovative means are used to create increased sales and increased profits.

A major disadvantage of this concept is the possibility that sales increases may be created while slighting or ignoring the resultant impact on costs and profits. This problem can be best handled through strong central controls.

Investment Centers

Investment centers usually maximize short term ROI on a year-to-year basis. Most ROI approaches consider the major factors of labor, material, capital, and so on. The major advantages of this approach are that it is a relatively simple concept for rating a department or division on several important factors such as investment and return on labor, material, capital equipment, and so on, and if an adept manager repeatedly produces high ROI he or she can rise rapidly in the organization.

There are also several disadvantages of the ROI concept used by investment centers. ROI measures only a single criteria, and it is usually based on short-run results and can hurt the company in the long run. It can also hurt a new manager if the previous manager had abused the concept to his or her advantage. There are several methods for calculating ROI, and depending on which method is used it can help or hurt the company. Recommended solutions to these disadvantages include requiring each manager to submit short- and long-range impact reports and carefully watching the level of ROI. If the level of ROI gets too high (over 20 percent after taxes is a rule of thumb some companies use), one should be suspicious and examine how it is being accomplished. It is possible that the high ROI is being accomplished by using concepts, means, methods, and practices that are detrimental to the company. For example, holding off purchase of new equipment might help improve short-term ROI but hurt long-term ROI and future company prospects.

Discretionary Expense Centers

Discretionary expense centers work on the basis of providing the best possible service within a given budgeted amount. This form of center is applicable to service and administration types of departments. The main advantage of this type of center is that it has a budget of a known amount and is given a fair amount of discretion in providing the best service within the budget.

Some of the disadvantages of the discretionary expense center approach are that the budget amount is fairly established for a given period of time; the budgeted amount may not be adequate to perform the desired or even realistic levels of service in a timely fashion; and it is difficult to hold a manager fully accountable for the results. Close monitoring is the best way to control this type of budget.

FINANCIAL RATIO ANALYSIS

Financial ratio analysis is another tool used by today's businesses to enable management not only to evaluate the company's progress from one period to another but also to compare its status and progress with other firms in the same or similar industries. There are many types of financial ratios, which can be divided into five major categories: (1) liquidity ratios; (2) debt management ratios; (3) asset management ratios; (4) profitability ratios; and (5) other ratios.

Liquidity Ratios

Liquidity refers to the ease with which an asset can be converted into cash. This is very important for a creditor to know, particularly if a company with which it is doing business is on "shaky ground" or should become bankrupt. Two ratios—the current ratio and the quick ratio—help show the liquidity level or change in liquidity of a company.

Current Ratio. The current ratio is a direct measure of the company's liquidity and is equal to the current assets divided by the current liabilities. Current liabilities are those liabilities normally liquidated as a part of the company's regular business activity. Current assets are those assets that will or can be readily converted into cash in the near future.

Upon calculation of the current ratio, one is able to see whether or not, under conditions of liquidation, a company is able to cover each dollar owed in current liabilities with better than a dollar's worth of current assets (usually a two-to-one ratio is desirable). Comparison of a given company's current ratio with the industry average can also be made. Changes in current ratio from period to period can also be observed.

$$\text{Current ratio} = \frac{\text{Current assets}}{\text{Current liabilities}}$$

Quick Ratio. Closely related to the current ratio is the quick ratio. This ratio shows the relationship between immediately available cash flows and immediate demands against these cash flows. It measures the firm's ability to meet short-term obligations from its most liquid assets. A quick ratio in excess of 1.0 means that the company has enough cash and liquid assets to pay off its obligations on a short-term basis. The quick ratio is equal to the current assets minus inventories, divided by the total current liabilities.

$$\text{Quick ratio} = \frac{\text{Current assets} - \text{inventory}}{\text{Current liabilities}}$$

Debt Management Ratios

Debt management ratios (sometimes referred to as financial leverage ratios) present information pertaining to the company's use of funds supplied by creditors. Financial leverage ratios help determine the amount of debt a firm is employing relative to equity, a firm's ability to raise debt, and the ability of a firm to pay debt when due. Six ratios falling into this category include the debt to assets ratio, the capitalization ratio, the debt to equity ratio, the times interest earned ratio, the fixed charge coverage ratio, and the burden coverage ratio.

Total Debt to Total Assets Ratio. This ratio is sometimes referred to as the debt to assets ratio or simply the debt ratio. The company's total debt is the sum of all current liabilities plus the long-term debt (that portion of the total debt that will not be paid in the current year). The debt ratio is equal to the total debt divided by total assets.

$$\text{Debt ratio} = \frac{\text{Total debt}}{\text{Total assets}}$$

Capitalization Ratio. This ratio shows the impact of the acquisition of new property and equipment and is equal to the long-term debt divided by long-term debt plus property and equipment.

$$\text{Capitalization ratio} = \frac{\text{Long-term debt}}{\text{Long-term debt} + \text{property and equipment}}$$

Debt to Equity Ratio. When the debt to equity ratio is high, the obligation of paying high interest charges may place a strain on the company's cash position. If this ratio gets too high (over 100 percent), then concern for company solvency may set in. This ratio is calculated by dividing the company's total debt by the stockholders' equity.

$$\text{Debt to equity ratio} = \frac{\text{Total debt}}{\text{Stockholders' equity}}$$

Another version of the debt to equity ratio is the long-term debt to equity ratio. A ratio of one-third long-term debt to equity is generally considered acceptable for a typical firm. This ratio is expressed as long-term debt divided by equity.

$$\text{Long-term debt to equity ratio} = \frac{\text{Long-term debt}}{\text{Stockholders' equity}}$$

Times Interest Earned Ratio. All companies pay interest on the long-term debt they carry. If short-term borrowing occurs, it is most probably shown in the accounting data as "notes payable" and is carried as a current liability. No matter how it is labelled or carried on the books, interest payments are legal obligations of the company and must be paid. The ability to pay this interest obligation is important to company solvency, and the times interest earned ratio shows directly how many times gross earnings will cover the company's interest charges. It is calculated by dividing earnings before interest and taxes (EBIT) by interest charges.

$$\text{Times interest earned ratio} = \frac{\text{Earnings before interest and taxes (EBIT)}}{\text{Interest charges}}$$

Fixed Charge Coverage Ratio. There are often other fixed charges in addition to interest that a company is legally bound to pay. These may include such payments as leases or rent. A measure of a company's ability to pay these obligations is completed by using the fixed charge coverage ratio. This ratio can be expressed mathematically as:

$$\text{Fixed charge coverage ratio} = \frac{\text{EBIT} + \text{rents and leases}}{\text{Interest} + \text{rents and leases}}$$

Burden Coverage Ratio. The burden coverage ratio helps determine a firm's ability to meet interest and principal payments. A low burden coverage ratio indicates that a large portion of the earnings have to be used to pay debt service. It can be expressed mathematically as:

$$\text{Burden coverage ratio} = \frac{\text{EBIT}}{\text{Interest} + \dfrac{\text{Principal payments}}{1 - \text{Tax rate}}}$$

Asset Management Ratios

Asset management ratios (sometimes called efficiency ratios) show the company's effectiveness and efficiency in handling its assets. A company's assets should be neither too high nor too low for maximum performance of the firm. Inadequate assets may result in decreased or missed sales opportunities, while excess assets normally decrease the return on total assets. Several ratios are helpful in analyzing and evaluating this delicate balancing act.

Inventory Turnover. This inventory turnover calculation helps determine how well inventory is handled and managed. Slow inventory turnover can result in high inventory storage and carrying costs. This ratio is expressed as the number of times inventory is turned over during the year and is determined by dividing sales by inventories.

$$\text{Inventory turnover} = \frac{\text{Sales}}{\text{Inventories}}$$

Average Collection Period (ACP). The ACP shows how well the company handles and collects its accounts receivable. It shows, on the average, how many days it takes to collect on an account. Too lax a collection policy can cost the company money; too aggressive a collection period can agitate and possibly lose customers. This ratio is calculated by dividing accounts receivable by average sales per day.

$$\text{Average Collection period} = \frac{\text{Accounts receivable}}{\text{Sales divided by 365}}$$

Average Payment Period (APP). The APP provides a view of how well the firm is paying its accounts payable. It is determined by dividing accounts payable by average purchase per day and is shown in days.

$$\text{Average payment period} = \frac{\text{Accounts payable}}{\text{Purchases divided by 365}}$$

Fixed Assets Utilization. Many of the funds utilized by a company to generate sales and earnings growth are invested in fixed assets such as property, plants, and equipment. The fixed assets utilization ratio (or fixed assets turnover ratio) helps examine capacity utilization and the quality and efficiency of the fixed assets and shows how many times fixed assets turn over in a year. It is calculated by dividing sales by net fixed assets.

$$\text{Fixed assets utilization} = \frac{\text{Sales}}{\text{Net fixed assets}}$$

Total Assets Utilization. Total assets utilization (or total assets turnover) helps determine the efficiency of total asset usage and the level of capital intensity. It is calculated by dividing sales by total assets.

$$\text{Total assets utilization} = \frac{\text{Sales}}{\text{Net total assets}}$$

Profitability Ratios

Company profit is important to everyone within the company and to those who deal with the company in any capacity. There are a number of ways to measure company profitability, such as sales profit margin, return on assets, return on equity, and return on invested capital.

Sales Profit Margin. One of the most commonly quoted profitability measures is profit margin as a percentage of sales. This is easily calculated by dividing net income by sales.

$$\text{Sales profit margin} = \frac{\text{Net income}}{\text{Sales}}$$

Return on Assets (ROA). This ratio, also expressed as a percentage, shows how the company's profitability is related to its total assets. It shows how much profit is made on each dollar of assets. ROA provides an incentive for managers to reduce costs and increase sales, and it demonstrates the capabilities of the divisional managers to use capital profitably from all sources, not just from stockholders as return on equity tends to do. ROA is calculated by dividing net income by total assets.

$$\text{Return on assets } = \frac{\text{Net income}}{\text{Total assets}}$$

Return on Equity (ROE). Stockholders who invest money in a company are interested in the profitability of their investment. This is expressed as return on equity. If maximum dollar profit is desired, ROE may be a better measure of profitability than ROA. ROE is determined by dividing net income by stockholders' equity.

$$\text{Return on equity } = \frac{\text{Net income}}{\text{Stockholders' equity}}$$

Returned on Invested Capital. Stockholders are always interested in how well the company capital is invested. There is considerable argument on just how this ratio should be calculated; however, for purposes of this book, it will be calculated as net earnings divided by long-term debt plus shareholders' equity.

$$\text{Return on invested capital } = \frac{\text{Net Earnings}}{\text{Long-term debt + Stockholders' equity}}$$

Limitations of Ratio Analysis. The various ratios discussed above are easy to calculate and provide valuable information about a company. Using these ratios, comparisons with other companies and the industry as a whole can be made, as can trends within the company.

In spite of these positive attributes of ratio analysis, the ratios can be distorted or skewed if inflation rates are severe in early or late years of extended period trend analysis. Also, if assets are old (or fully depreciated) or expensive new assets have just been acquired, then some of the ratios involving assets might be distorted or skewed. All of these factors must be taken into consideration when undertaking ratio analysis, and experience and judgment should influence the results to avoid an incorrect or misleading conclusion.

Cash Flow

Although cash flow is not strictly a financial ratio, it does measure the effect of a single transaction or a group of transactions on cash. Cash flow answers the question of how much cash is generated by the company's income for the fiscal period under consideration.

Although cash flow has been defined for the purposes of this book, there is no standard definition of cash flow. Therefore, whenever the term cash flow is used, the reader should attempt to determine the specific meaning being used for the particular application.

Cash flow is higher than net income by the amount of depreciation. Depreciation is deducted as an operating expense, thus lowering net income; however, depreciation does not require an outlay of cash. Deferred taxes, depletion, and amortization also contribute to a difference between net income and cash flow.

Other definitions of cash flow use the working capital concept or the cash approach. The cash approach is more conservative in that it takes a more limited view of the pool of funds. The cash approach shows if increases in inventories or receivables are using up the operating funds; this may go unnoticed if the working capital approach is used.

Cash flow is also defined as funds from operations before nonrecurring items. If cash flow is defined in this manner, however, and if a substantial increase in receivables and/or inventories occurs, then cash shortfall from operations in that period may not be apparent. A more conservative approach is to define cash flow as the adjusted funds from operations before nonrecurring items that come from a cash basis; this approach shows if the company has cash flow problems from operations when receivables and/or inventories are increasing.

For purposes of this book, cash flow will be defined and calculated as follows:

Cash flow $= \text{NI} + \text{D} \pm \Delta \text{WC} \pm \Delta \text{I}$

where

$\text{NI} =$ net income

$\text{D} =$ depreciation

$\Delta \text{WC} =$ change in working capital

$\Delta \text{I} =$ change in investment

Working capital is defined as current assets (cash, accounts receivable, inventories, etc.) minus current liabilities (notes payable, accounts payable, accrued liabilities, current long-term debt, etc.), and investments include property, plant, equipment, and other assets. Increases in working capital or investments should be subtracted from cash flow because these positive uses of funds require cash, thus reducing cash flow from continuous operations.

FINANCIAL COMMITTEES

Most companies today have a number of established financial committees that aid in the financial management of the company. Some examples of these committees are:

1. the finance committee, which deals with accounting policy and procedures, contracts, corporate taxes, dividend policy, depreciation policy, and so on;

2. the capital appropriations committee, which deals with selecting projects that best meet the company needs, oversees uniform evaluation of capital projects, eliminates duplication of projects, and controls the expenditure of funds;

3. the budget committee, which recommends, approves, and oversees the budgets;

4. the pension and retirement committee, which establishes and implements company policy on various monetary employee fringe benefit programs;

5. the salary committee, which establishes and implements salary structure and policy; and

6. the general accounting committee, which is responsible for seeing that company funds are honestly and efficiently used in accordance with established policy.

The membership of these committees is made up of top officials of the company.

COMPANY EVALUATION

Finance and accounting are deeply involved in all monetary decisions that take place within a company. They must, therefore, work closely with all other functional areas within the company. Table 8.1 helps evaluate how well finance and accounting departments accomplish these tasks in the areas of planning, organizing, directing, and controlling.

Table 8.1
Typical Strengths and Weaknesses in Planning, Organizing, Directing, and Controlling Finance/Accounting

	Strengths	Weaknesses
PLANNING	Top management is committed to a strong financial and accounting program.	No strong commitment exists within the company for a strong financial and accounting program.
	There is an official planning committee to develop short, medium, and long-range accounting and finance plans.	No planning committee exists to develop or review accounting and finance plans in an integrated manner.
	Accounting and financial plans are periodically reviewed and kept current.	Accounting and financial plans, once generated, are seldom or never reviewed or updated.
	All accounting and financial plans are consistent with company strategy and goals.	Accounting and finance planning is inadequate in many areas.
	All accounting and financial plans are coordinated and integrated between all functional areas.	Accounting and financial planning is not coordinated or integrated between functional areas.
	Adequate equipment and competent people are employed and utilized in the accounting and financial functional areas at all times.	Equipment and personnel skills are updated only when absolutely necessary.
ORGANIZING	Accounting and finance report directly to the president through a vice president.	Accounting and finance operations report to a manager or director level.
	Competent and efficient people are assigned to each accounting and finance position.	Clear lines of responsibility and authority are not established in either accounting or finance.
	Accounting and finance are organized in a manner to quickly respond to any accounting or financial emergency while maintaining routine task requirements.	Accounting and finance are not able to cover both regular and emergency situations at the same time.
	Accounting and finance are organized in a manner to take care of all accounting and financial needs at all times.	Accounting and finance needs are handled in a crisis type reaction mode most of the time.
	Accounting and finance are organized to take advantage of the latest equipment and techniques.	Latest equipment and techniques are seldom available within accounting and finance.

Table 8.1 (Continued)

	Strengths	Weaknesses
DIRECTING	A competent vice president reporting directly to the president heads up accounting and finance.	The accounting and finance operation is headed up by a managerial level person.
	MIS systems are used to track, coordinate, and direct budgets and other accounting and financial information on all projects.	MIS systems are used to a minimum in any accounting and financial situation.
	Excellent coordination and interface exist between accounting and finance and all other functional areas of the company.	Inadequate coordination and interface exist between accounting and finance and other company functional areas.
CONTROLLING	Accounting and finance operations are coordinated and integrated within those of other operating departments through use of MIS.	Accounting and finance operate loosely but fairly independent of other company functional areas.
	Accounting and finance operations are monitored and coordinated from a central location with local responsibility.	Accounting and finance operate separately from each different program with no central coordination or control.
	Accounting and finance control reports are properly designed, easy to use, and timely.	Accounting and finance control reports are inadequate in both information and timeliness.
	Adequate and sufficient accounting and finance controls exist at all levels and over all financial data.	Inadequate accounting and finance controls exist in much of the financial data.
	Equipment, facilities, and procedures are constantly reviewed and updated to insure maximum efficiency of accounting and finance operations.	Equipment, facilities, and procedures are only changed or updated when absolutely required.

9

Management Information Systems

In today's business world, information systems are an absolute necessity, regardless of whether the business is small, intermediate, or large in size and scope. Management information systems (MIS) are a system or a combination of systems (usually computers) that communicate information for management purposes in a business. In simplest form, MIS consists of input, processing, output, storage, feedback, and control, and it is responsive to the internal and external environments in which it operates.

MIS is used in many functional areas of business, such as research and development, engineering, marketing, accounting, finance, legal services, production operations, and human resources. From an applications standpoint, MIS is used for business and personal services, banking and finance, manufacturing, strategic and tactical plannings, operations control, record keeping, manufacturing, utilities, insurance, transportation, retail operations, health care, printing and publishing, distribution, and many other applications too numerous to mention.

The information supplied to the business managers by these systems must be timely, accurate, complete, concise, and crucial. It must be available for the purposes of strategic, tactical, and operations management.

Although the information systems discussed in this chapter are all loosely classified as MIS, they can be more correctly and precisely broken down into two categories—operations information systems and management information systems—with each of these further divided into several subsystems. Operations information systems include process control systems, transaction processing systems, and automated office systems. Management information systems include management reporting systems, decision support systems, executive information systems, expert systems, and other knowledge-based systems.

THE COMMUNICATION AND INFORMATION ASPECTS OF MIS

Communication is the conveying of meaningful information from one person to another in either written, oral, or visual format. This information is received and interpreted by a receptor after traveling through a medium of "static" or "noise." This may be created by the sender or the receptor who does not fully understand what the other person needs or wants, inadequate software or hardware, inadequate or incorrect input or output, too much information, or misinterpretation of the information.

Conveyance and transfer of information is the essence of communication. In the case of MIS, managers are concerned with the acquisition and transmission of information that will increase or enhance their knowledge of current business. As far back as 1966, John Deardon classified the various types of information found in business operations and necessary for business planning into five major groups:

- *Action versus nonaction information.* Action information requires that the receiver do something. Nonaction information may advise that a certain action has taken place, or it may provide general information that is helpful but requires no action.

- *Recurring versus nonrecurring information.* Recurring information is generated at regular or periodic intervals. Nonrecurring information is a one-time event, such as a special study conducted to help in a management decision.

- *Documentary versus nondocumentary information.* Documentary information is retained and preserved in material form, such as written literature and magnetic tapes or disks. Nondocumentary information is transmitted orally or received through visual observations.

- *Internal versus external information.* Quite simply, internal information comes from within the company, and external information comes from outside the company.

- *Historical information versus future projections.* Historical information is generated from past activities and might be stored and used to help make future projections. Future projections are self-explanatory.[1]

Most information systems use a combination of these types of information and embrace a number of disciplines, tools, and techniques.

Figure 9.1
Business/Information Systems Relationship

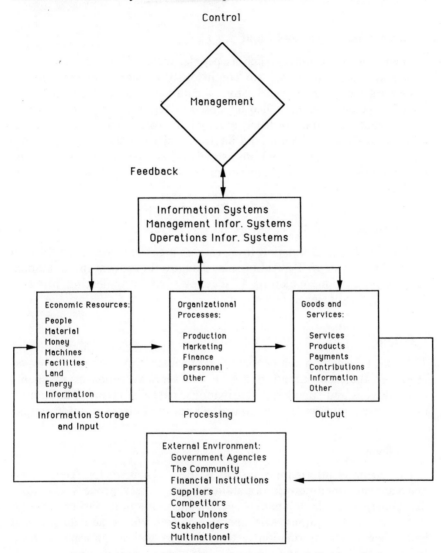

Control

Management

Feedback

Information Systems
Management Infor. Systems
Operations Infor. Systems

Economic Resources:

People
Material
Money
Machines
Facilities
Land
Energy
Information

Information Storage
and Input

Organizational
Processes:

Production
Marketing
Finance
Personnel
Other

Processing

Goods and
Services:

Services
Products
Payments
Contributions
Information
Other

Output

External Environment:
Government Agencies
The Community
Financial Institutions
Suppliers
Competitors
Labor Unions
Stakeholders
Multinational

THE BUSINESS SYSTEM

Without going into the detailed arrangements and flow of information in information systems for different applications, Figure 9.1 shows in general terms the information flow within the business/information systems relationship. This is an integrated system continuously processing, updating, and refining information as it is needed.

Information Storage and Input

Input data on resources such as people, material, money, machines, facilities, land, and energy are continuously updated and fed into the system on a real-time basis. Historical data for trend analysis and other quantitative analyses may also be stored or fed into the system as part of the input. Last but not least, external environmental factors such as data on local, state, federal, and international government agencies; the community; financial institutions; suppliers, competitors; labor unions; stockholders; multinational operations; and so on may also be input into the business system.

Processing

Many types of information from various areas are processed through the business system. Typical of such data are those from the functional areas of production, marketing, finance, personnel, engineering, research and development, legal, and so on.

Output

Output information can be varied and formatted in innumerable ways. However, the basic outputs revolve around services, products, payments to employees and suppliers, contributions, payrolls, financial data, dividends, taxes, interest, and various other selected pieces of information.

Feedback

The business information system is the mechanism for feedback to management. Operations information systems collect, process, and store data generated by the company's operational transactions during its everyday course of operations. MIS operates on and refines the data supplied by the operations information systems and also gathers information from the external business environment. MIS then provides information to management for decision-making purposes.

Control

Management at all levels is involved in planning, organizing, directing, and controlling. Managers are able to control the operations of the business through the feedback provided by information systems.

External Business Environment

Any given company or corporation is a subsystem of the total business environment. It contributes to the environment and is also influenced by this same environment in an open loop system, to which it must adapt its operations. How well the business is able to adapt competitively to this external environment strongly influences the growth and even survivability of the company in future years.

FUNCTIONAL AREAS OF OPERATION AND APPLICATION

Information systems can be, and in many companies are, used in every possible functional area within the company, including research and development, engineering, manufacturing, marketing, finance, accounting, and human resources. A brief list of applications in four functional areas is given below to present an idea of the use and application of these functional area information systems. An operational flow diagram is also presented to show how in one of the functional areas (human resources) information systems operations might take place.

Production Operations

The production operations functional area is responsible for all operations in the planning, monitoring, operation, and control of the processes that produce goods and/or services. In production operations, information systems are used extensively for such things as computer-aided design (CAD), computer-aided manufacturing (CAM), material requirements planning (MRP), just-in-time inventory control (JIT), purchasing and receiving, process control, numerical machine control, robotics, capacity requirements planning (CRP), plant maintenance, shop floor control, and physical distribution planning.

Marketing

After the production facilities manufacture a product or develop a service, it must be marketed. Marketing identifies the markets to be served and selects, distributes, and prices the products and services to be exchanged with the customer for orders and cash. In order to fulfill these requirements, marketing-oriented information systems perform such operations as market research, product management, sales forecasting and management, advertising and promotion, sales order processing, diagnosing performance, pricing strategy, and marketing management.

Accounting

Accounting information systems are perhaps the oldest and most widely used of all business information systems. Computer-based accounting information systems record and report the flow of funds through the company on a historical basis and produce financial statements and data such as the balance sheet and income statements.

In order to keep track of, process, and control accounting department operations, accounting information systems perform such tasks as budgeting, billing, accounts receivable, accounts payable, payroll and labor analysis, general ledger, cost accounting, fixed asset accounting, tax accounting, and billing and sales analysis.

Human Resources

Among other things, the human resources function performs the operations of recruitment, placement, evaluation, compensation, and training and development of personnel. As a part of this process, the personnel information systems operation performs personnel record keeping, employee skills inventory and analysis, payroll and labor analysis, salary levels and distribution, compensation analysis, and personnel requirements analysis and forecasting. Figure 9.2 shows how an information system in the human resources area can be used to collect, track, evaluate, and point out necessary personnel control information.

INDUSTRY AREAS OF OPERATION AND APPLICATION

In addition to understanding how information systems are applied to specific functional areas within a company, it is also necessary to understand that information systems have a variety of different applications in different industries.

Insurance

Some of the applications of information systems in the insurance industry include customer billing, reserve calculations, premium accounting, external reports, investment analysis, actuarial analysis, cash flow analysis, and policy approval or negation.

Utilities

In the utilities industry, information systems perform such tasks as customer billing, accounting, inventory control, meter reading, power

Figure 9.2
Personnel and Human Resources Information System

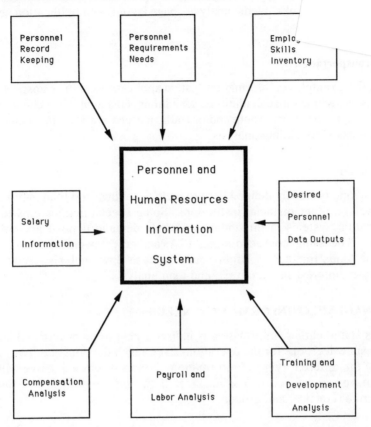

level loading (line and generator), rate analysis, financial models, and operational simulation.

Health Care

The ever-expanding health care industry uses information systems extensively for patient billing, inventory accounting, patient history, health care statistics, patient monitoring, computerized diagnostics, nurse station automation, room availability and utilization, laboratory/operation scheduling, and many other applications.

Printing and Publishing

The printing and publishing business is becoming more sophisticated, complex, and competitive each day. Some typical information system applications in this industry include payroll, accounting, circulation, class-ified ads, automatic typesetting and printing, desktop publishing, custom-published textbooks, media analysis, page layout, and publication sched-uling.

Transportation

A few examples of information system applications in the transportation industry include rate calculations, scheduling, cost analysis, vehicle main-tenance, reservations, route and/or traffic pattern analysis, tariff analysis, and breakeven loading analysis.

Banking

Banking is loosely defined here to include savings and loan institutions as well as other financial institutions. Some special applications for in-formation systems in this industry include demand deposit accounting, check processing, cost accounting, IRAs and other special accounts, elec-tronic funds transfer, portfolio analysis, cash flow analysis, credit card analysis, interest rate analysis, and loan analysis.

MANAGEMENT INFORMATION NEEDS

As stated earlier, information is indispensable to managers making re-sponsible decisions for the operations over which they preside. However, all of the different types of information systems discussed above will not be of any assistance to the manager if the information is not timely, accurate, concise, and crucial.

Timeliness

Information must be supplied to the manager when it is needed, not days, weeks, or months after the fact. For example, a computer printout on a quarterly basis of how close a person is to meeting all areas of his or her sales and profit budget is of little value if some area within the budget has gone far astray within that time period; the year is one-fourth over before the discrepancy is seriously noted or caught and necessary corrective action can be taken. A weekly or at worst a monthly printout of the budget progress would provide timely information of any deviations from the standard that needs closer scrutiny and action.

Accuracy

Information must be accurate and free from errors. Inaccurate infor-mation may be more harmful in the decision-making process than no information at all since it could lead to an erroneous conclusion. Accurate information requires the right hardware and software programs, correct data inputs and outputs, and an understanding of how to interpret the output.

Completeness

Not only must the information received be accurate, but it must also be complete to prohibit incorrect conclusions. One manager in a well-known company received computer printouts of his program's progress as compared to his budget on a monthly basis. He was pleased with his progress because the printout indicated that he was repeatedly running the program a little better than budget. However, several months into the program he received his computer budget printout update and discovered that not only was he considerably over budget, but he was outside of the company's permissible variation from budget. Upon performing a variance analysis on the data, he discovered that there had been a $50,000 increase in material over the previous month's computer printout; he thought that there had been no such recent purchase, so he continued his investigation. He found out that the software program was set up so that purchases for equipment and material were not charged against the budget until the equipment or material had actually been paid for. Thus, purchase order releases on long-lead items did not show up as expenditures on the computer printout of the budget status for several weeks or months after the money had been committed. This procedure resulted in an incomplete and inaccurate budget report to the manager. The procedure and the software were changed to show these charges against the budget but that they were not yet paid.

Conciseness

Only the information needed or wanted should be printed out and distributed. This should cover the critical factors needed to make a decision. It is all too easy to print out reams of data that are meaningless and confusing to the main issue under consideration and flood the manager with more paper and information than can possibly be used in an intelligent and meaningful manner. The data supplied should also be tailored to the person or group needing it; unfortunately, it is a common practice to supply every manager in the company with the same 200 pages of printout and then let them sort through the data to try and find and assemble what they need. This is not the purpose of information systems nor the job of the busy manager to do this.

Crucial Factors

Managers need information on key factors that are crucial to the success of their programs and the future of their company. These crucial items must be identified by and supplied to the managers in a timely, accurate, complete, and concise manner. This information should be primarily in the areas that will help the managers meet their objectives and those objectives established by the company.

INFORMATION SYSTEMS DATA SUPPLIED TO DIFFERENT LEVELS OF MANAGEMENT

When discussing levels of management, many authors, consultants, and businesspeople break it down into three major levels: the strategic management level, the tactical management level, and the operations management level. The planning and strategy responsibilities of these three levels have been previously discussed in Chapter 2, "Corporate Planning and Strategy Formulation and Implementation."

The information requirements for each level of management are closely related to the types of activities that they perform. The strategic management level normally requires more summarized, condensed, special one-time internal operations reports; forecasts; external impact reports; simulated projections; inquiry reports; and so on. The operational management level, on the other hand, in order to run its day-to-day operations may require more regular or periodic internal reports, procedure manuals, current and updated historical data on budgets, and other detailed information. Information supplied to the tactical management level includes regular internal and external reports, exceptions and variance reports, simulations, forecasts and historical data, special inquiry reports, and any other data or reports they deem necessary to perform their jobs effectively and efficiently.

MANAGEMENT INFORMATION SYSTEMS AND OPERATIONS INFORMATION SYSTEMS

Although there are distinct differences between the tasks performed by MIS and OIS, most people loosely refer to all of them as management information systems or simply information systems.

Operations Information Systems

Operations information systems process data generated by the company and used in its business operations. Three major subcategories of operational information systems exist.

Process Control Systems. One of the functions of OIS is to produce routine decisions that control an operational process. These are called programmed decisions because they are automatically programmed based on established decision rules. These decision rules outline and establish the actions to be taken when confronted with a certain event or set of events. Included in this category of systems are the process control systems, which automatically adjust, through use of computers, the production process when various decisions are met. For example, an automated paper-producing factory uses such a system. In the making of paper products, such as napkins, paper towels, and toilet paper, the wood-pulp/chemical transformation process into paper involves almost 100 crucial decision steps. These systems monitor the physical process, collect and process the data detected by the sensors, and make real-time adjustments and changes in the process from the beginning to the final product. Many production operations systems also fall into this category.

Transaction Processing Systems. Transaction processing systems, which evolved from manual information systems, were one of the earliest forms of information systems and are now often referred to as electronic data processing (EDP) systems. These subsystems process data that arise from various business transactions such as sales, purchases, and inventory charges. In addition, they can make adjustments to the records in a file or database. These systems produce numerous types of information for both internal and external use, such as customer statements, sales receipts, employee paychecks, dividend checks, tax forms, purchase orders, financial statements, and so on.

Automated Office Systems. Automated office systems collect, process, store, and transmit data and information in the form of electronic office communications; this replaces the old manual communications systems that generated excessive office paperwork. Included in this category of information systems are word processing, desktop publishing, teleconferencing, electronic mail, micrographics, electronic calendars, and records management.

Many of the automated office systems today are a combination of computer and communication systems and might include such capabilities as electronic messaging, distributed databases, interactive computing, high-level graphics transmission, videotex, digitized voice, teleconferencing, voice storage and forwarding, and many other operations.

Management Information Systems

MIS is designed to provide the needed information to support managers in making intelligent and efficient decisions. Although growing rather by piecemeal and haphazardly during the 1960s and early 1970s, MIS is now both efficient and effective. Today, MIS emphasizes the orientation of business information processing in the direction of management. It it directed toward the support of management decision making and not just the processing of data generated in the business organization. It serves as a framework for organizing and integrating business computer applications and communication networks. It is an interrelated and integrated computer-based information and communication system and not just a group of independent data processing systems.

There are a number of subsystems under the classification of management information systems. The major MIS subsystems, based on their information outputs, are management reporting systems, decision support systems, executive information systems, expert systems, and knowledge-based systems.

MIS is becoming more important each day. With the rapidly changing and increasingly complex business world and explosive expansion of multinational trade, top managers need rapid, efficient, and effective management information to help them make strategic and tactical decisions in marketing, finance, production, engineering, personnel, and any other areas in which they are involved. No single system can supply all of the information needed for making crucial decisions; therefore, it is not uncommon to see in use a combination of the following MIS subsystems.

Management Reporting Systems (MRS). The computer-based management reporting system can provide information to satisfy the timing requirements of most managers in almost any form. The system configuration requires hardware in the form of management workstations, properly designed application software packages, and personnel resources in the form of information specialists. These resources are configured and integrated to obtain the information needed by the managers, in the time and format required by the managers. To accomplish these tasks:

- *Input data*, which has been generated by the operations information systems and the business environment, is collected and fed into the processing computer.

- *Processing* is performed by a computer system, which transforms the data into the desired format.

- *Storage* data from a database (consisting of historical records, forecasts, budgets, plans, standards, models, decision rules, etc.) is also fed into the processing computer, when and where needed, to be processed in conjunction with the input data. Internal, external, and personal data are used. The processed data may also be returned and stored in the database as new or updated data.

- *Output* information from the computer system processor, necessary to support the decision-making process of the manager, can be provided in a variety of forms. This information can be supplied on demand, on a predetermined schedule, or when specified conditions occur. It can be displayed in visual format or in printed report format.

- *Control* levels and types vary as a function of the manager's needs and desires.

Decision Support Systems (DSS). Decision support systems are interactive computer-based information systems. These systems use decision models and specialized databases to supply information used to support specific decisions that must be made by the individual managers.

DSS offers managers interactive responses on an as-needed or as-required basis. Information is given in an interactive exchange session between a manager and a computer through the use of an interactive modeling software package. For example, an electronic spreadsheet package might be used. The manager may not want or demand a specific answer but may want to examine a number of alternative proposals and tradeoffs between people, machines, facilities, and services on a certain project or task about which an eventual decision must be made. By exploring possible alternatives, information needs do not have to be specified in advance.

There are quick response systems that can help the manager solve semistructured and unstructured problems. These systems normally use decision models that require the manager to supply his or her own insights and judgments as part of the decision-making process.

The decision support system components, all of which are interactive, consist of a manager, an executive workstation in the form of a personal computer or computer terminal, database management software, model base management software, dialogue generation and management software, a DSS external database and a manager's personal database, and a model base that includes a library of models and analytical techniques.

Executive Information Systems (EIS). Executive information systems are management information systems especially tailored to the strategic information needs of top management. EIS must provide top management with immediate and easy access to key information pertaining to the accomplishment of the company's strategic objectives. Because of top management's workload and limited time availability, these systems must be easy to understand and operate on a real-time access basis. Data should be displayed in easy-to-understand format and preferably in graphics. The data must be current and formatted to the preference of the top management using the system.

EIS components include a top executive, an executive workstation in the form of a personal computer with interactive graphics, an EIS generator, DSS software, database management software, communications software, an external database, an internal operations database, and a special management database.

It is expected that the use of EIS will grow rapidly as more top executives become aware of its availability, feasibility, and decision-assisting benefits.

Expert Systems. An expert system is a computer-based system that applies knowledge about a specific complex area of application where it can act as an expert consultant. With the development of artificial intelligence, computer-based expert systems are being designed to walk, talk, see, hear, feel, and think. This is resulting in intelligent computers (sometimes referred to as knowledge-based systems) and advanced robots, some of which are in use today in such areas as medicine, chemistry, engineering, and geology.

Integrated Information Systems

In the real, operating business world of today, the information systems used by most competent, aggressive companies usually combine and integrate a combination of the information systems discussed above. In fact, most designed and installed information systems produce information to support management decision making at all levels, as well as perform recordkeeping and transaction processing chores.

Almost every business-oriented periodical or magazine discusses the use, advantages, and growth of integrated information systems. Stuart Ganners, in *Fortune* magazine, discusses the four waves of growth in computers.[2] Mainframes have progressed from 77 percent of computer sales in 1971 to a projected 10 percent of sales in 1992. Minicomputers peaked at 71 percent of sales in 1976 and are projected to drop to 4 percent of sales in 1992. Personal computers peaked at 51 percent of sales in 1984 and are projected to drop to 10 percent of sales in 1992. Workstations and network computers began to increase in sales in 1979 and are projected to account for 76 percent of sales in 1992.[3] Joel Dreyfuss, also in *Fortune* magazine, presents an article on managing by computer groupware.[4] The groupware system is composed of three major groupings of information systems. The first group, called the workgroup, contains a central electronic calendar that keeps the executive in the workgroup organized and on schedule by tracking strategic objectives and goals, arranging meetings, reminding managers of critical events, and advising when a program is not on schedule or budget. The second group has a mainframe at its core and connects the workgroup with remote operations through an electronic mail network by moving messages, reports, and other correspondence between headquarters, branches, subsidiaries, and multinational offices. The third group of information systems processes all data relevant to the business—sales, inventory, financial data, cash flow, marketing reports, and so on—and makes the information immediately available throughout the organization.[5] Much of this information will be available to computer-savvy managers through the use of personal computers in their offices. According to the Gartner Group, a Stamford, Connecticut, market research firm, the number of personal computers in offices is expected to quadruple to 46 million by the year 2000.[6] A special advertising section of a November 1989 *Fortune* magazine presents and discusses several arrangements of workstations and networks and how they can enhance personal and group productivity.[7]

With all the information systems available, how can a company be certain that the information system arrangement it purchases today will meet the needs of the future? One can never be totally certain. Hans T. Koppen and David S. Linsey feel that the risk of purchasing a system that will shortly become obsolete can be minimized by carefully thinking through the present and future company application needs and then measuring them against the existing capabilities of today's hardware and software.[8] They then offer a checklist of what to look for when purchasing the next information system, including "multivendor convenience; RISC processing; workstation graphics; mainframe utility; storage systems; database management; multimedia databases; and UNIX compatibility."[9]

COMPANY EVALUATION

Management information systems are used in an integrated and coordinated manner in a well-operated company. All functional areas are involved in information inputs and outputs and the processing and usage of the generated information. Table 9.1 can help determine how well MIS is performing these tasks in the areas of planning, organizing, directing, and controlling.

NOTES

1. John Deardon, *Computers in Business Management* (Homewood, IL: Dow Jones–Irwin, 1966).

2. Stuart Gannes, "IBM and DEC Take on the Little Guys," *Fortune* 118, no. 8 (October 10, 1988): 108–114.

3. Ibid., p. 108.

4. Joel Dreyfuss, "Catching the Computer Wave," *Fortune* 118, no. 7 (September 26, 1988): 78–82.

5. Ibid., p. 78.

6. Ibid.

7. "Workstations and Networks—Enhancing Personal and Group Productivity," *Fortune* 120, no. 11 (November 6, 1989), Special Advertising Section.

8. Hans T. Koppen and David S. Linsey, "Can Your Computer Go the Distance?" *Research and Development* 31, no. 36 (June 1989): 55–57.

9. Ibid., p. 55.

Table 9.1
Typical Strengths and Weaknesses in Planning, Organizing, Directing, and Controlling Management Information Systems

	Strengths	Weaknesses
PLANNING	Top management is committed to a comprehensive integrated MIS effort throughout the company.	Little or no emphasis is made by top management to use or integrate MIS efforts within the company.
	There is an official planning committee to develop short, medium, and long-range MIS growth and usage plans.	No planning committee exists. Computer installation and growth is in a nonsystematic, uncontrolled manner.
	MIS planned employment and usage follows a logical growth pattern.	Little or no effort is made to follow a logical growth pattern in the usage or employment of MIS.
	All MIS growth and usage plans are coordinated between all functional areas within the company.	The company is content to be a follower.
		MIS growth and usage planning on a coordinated or integrated basis does not exist.
ORGANIZING	The head of MIS reports directly to the president through a vice president.	The MIS group, if it exists at all, is a subsection of marketing, accounting, finance, or manufacturing.
	Competent and efficient people are assigned to all areas of MIS usage.	Clear lines of responsibility and authority are not established for deployment or usage of MIS personnel.
	MIS personnel are organized in a manner to quickly respond to any information need, routine, or emergency.	MIS personnel cannot cover both routine and emergency information demands.
	MIS is organized in a manner to handle any and all information needs at all times.	At best, only routine MIS information tasks can be handled.
	MIS is organized in a manner to take advantage of the latest equipment and techniques.	The latest MIS equipment or techniques are seldom available or employed.
DIRECTING	A competent vice president reporting directly to the president heads up MIS.	The MIS group is headed up by a management level person under marketing, finance, accounting, or manufacturing.

CONTROLLING		
Excellent coordination and interface exists between MIS and all other areas of the company		Inadequate coordination and interface exists between MIS and other areas of the company.
MIS is used to help direct and coordinate all programs within the company.		MIS is used only to run a specific, limited number of programs.
	MIS is used to coordinate and integrate all programs within the company to insure compliance with company strategic goals and objectives.	MIS is not used to track or coordinate company programs.
	MIS is used to monitor and coordinate programs from both central and local locations.	MIS is not used to monitor or coordinate any company programs.
	MIS output data are timely, accurate, concise, and crucial so that accurate real-time assessments of program status can be obtained.	MIS output data is released on a periodic scheduled time basis.
	Equipment, facilities, and procedures are constantly reviewed and updated to insure maximum efficiency in MIS operations.	MIS equipment, facilities, and procedures are only changed or updated when absolutely required.

141

10

Organization Structure and Human Resources Management

You cannot teach a man anything. You can only help to find it within himself.

Galileo

A key aspect of the directing function of management is development of subordinates. Closely allied to this goal are the processes of communication, motivation, and goal attainment. Within any given situation, effective motivation of individuals to accomplish company goals and yet still yield a fair measure of individual objectives requires great skill in human resource management. Galileo's observation in the early seventeenth century forecast, as did so many of his touches of genius, the complexity of the discipline of human resource management. The Japanese answer to the Galilean method of development is a Zen retreat in a Buddhist temple, where "finding it within" involves concentration on *koan* or "mind-breakers" designed to act as an aid to concentration (for example, what is the sound of one hand clapping?).[1]

Faced with such esoteric approaches to the human resource function, it is no wonder that both the managing practitioner and one attempting to analyze its effectiveness may well be confused if not totally frustrated. People-oriented skills include the ability to understand the individual needs of group members, to build morale, and to motivate all members to accept organizational goals as their own while accomplishing them in accordance with a plan to which there is joint input. Expertise to accomplish the above, especially while giving some credence to the 'new' concepts which remove much of the direct cause/effect relationships expected from traditional management concepts, is hard to find. Adding to the difficulty of analysis, traditional management beliefs tend to prove effective in the short run. Fear is an effective tool for immediate control but only in situations with a short-term horizon. Surveillance, frequent inventories, and limited spans of control are effective but costly tools to insure compliance. Leadership skills must be not only effective but efficient. The cost penalties from inefficient, short-run management direction represent one of the key factors that needs to be considered in the process of functional evaluation.

SCOPE OF ANALYSIS

Limiting the scope of those areas of human interactions considered vital to accomplishing the goals of the organization is both essential and difficult. Each situation has unique aspects. Essentially, what needs to be placed under the microscope of analysis are the active processes carried on by members of the organization. People are the catalysts in effective discharge of most aspects of marketing, manufacturing, and other company functions. What are the rules which seem to guide these processes? How consistently are these rules followed? How logical is the design of the structure within which these processes are conducted? What are the skills and qualifications of those who conduct these processes that are so critical to goal accomplishment?

These questions may still represent a near overwhelming challenge in terms of reaching a definitive conclusion as to the efficiency or effectiveness of the people running an operation. This feeling of overwhelming complexity is normal and even expected. The matrix of possible human interactions is unlimited. If, however, the actual mainstream processes of planning, organizing, directing, and controlling human resources conflict with the logic and effectiveness of those actions, it is possible to develop an overall evaluation of those actions needing change, modification, or elimination. It is toward this objective that the efforts of those using these concepts are directed. In most instances, this process of change consumes only a reasonable amount of time and effort.

ORGANIZATION CULTURE: FIRST POINT OF INQUIRY

Extending as it does into every aspect of the organizational environment, the human resource function does not fit the normal requirements of the exception concept. This means that acceptable deviations from the norm are accepted. Setting standards of deviation from the norm that trigger an alarm for management action seldom work as desired. The basic problem for setting such standards is the lack of consistency from situation to situation. Thus a broad, macro approach to issues related to people in organizations is required.

A first point of inquiry, valid in almost every case and generally efficient, is to look closely at the culture of the organization. For purposes of this book, "culture" means the beliefs, customs, skills, knowledge, and habits of the unit, be it large or small. As an effective means of answering the many questions concerning the culture of a body of people, consider the following:

1. *What attributes are most valued in members?* The value placed upon creativity or conformity is stressed here. Of special importance is the treatment of those who question conventional wisdom.

2. *Who or what is most valued?* Are people more valued than bottom-line figures? Here questions of short-run and long-run considerations come into play, but the primary issue is the expendable nature of people in relationship to financial or production goals.

3. *How are leaders who develop their subordinates rewarded?* Relatively few organizations give more than lip service to their managers for the effort spent in development of subordinates. Answers to this question are not easy to find. Often it is the testimony of grateful subordinates that gives credence to efforts of supervisors who act as mentors and teachers. At other times, it is an overall record of competent, professional executives and managers at all levels. Managers who care for their subordinates reflect upon the organization as a whole.

4. *Is pride in the organization a strong reality?* The pride of Honda of America employees is evident to any visitor at the huge Marysville, Ohio, facility. Shoichiro Irimajiri, president of Honda of America, wastes no opportunity to talk about the "winning difference" at Honda. Each employee is given a thorough indoctrination in the Honda superordinate goal dedicated to producing products of the highest efficiency at a reasonable price.[2] The primary method of communicating Honda's philosophy is through its products. Employees apparently fully embrace this philosophy, which is reflected in the Honda Accord automobile primarily produced at the Marysville plant and the best selling automobile in the United States in 1989, toppling Ford Escort from its seven-year reign.[3]

Analysis of culture as part of the human resource function does present a challenge to those individuals attempting to determine the quality of this most critical area. The four areas of concern in this area—pride, mentoring, the most valued attributes in personnel, and the most valued qualities within the organization—represent only a beginning in the process of analysis. It is, however, a most critical area of research. Finding in an organization that people are basically expendable, conformity is encouraged, only lip service is given to training and development, and that pride is a missing commodity both in terms of self and in the organization will of necessity result in the most pessimistic view of the future. Finding serious weakness in any two of the above variables makes the evaluation far more difficult and complex. Here, at the outset, there is a need to overlay perceived methods of personnel management against the objectives of the subject organization.

A word of encouragement is offered to those discouraged by this seemingly daunting task. The leverage reflected in a solid, thoughtful consideration of cultural variables is enormous. Concerns raised in analysis of cultural variables are often magnified when the more ordinary aspects of human resource management are reviewed, such as systems of motivation, selection for promotion, retention of key personnel, and how well new individuals are indoctrinated into the organization. The discussion of this topic could be continued, but the basic issue becomes one of determining the quality of each of these functions and thus the probability that the goals of the organization will be discharged with both effectiveness and spirit.

When using analysis of the human resource function as a tool for evaluation, one should consider the following basic elements of reorganizational culture as positive or negative variables:

a. *Shared assumptions*. The range of shared assumptions in an organization is practically without limit. The key to effective analysis is to focus upon those assumptions critical to workforce motivation and productivity. A most critical factor in this area is a shared belief that top management values its employees and considers them critical to success and survival. When the opposite belief is true—that top management views its people as expendable—the impact upon creative output is extremely negative.

b. *Ritualized practices*. For most U.S. firms, regularly scheduled golf or tennis matches take the place of social drinking afterhours among the Japanese. The foundations, if not a complete framework, for numerous programs are often born on the green or on the court. Is such practice detrimental to corporate efficiency? Not in the least. Can such practice when institutionalized to the point that it becomes a cultural way of life be dangerous? Yes, without question. Decision making in such informal environments is great for those of the inner circles of top management, but an organization is made strong and viable through the input of all its members. Following such procedures and customs, which at the outset exclude nonathletic types, means that important voices are not heard or included in what may be the initiation of important matters of company policy or strategy. The investigator of corporate culture needs to be sensitive to such practices and their implications for good and evil. While identification of the nature of such cultural practices may be difficult at first, it is surprising how readily those who have suffered from such practices are willing to identify them in surprisingly vivid detail.

ORGANIZATION STRUCTURE AND DESIGN

In evaluating relationships between the stationary organizational structure and task relationships, an analyst is often presented with a wealth of opportunities for system improvements. Organization design is rarely fully appropriate for the current mission. Alfred P. Sloan, Jr. is considered the father of the divisional unit profit center concept, originating the concept in the 1920s.[4] Sloan's legacy of relatively autonomous divisions is widely credited for the success of General Motors. Yet, under Roger Smith, major efforts have been made to restructure the traditional divisions within the past structure, which is often blamed for many of the ills of General Motors. In a singularly caustic review of the GM system, Ross Perot likened Sloan's system and structure to the Old Testament—frozen in place thousands of years ago. Perot went on to identify the traditional divisional system as a "blanket of fog that keeps these people from doing what they know needs to be done."[5] Smith, undoubtedly stung by Perot's charges, cited three years of restructuring initiated in 1985, which was designed to give GM people more authority, delegation, and participation. Smith, however, defended the GM committee structure as necessary for coordination. "You can't run it by the seat of your pants," he stated.[6]

Definition of Structure—in the Dynamic Sense

In the simplest sense, structure deals with the components or parts of an organization as they are interrelated in an established system. A key factor is that this structure of a social system is not readily visible, even in attempts to illustrate it in the most up-to-date and graphic charts. No two-dimensional chart is able to duplicate the complexity of the dynamic processes that constitute the social system of an organization. It is this dynamic, changing complexity that causes many smaller firms to give only lip service to any formal effort at duplicating the full structure of the firm. At best, an organizational chart is merely the first step in the analysis and definition of an organization's formal structure. It is necessary also to consider the following:

1. The patterns building from formal relationships such as position or job descriptions and the chart itself.

2. The way in which the formal positions or tasks are assigned to various departments and how these separate activities are then coordinated (differentiation and integration).

3. Special evaluation of power, status, and hierarchy (authority system).

4. Documents setting forth formalized policies, procedures, standards, and other control elements designed to guide the activities and interrelationships of members of the organization (administrative).

A significant amount of reading, discussion with various parties, and integration of such findings is required for a useful picture to emerge. To be of any use, this picture must then be overlayed against the goals of the organization in question, its environment, and target markets. If such goals and strategies for attainment are not readily apparent, this presents an additional problem in clearly defining the required organizational structure. To eliminate this problem from the discussion, such well-defined goals are assumed to be among the resources available to the analyst.

Formal and Informal Organization

Management typically plans with some care the organizational structure, which can be represented by a printed chart and supported by manuals, position descriptions, and flow charts. Thus, the formal structure is representative of the explicit wishes of senior management. People within the organization are expected to communicate, interact, and hopefully cooperate within this pattern of relationships.

However, for reasons that may not represent a calculated desire to circumvent these managerial efforts and in actual practice may have at their roots a desire to fix what is viewed as a defective document, spontaneous interactions by organizational members take place. These interactions are popularly classified under the wide umbrella termed the "informal organization." The positive intent of these deviant participants removes much of the criticism of informal practice and even moves some to say that informal relationships are vital for the effective functioning of the organization.[7]

Verification of this positive intent and impact becomes the challenge for one investigating the nature and extent of informal excursions from the stated patterns of the formal structure. A primary objective of such investigation is the determination of the extent of damage inflicted by informal patterns of behavior. The web-like pattern of sidewalks and paths on a college campus is an example of the interactive process of formal and informal processes. In the case of sidewalks, buildings, and grounds, builders plan and construct patterns of walks designed to be both functional and attractive. Students who are far more concerned with functionality than beauty soon develop informal routes off of the sidewalks. When the endorsement of these informal shortcuts becomes too strong to ignore or repair, a new segment of concrete appears that represents the formal acceptance of the voice of the people.

Traditionally, management theory focuses on the formal structures of organizations. Those students of management who have deeply focused on the neoclassical concepts of human relations have focused on interpersonal relationships and, thus, on the informal organization. Some years ago, Peter M. Blau and W. Richard Scott, in their definitive study of formal organizations, came to the conclusion that the two camps were really dependent upon each other.

It is impossible to understand the nature of a formal organization without investigating the networks of informal relations and the unofficial norms as well as the formal hierarchy of authority and the official body of rules, since the formally instituted and the informally emerging patterns are inextricably intertwined. The distinction between the formal and the informal aspects of organizational life is only an analytical one and should not be reified; there is only one actual organization.[8]

The role of analysis in evaluating formal and informal aspects of structure is to keep in mind the reality that there is no separation of the two in terms of goal attainment. In well-motivated groups, informal actions may be the key to successful actions. In fact, it is often the case that strongly motivated groups must be constrained not because of lack of goal attainment but because of their abilities to disrupt the flow of limited assets as decreed by the formal planning structure. As might be expected, some of the most difficult tasks facing an analyst investigating overall aspects of organizational effectiveness are found in this area of formal and informal structures. Interaction of the aspects of this system is pervasive. Analysis of the most glaring examples is possible; the other, less obvious examples must in most cases be evaluated through extrapolation and the insights of the investigator.

Organizational Charts

Until a better system is developed, structural relationships in organizations will continue to be depicted by charts that specify the formal authority and communication networks as agreed upon by those in power at the time of chart publication. For most large, hierarchical structures, significant changes in designated patterns occur by the end of the first quarter following publication. For some firms, the administrative costs of maintaining currency and reprinting on an annual basis are such that a moratorium is placed on revisions before two- or three-year phase points.

The realities of economics and organization dynamics delegate a chart that proports to depict structure to the status of an abstract model, which is widely recognized as imperfect and, therefore, of limited value. Even in the terms of formal structure, important relationships are often not depicted. Task force teams, of critical importance in matrix structures, are rarely indicated on charts. No informal relationships, even the "dotted line" staff channels are rarely indicated for all to see. The degree of authority of a superior over a subordinate, especially power to hire and fire, is not indicated. Key lateral relationships between peers are basically of no concern to those constructing such a model. For new hires, the process of ferreting out lateral relationships necessary for accomplishing their job is a continual frustration. In large firms, it often takes a year for new personnel to become comfortable with the authority and communication.

Limitations accepted, the typical organization chart still represents the most useful starting point for analysis of structure. Granted, it is usually overly simple and fails to consider a significant number of important relationships. However, it is still of great value, particularly when these imperfections are fully considered and used as starting points, not as the final word.

Appropriate Structural Design

Deciding on the appropriate structural design is best approached by examining series of facets related to the nature of the organization under consideration: its mission or objective, its personnel, its technology, and its size. Also of great importance is the external environment in which the organization must operate and exist. Finding negative aspects among the above organizational components is quite easy and rather common. Few executives admit to being well satisfied with their structure and for the best of reasons: lack of efficiency, ineffectiveness, and failing to accomplish the mission of the organization. The difficulty in preparing a chart that precisely depicts the true nature of structure has already been indicated. If a representative blueprint of structure is not available, then a determination of whether or not the organization effectively deals with such key variables as specialization and coordination is, at the very least, required.

In a significant number of cases, even a hint that structure is ineffective should be sufficient to start a process of reorganization. Three popular forms of restructuring are: (1) eliminating scalar levels of functional departments; (2) reduction of headquarters size; and (3) matrix departmentation.

Of these three approaches, matrix departmentation or matrix organization is the most complex and difficult to operate effectively over time. It combines functional and divisional structures within the same part of an organization to create a matrix of cross-functional teams on a permanent rather than temporary basis. The system violates concepts of unity of command and can potentially impose high levels of stress on those operating within such a structure, especially for extended periods of time.

Why, then, should the matrix form of structure be considered? The advantages are several. First, it can formalize an existing informal system that has been developed to serve the needs of its organization. The flexibility offered by a matrix system serves to accommodate cross-national differences. It may also stimulate interfunctional cooperation and in common applications ease growth in new product or service applications. It is accommodating to task force teams that require significant flexibility.

On the down side, from the human resource management perspective, matrix systems present problems that seem to fester over time. Perhaps the most serious of these is the loss of control over managerial development. Career paths become blurred when so many promotions or assignments are lateral. Although experience is valued, organizations promote not so much on the accumulation of experience at the same level of difficulty as for mastery of successive levels of more difficult, more advanced experiences. Evaluation of career paths through the complex two-boss systems is difficult at best. Power struggles, now absent from conventional structures, seem manifest in matrix structures as functional and program managers each strive for advantage in their personal respective arenas. Of significant impact in an area striving for cost efficiencies, matrix systems add overhead, such as extra salaries for program managers and operations made more complex than necessary and inefficient use of high-salary personnel whose skills are only partially utilized by their matrix teams. Analysis of cost and effectiveness, while difficult at best in structural analysis, becomes absolutely profound in the case of matrix systems. Usually it is fatigue on the part of personnel, not cost analysis, that triggers a return to more conventional forms of structure.

Reduction of the size of headquarters staffs represents an interesting study of contrast. Schlumberger, Ltd., a dominant figure in the oil business employing some 70,000 people worldwide, retains less than two hundred employees in both their Paris and New York offices combined. Other highly successful firms, such as specialty steel marker Worthington Industries, maintain a headquarters of less than one hundred personnel. Individuals driving past Worthington's headquarters will be hard pressed to count a dozen vehicles in its parking lots at a time; executives are expected to be out with customers or in the factories with the workers. Output, service, and quality are the priority messages sent downward through the organization when headquarters staffs are lean. Large headquarters staffs housed in palatial surroundings send a mixed signal to the workforce. Ross Perot states that if he were to control GM, he would close the 14th floor of GM headquarters where the senior executive offices are located. All executives would work in car manufacturing plants and other production facilities. Huge staffs, he maintains, act as buffers shielding the people running the company from the reality of lower corporate levels. When such staffs are abolished, lines of communication are open.[9]

The third method of organization redesign currently enjoying great popularity consists of cutting out levels of functional structure. "Smashing the corporate pyramid" is the popular term, and the Nucor Corporation has become a popular example of this form of restructuring. Under their CEO, F. Kenneth Iverson, the faltering company restructured with only four scalar levels of management. Decentralization was stressed and made necessary by this restructuring. Sales and profits have enjoyed extraordinary growth—some 1,250 percent over a ten-year period.[10] Nucor's actions apparently were well planned and executed. Unfortunately for many firms, the term "smashing the pyramid" is a most appropriate analogy. Elimination of functional levels by a certain firm in which this author was consulting increased the span of control for manufacturing supervisors from an average of eight or twelve employees, a demanding level in itself, to a nearly unmanageable level of high twenties to low thirties. In addition, the load upon the supervisor of these managers was of such magnitude that only an hour a week was allocated to each manager for general discussion and interaction.

The objective of small corporate staffs positioned upon lean, flat structures is greater efficiency and rapid communication. How lean and how flat a firm can become is not subject to analysis by formula. The question is often asked, "How deeply can staff operations be cut?" In many situations the answer is, "Cut until productivity is suffering." To maintain adequate control over divisionalized structures, to insure that cuts have not moved from fat to muscle and then to bone, requires knowledge of the impact of organizational surgery. Too often this knowledge, especially in terms of human resources impact, is inadequate. The process of obtaining feedback from areas of impact is further complicated by maintaining confidentiality over reorganization plans. In most situations, word of impending change is out well before most of those officially involved are introduced to the plan. A strong case may be made for the involvement of the total organizational body, which will be impacted by change. Involvement to the fullest extent reduces personnel stress, serves to enhance the quality of change, and, most importantly, results in the retention of key personnel.

DEVELOPMENT AND MOTIVATION OF ALL PEOPLE WHO INTERACT WITH THE ORGANIZATION

Each year, major business publications present their versions of America's most admired corporations and their leaders. *Fortune* researches the key variables that build a winning reputation. Appropriate to this discussion, the first in-depth look at leadership in the 1990s identified the "ability to attract, develop, and keep talented people" as the most critical attribute in building a winning reputation.[11] Boeing, often cited as one of the top ten places to work, is very solid in employee development. This is not a recent conversion but a reflection of decades of attention to the needs of its people. As Frank Shrontz, chairman and CEO, recently noted, employee training and process enhancement rank equally with a $690 million investment in equipment and facilities as the key to improved productivity.[12]

Traditionally, analysis of leadership and motivation variables has focused on employees of the organization and those in the leadership chain. Today, more successful companies are emulating the philosophy of Worthington Industries. The philosophy of this highly successful firm deals in some depth with customers, suppliers, managers and support groups, citizenship, communication, and "all Worthington people."[13] Placing second only to Philip Morris for quality of management in the *Fortune* poll, Wal-Mart Stores stands far above larger competitors Sears and K-Mart in perceived quality of management, which is the trait in shaping a positive reputation currently considered second only to attracting and keeping talented people. Of course, the direct relationship of one variable to the other is apparent. Wal-Mart encourages responsibility at the lowest possible level. All managers of the approximately thirty-four departments within a typical Wal-Mart are expected to run their operation as if they were running their own business. Says President David Glass, designated successor to Sam Walton, "Instead of having one entrepreneur who founded the business, we have got 250,000 entrepreneurs out there running their part of the business."[14]

The accomplishments of Boeing, Wal-Mart, and Worthington Industries are impressive, and such recognition as one of the top ten places to work is gratifying to each firm's management group. The durability of such recognition is, however, sometimes transitory. Wang Laboratories was a favorite of Thomas J. Peters and Robert H. Waterman in the bestseller *In Search of Excellence*. In their survey of excellent companies, Wang passed all hurdles for excellent performance from 1961 to 1980. Boeing and Wal-Mart were also recognized in the same survey.[15] By 1990, however, Wang Labs ranked next to last among admired U.S. companies, garnering a score of 3.08 out of a possible 10.[16] What can happen to a well-respected, well-managed firm in the relatively short time span of ten years? In the case of Wang, what happened is complex. There were mitigating circumstances, but in the end, the founder of Wang himself was forced to admit that he made poor decisions and delegated leadership positions based on family rather than ability. A son was dismissed, and the founder attempted a partial return, but the damage had been done. As Peter Drucker is fond of saying, leadership "is work."

Leadership is not only work, it is difficult. Most principles of management appear simplistic to the uninitiated. Leonard R. Sayles observes that "the principles of management neglect everything that's problematic in converting good intentions into good results. The middle ground, between motive and results, is both the critical and the neglected area of training."[17] There are few in management positions in Western culture who do not want to manage well. Yet, for reasons that may be directly related to Western culture, many do not manage or lead well, especially when compared to Japanese competitors.

Many reasons for inferior performance relate back to the key variables discussed in the early segments of this chapter: pride, mentoring, personal attributes and qualities, and the contradictions imposed upon people in organizations through inappropriate structure and design. Though customs and practices may contribute to the feeling of rank and importance of certain members of the hierarchy, they also serve to subdue the positive, productive impulses of much of the workforce. Returning to the basic subject of development and motivation, subordinates must be given information that results in a clear understanding of jobs and boundaries. Descriptions of jobs and tasks are helpful, but precise specifications are of greater value to the position incumbent. Once clear boundaries are established, excitement and motivation follow naturally. Unfortunately, jobs do inevitably overlap and boundaries become blurred. Those charged with the preparation of written specifications often choose to ignore such overlap, assuming that such grey areas will be solved by the passage of time or the natural interactions of those faced with such organizational inadequacies. Frustration results from such imposed friction, as well as the decay of positive relationships so important to goal achievement.

The presumption of this analysis is that motivation of organizational members relates more to the structural conditions within an organization and how it is designed for goal attainment than to various programs designed to "turn people on to work." Frederick Herzberg's well-known restatement of Abraham Maslow's "need hierarchy" holds that lower-order (extrinsic) needs, such as pay and benefits or working conditions, do not truly motivate, primarily because in most organizations these needs are satisfied. Higher-order (intrinsic) needs, such as job challenges, accomplishment, and sensing achievement, are never fully satisfied and, thus, are continually motivating.[18] If we accept the full implication of this theory, then intrinsic or motivating forms of job satisfaction can be obtained by the employees themselves. In fact, management is hard pressed to do much more than provide the conditions through which their membership is able to find challenge, seek accomplishment, and internalize a feeling of self-actualization or achievement. Extrinsic needs, or the lower-order, "hygienic" areas of job satisfaction, must be serviced by the administrative aspects of organization and management.

Successful organizations, according to the self-motivating interpretation of Herzberg's model, enjoy a management capable of providing a long-lived, behaviorally healthy atmosphere for their employees. Within this environment, need satisfaction of the highest order is obtained by following procedures and targeting on objectives that are internalized rather than ordered. In such situations opportunities for satisfaction are not limited by economic ceilings or coercive competition. The higher-order needs or motivations are those in which open access is controlled by the individual member. Supervisors fulfill the ideal role of facilitators or servants to subordinates, aiding and facilitating them to reach goals within an organizational context.

BUILDING TALENT

Leaders of the most admired U.S. corporations develop their talented people in a facilitating environment that includes the finest tools available. Merck, the most admired U.S. firm in *Fortune*'s 1990 survey, has a stable of scientists that Harvard and MIT are trying hard to tap. Research facilities at Merck's Rahway, New Jersey, headquarters are lavishly equipped. More R&D dollars (some $755 million in 1989) are invested in the development of new products at Merck than at almost any other pharmaceutical company.[19] Star performers at Merck are allowed freedom to pursue extracurricular projects—a popular option with many top-rated firms. At Rubbermaid, another top-rated firm in the 1990 survey, President Stanley C. Gault acts as a corporate cheerleader, as well as the number-one quality controller. Gault is passionate about quality because he is passionate in his pride for his firm. Many observers feel that the infectious pride in quality products is a key factor in motivation of Rubbermaid people. Consequently, Rubbermaid enjoys a reputation for some of the best-made products in the United States. This same level of pride and enthusiasm is evident at quality companies such as Boeing Commercial Air and Hewlett-Packard. Boeing is noted for employee development. Every new employee is given an eight-hour first-day orientation. Total quality concepts are stressed at these early sessions along with the concept of continuous improvement. After job assignment, new hires are given extensive awareness training in total quality control and statistical process control. Quality circles or management quality improvement teams are an expected part of each employee's further development.[20] Hewlett-Packard, another firm noted for its motivated workforce, encourages risk taking. Engineers and others within the firm are given technical and intellectual freedom within their operations. The key to a risk-taking environment is the actions directed at employees who fail. According to Harold Edmondson, Hewlett-Packard vice president of manufacturing, "If someone fails, it's no disgrace or discredit, if he or she had made the effort in an ethical, positive and intelligent way. . . . We don't want people so afraid of failing that they don't set high enough goals."[21]

COMPANY EVALUATION

Organizational structure and human resource management systems are reviewed in this book as one subject area. The critical dependence of organizational quality on the effective design and application of these functions is a proven fact, especially in terms of organizational de-layering, headquarters reductions, and dependence on autonomous work and task force teams for quality and competitive strength. Table 10.1 identifies areas of critical importance when conducting an evaluation in this area.

NOTES

1. John Stevens, "Echos from the Past," *PHP Intersect* 1, no. 8 (August 1985): 46.

2. Shoichiro Irimajiri, "The Living Difference," speech delivered at Stanford University (Marysville, OH: Honda of America Manufacturing, Company Publications, April 7, 1987).

3. "Milestone," *Fortune* 121, no. 3 (January 29, 1990): 16.

4. James G. March, ed., *Handbook of Organizations* (Rand McNally, 1965), p. 401.

5. Ross Perot, "The GM System Is Like a Blanket of Fog," *Fortune* 117, no. 4 (February 15, 1988): 50–51.

6. "Roger Smith Replies to Ross Perot," *Fortune* 117, no. 4 (1988): 50.

7. Fremont D. Kash and James E. Rosenzweig, *Organization and Management*, 4th ed. (New York: McGraw-Hill, 1985), p. 235.

8. Peter M. Blau and W. Richard Scott, *Formal Organizations: A Comparative Analysis* (San Francisco: Chandler Publishing Company, 1962), p. 6.

9. Ross Perot, "How I Would Turn Around G.M.," *Fortune* 117, no. 4 (February 15, 1988): 46.

10. "Iverson: Smashing the Corporate Pyramid," *Business Week*, January 21, 1985, p. 71.

11. "Leaders of the Most Admired," *Fortune* 121, no. 3 (January 29, 1990): 40.

12. "Boeing Is Big on Employee Development," *Manufacturing Engineering* 103, no. 1 (July 1989): 40.

13. *Worthington Industries Philosophy* (Worthington, OH: Worthington Industry Publications, 1988).

14. "Leaders of the Most Admired," p. 46.

15. Thomas J. Peters and Robert H. Waterman, Jr., *In Search of Excellence* (New York: Warner Books, 1982), p. 20.

16. "How All 305 Companies Rank," *Fortune* 121, no. 3 (January 29, 1990): 66–67.

17. Leonard R. Sayles, *Leadership* (New York: McGraw-Hill, 1979), p. 7.

18. Frederick Herzberg, *Work and the Nature of Man* (Cleveland, OH: World Publishing Company, 1966), p. 72.

19. "Leaders of the Most Admired," p. 40.

20. "Ten Top Places to Work," *Manufacturing Engineering* 103, no. 1 (July 1989): 37.

21. Ibid., p. 45.

Table 10.1
Typical Strengths and Weaknesses in Planning, Organizing, Directing, and Controlling Organizational Structure and Human Resource Function

	Strengths	Weaknesses
PLANNING	CEO provides leadership and challenges which stretch but are attainable.	Challenges and leadership at the top levels basically take the human factors for granted and not as a key factor for success.
	Human resources are considered as a critical element and constraint on all plans.	Skills, staff demographics, and style are not considered the equal of strategy structure and systems in goal accomplishment.
	Necessary time is allowed for recruitment, training, and development of personnel.	The significant majority of management time and funding for production/service improvement is allocated to technology and automation.
	Plans are well communicated to all organizational levels at the earliest possible date, the only exception being critical need for corporate security.	Adequate time for key impact changes such as re-organization is not provided.
		Contingency plans are inadequate, outdated.
ORGANIZING	Organizational structure is appropriate for mission accomplishment.	Structure is outdated and inappropriate for current mission.
	Organizational structures are revised as necessary, but only with careful review for impact upon people.	Changes to structure are made by executive task force, with little overall input.
	Job descriptions and specifications are kept current and appropriate.	Lateral relationships, "dotted-line" staff linkages are not formally considered in structure analysis.
	Lines of communication and coordination are considered in organizational design.	Span-of-control numbers are not checked or analyzed in terms of subordinate needs or supervisory time.
	Committees are considered part of the formal structure of the organization. Duplication of efforts are recognized and avoided.	Authority and responsibility are not appropriate for both functional and scalar positions.
DIRECTING	Communication of strategy, objectives, and policy is frequently accomplished in a clear and understandable manner.	Communication of matters of importance and concern to the workforce is guarded, infrequent, and often fragmented.

158

Senior executives are visible and available to all members of the organization. Not only are doors open, but these leaders appear on the turf of workers and subordinates.

Development of subordinates is not only encouraged, but evident abilities in the area are a requirement for promotion.

CONTROLLING

Near zero tolerance for poor quality or service is instilled in the workforce.

"Soft" measures of performance are recognized and rewarded, as are quantitative figures and data.

The tradeoffs between control and creativity are recognized and reflected in policy.

Attention to quality improvement with respect to the duty of each organizational member is well communicated.

Development of subordinates, while given space in performance review documents, is not considered as a key factor in assignments or promotion.

Actions by senior management, along with benefits such as "golden parachutes" are exceedingly generous while pressure for wage concessions and layoffs is placed on lower staff and hourly employees.

Quantitative data is used in performance evaluation to the near total exclusion of qualitative data.

Team efforts are controlled through standards which are basically a multiple of the number of team members times individual figures.

Limited guidance is provided relating to ethical issues, standards of service, and replacement of defective products.

Standards of evaluation are poorly communicated to the workforce. As a result, personnel selected for negative personnel actions are often not aware of their unsatisfactory performance.

159

11

Organizational Interface, Takeovers, Mergers, and Acquisitions

Years of consulting in the areas of organizational culture and productivity can result in a classic case of déjà vu. Between units of the same department, departments of the same division, and divisions of the same organization, one encounters an insidious repetition of the following behaviors:

—failure to assist anyone in any area due to a lack of confidence about future cooperation

—a belief in the other's ineffectiveness

—artificial boundaries between like functions

—a few joint activities but little mutual understanding

The list could go on, but the impact of each element is basically the same. Barriers to productive activity become ingrained in the fabric of the particular functions or units. A consultant can be engaged at some cost to correct ingrained problems, which in early stages could be readily avoided altogether but once established require time, effort, and possible removal and replacement of personnel. In some cases, the only solution may be near total replacement of upper management or sale/takeover of the corporation.

ACTIVITY INTEGRATION, THE ELUSIVE GOAL

A critical consideration in the design of organizational structures is the smooth coordination of activities. A key objective is overall unity of effort among the various subsystems as they focus together on the accomplishment of the organizational objective or group task. "Interface" is the term that best describes this objective. *Webster's* defines "interface" as "a point or means of interaction between two systems, disciplines, groups, etc."[1] Both the point and the means of interaction are important. There must be a means to achieve interface, but there must also be a point at which it occurs. It is often the intent of units to interact, cooperate, and coordinate, but they never determine where or at what point this interaction or interface will occur. The opposite is equally frequent; points of full interface with contributing units are established, yet no effective mechanism is devised to proceed toward this goal.

Why is effective interfacing such a problem for organizations in our culture? According to Leonard R. Sayles, a source of this problem is that new executives anticipate a simple, rational, clearly bounded world and instead encounter a vague, ambitious, "systems" world.[2] The concept of interface is adapted from systems theory, which is an open, flexible concept of organizational structures and interaction. It also places emphasis upon system integration; without such integration the system is, for the most part, inoperative. Comparison of American and Japanese cultures reveals interesting differences among the various groups to which one is held responsible. Americans tend to view collectives as negative, as something that inhibits initiative and delays progress. On the other hand, the excuse "it didn't happen on my watch" simply does not cut any ice in Japan. As an illustration of this cultural variance, the following orders of the day, given by Admiral Lord Nelson in 1805 in the battle of Trafalgar against the French and Spanish and by Admiral Heihachiro Togo 100 years later in the battle of Tsushima Strait in the Russo-Japanese War, are cited by Jiro Tokuyama of the Nomura School of Advanced Management:

Lord Nelson: "England expects every man to do his duty."

Heihachiro Togo: "The future of our nation and our empire depends upon the performance of each of you."[3]

Of the two exhortations, Togo's is clearly far more demanding and systems oriented, embodying the principle that there is no limit to the duty each individual Japanese owes to the group.

Mechanisms for Interface

Structural mechanisms are most popular in American culture. Their general methods of achieving coordination, suggested by Joseph P. Litterer, are directive, voluntary, and facilitated.[4] In the most favored form of directive coordination, *hierarchical coordination*, various activities are linked by placing them under a central authority. Normally such functions are coordinated by a president or chief executive officer. In the days of more simplistic organizations and a more pliable workforce, this form of integration was sufficient—it apparently worked. As we saw in the space shuttle Challenger disaster, the nonhierarchical coordination of NASA, in the form of its many levels and specialized departments, served as a near perfect filter to the upward movement of critical concerns for the life and safety of the crew.

Although the typical pyramidal chart indicates one central position that is a focal point for coordination of all the key activities, realization of this objective is nearly impossible in large organizations. Assuming that there is delay of interaction until such a central point is established, and assuming that it will be effective at that time, there could very well be an unacceptable delay in the taking of action. Major problems of communication exist among the scalar levels of a large hierarchy that make it close to impossible for individuals at or near the top to have information necessary for the coordination of activities at lower levels. Thus, interface throughout a large hierarchical structure must be supplemented by other formal and informal means.

A second mechanism for coordination is *administrative*. The horizontal flow of routine work is easily integrated through work procedures such as memos with routing slips. If these procedures are programmed or routinized, other special structural means for coordination may not be necessary. Over time, however, there is danger that such routine procedures may become institutionalized and a detriment rather than a facilitator for interface. For the more nonprogrammable situations, committees and task force groups are required to supplant administrative procedures that are more inflexible in nature. Committees as a mechanism for interface present unique problems of their own. These will be covered in detail later in this chapter.

The third mechanism suggested by Letterer, *voluntary means*, cuts through many of the structural constraints that limit integration, but it presents a more difficult challenge to management. This approach involves the willingness and ability of individuals and groups to find means outside the formal mechanisms that will integrate their activities with others. The most desirable and important type of integration is that which transcends organizational barriers. Such voluntary coordination requires that the individual involved have sufficient knowledge of goals and adequate information concerning the specific organizational problems of coordination. In addition to possessing this knowledge, employees must be motivated to do the right and necessary actions on their own. Achieving such voluntary coordination is one of the most important and difficult problems facing management. There is a fear of unleashing actions beyond the control of the formal structure, yet it is the inadequacy of this very structure that requires individual initiative. This problem is especially acute for the organization facing rapidly changing environmental and technological factors. The traditional hierarchical structure in a stable environment can rely to a significant degree on established procedures to insure coordination. But when faced with turbulence, as are most of today's organizations, different mechanisms may be necessary to facilitate integration.

INTERFACE DYNAMICS

Studies of coordinating mechanisms in large contemporary firms reflect the relative consistency of the problems begging for creative movement toward effective integration. One of the largest investigations into the nature of interface programs looked at the top 1,000 Japanese firms in 1985. Results of this study indicate that five factors significantly affect the existence and selection of coordination mechanisms. In order of importance, these are:

—importance of technical factors
—organizational climate (adaptability)
—progressiveness of departments, especially information services
—resources of key departments
—computer experience of users[5]

For Japanese firms, effective interface is an objective of the highest priority. Such attention to interface is considered a key reason why Japanese corporations adjust so quickly to energy crises, currency fluctuations, microelectronic revolutions, and many extraordinary advances in production technologies.[6] Kenichi Ohmae maintains that interface problems are why so many Western companies fail to react to environmental changes in an effective, competitive manner. Often such cases of competitive breakdown happen at functional interfaces. The following queries are cited by Ohmae as typical examples of such problems faced by organizations:

• At the interface between engineering and marketing and possibly between other functions as well: Should Company A install computer-aided design (CAD) to free up and reassign some engineers into marketing so as to develop product concepts closer to the actual needs of the end users?

- At the interfaces between R&D, engineering, and purchasing: Should Company B manufacture large-scale integrated (LSI) circuits internally to protect the confidentiality of the circuit design, or should it purchase them from outside to take advantage of other manufacturers' economies of scale?

- At the interfaces between international, personnel, legal, production, and possibly other matters: Should Company C consolidate its overseas production plants and invest in a modern production facility at a single location?

- At all interdepartmental interfaces: Should Company D allow each operating division to establish its own international operations, or should it provide a corporate presence to host divisional growth in each country entered?[7]

Single, definitive answers to the above examples of interface questions are seldom, if ever, available. It is equally certain that satisfaction of all concerned parties will fall short of ideal. U.S. companies with their rigid functional and scalar structures are not well designed for dealing with interface issues. More loosely defined structures in the mode of Rensis Likert's "linking pin" concept, where each manager's area of responsibility slightly overlaps others, are better equipped to identify and deal with interface issues.

A study of Canadian public health organizations further supports the concept of overlapping functions as the key to more effective interface. The results of this study show that independence of groups within an organization is associated with failure to assist other groups, ineffective total outcomes, lack of confidence about future cooperation, and a belief in the ineffectiveness of other groups. Cooperative goals between and within units fosters positive expectations, exchange of information and resources, productivity, cohesion, and morale.[8]

The importance of technical factors can intensify interface problems. One of the most frequently noted areas of integration difficulty is in the data processing function, in which two areas of interface difficulty emerge. One area, that of integration with corporate management as a whole, has continued to present problems of integration since the advent of the discipline. One study of integration friction summarizes the standoff between data processing management and top corporate management. The upper scalar levels of organization perceive data processing management as "uncommunicative, unresponsive, and unpredictable." The opposite side of this area that cries out for interface of the highest level, the data processing managers, finds upper-level managers to be "insensitive, manipulative, demanding, and out of touch."[9] Attempts to manage this problem area fall into three general categories: manipulative, abdicative, or strategic. Manipulative managers use data processing resources and personnel as instruments to block the progress of rival departments while advancing their own positions. The abdicative group takes a hands-off approach and lets the data managers act independently. The most beneficial style, especially from the objective of improved interaction and goal attainment, is strategic. Strategic managers acknowledge a commitment of corporate management to data processing plans and clarify the relevance of their work.[10] Such clarification is basic to developing confidence and esteem between parties while providing the key lubricant (information) to successful interface, especially in technical areas.

As prominent as the problems of interface between data processing and the traditional functional areas of management are, it is becoming nearly as difficult to integrate the tasks of telecommunications, voice communications, and data processing. No state of consensus exists regarding the appropriate and effective method for consolidating the tasks of telecommunications and data processing departments, according to users at a national computer conference.[11] According to half of the users' companies, the two departments operate autonomously, with telecommunications reporting to data processing in a majority of the remaining cases. In contrast, the U.S. Air Force has both departments report to the Air Force Communications Command.[12]

Closely related to this problem is the transformation required when users must integrate previously stand-alone microcomputers into corporate information systems. As new, more powerful technology comes on-line, the question arises as to who should control, manage, and integrate this technology. Some professionals feel that management information systems departments should not be in charge of remote workstations. MIS has tried to manage resources located in user environs before, and the results have been less than ideal.[13] From the integration perspective, although microcomputers may be, and in fact often are, linked to global corporate networks, most of the processing they do and the output they produce is used locally. Needs at the global level are sufficiently unique that central control of applications and processing capability is simply not practical. As this example illustrates, a large cultural gap remains between most information service professionals and most corporate microcomputer users.

A logical step in integrating data processing and telecommunications is in the area of voice communications. Basically, there is no single, inexpensive, and straightforward method for integrating voice and data. Review and analysis of this area indicate that few users have made much progress in such interface activities.[14] An organizational structure that separates voice and data communications functions may represent a significant barrier to integration. With separate managers, budgets, and reporting, interface factors such as joint planning and purchasing are minimal. The historical dominance of data processing departments and a somewhat negative view of needs for voice communications present continuing obstacles to the integration of these technologies. The city of Fort Collins, Colorado, sidestepped the issue by combining these functions in a department of Information and Communication Systems.[15] However, allowing each function to retain its autonomy under a combined administrative department basically delays the day of reckoning. At some point, in the interests of efficiency and integration, artificial functional divisions must give way.

A not too distant series of historic events vividly portrays the fallacy, the problems, and the dangers associated with placing obstacles in the way of technology integration and why these artificial functional divisions must give way if technology integration is to take place and be productive.

U.S. military aviation pioneer General William "Billy" Mitchell, in spite of almost insurmountable obstacles, revolutionized modern warfare. He served as head of the combined Allied air force in Europe during World War I and emerged from the war as a highly decorated brigadier general. Upon his return to the United States after the war, he actively campaigned to develop an independent air force and a unified Department of Defense. The Navy violently opposed a merged Army and Navy air force command and Mitchell was assailed by a degree of vituperation that history does not record ever having been surpassed in any controversy. Mitchell pursued his objective and challenged the vulnerability of Navy battleships to attack by air. His challenge provoked worldwide repercussions and violent indignation among the Navy's admirals. As a result of Mitchell's agitation, the Navy performed its own bombing tests on the battleship *Indiana* to demonstrate the improbability of a modern battleship being either destroyed or even put out of action by a bomb. Undaunted, Mitchell reiterated his convictions, which made him a national figure, and Congress passed a joint resolution to permit him to perform his tests on two German prizes of war, one of which (the *Ostfriesland*) was described by many Navy experts as unsinkable. On July 18, 1921, the assembled Atlantic fleet watched as six army bombers, directed by Mitchell, and limited to small 600-pound bombs by the Navy as part of stacking the deck in the Navy's favor, sent each ship to the bottom in about a half hour. In spite of this demonstration, Mitchell found himself opposed at every turn by a military and Navy hierarchy who were not disposed to give up their traditions.

He, however, continued to struggle to develop the U.S. Air Force and succeeded in establishing all of its basic policies. He tirelessly worked to bring about an air department separate and coequal with the Army and the Navy. As a result of his efforts, and the ire he generated among hierarchy, he lost his post as assistant chief of the air service, he was demoted to the rank of colonel, and in April 1925 was assigned to a minor post in a remote area of Texas.

Chagrined and indignant, Mitchell, accused the war and Navy departments of "incompetency, criminal negligence and almost treasonable administration of the national defense." President Coolidge ordered him to be tried by court martial. He was tried and on December 17, 1925, was found guilty of making statements to the prejudice of good order and military discipline. He was sentenced to be suspended for five years.

Mitchell felt that he had been unjustly maligned and continued his crusade after his resignation from the Army in January 1926. He undertook a career of writing and lecturing to promote his beliefs and made numerous predictions about what the social and political consequences would be if he were not listened to. He warned that an attack from the Japanese could be expected "some fine Sunday morning" and that the Japanese would invade the Aleutian Islands; both of these happened in 1941.

Mitchell died February 19, 1936, shortly after the House of Representatives refused to reinstate him to the list of retired Army officers. He did not live long enough to witness his vindication. When the U.S. entered World War II in December 1941, his predictions swept the country with amazing force. A separate Air Force was established, and in 1945 the Senate voted to grant posthumously to Mitchell the Congressional Medal of Honor and promoted him to the rank of major general.

Perhaps the failure to integrate the functions of data processing and telecommunications is not as dramatic as the story of Billy Mitchell; however, it is similar in that if it is not accomplished, it will result in serious consequences.

In case after case the failures of integration within organizational structures can be documented. Hospitals are particularly susceptible to interface deficiencies. Cost considerations require consolidation and integration of patient-related clerical activities to maximize effective delivery of health care services, yet such objectives are hindered by boundaries between functional entities.[16]

In today's environment of mergers and acquisitions, a whole range of diplomatic skills are necessary, especially with regard to integration. A particularly difficult political situation occurs when one firm acquires another. Tact and sensitivity are essential in such cases. Divergent corporate cultures are essential to this problem, but even more basic is the excessive degree of specialization and independence exhibited by functions that lose sight of the concept of integrated service to their organization.[17] In the current competitive world environment, companies wishing to deliver high-quality products and services to their customers and gain a competitive advantage must recognize the concept of maximum interface between departments, functions, and scalar levels. Studies have shown that successful interdepartmental collaboration significantly affects a firm's productivity. Employees who believe their objectives are cooperative interact effectively, make progress on tasks, and strengthen their work relationships. Ineffective interaction proves costly to the organizations and to their employees.[18] Other studies show that ineffective interactions result in more than $10,000 being spent per employee per year. When periodic projected delays of as much as $750 per day (due to idle equipment and inflation) are also considered, the total reaches $35,000 per employee per year. Ineffective interaction among departments is particularly costly. Even if the managers' estimates are too high, these results underline the fact that teamwork is critical and that the inability to work together undermines productivity and profit.[19]

It is not uncommon for the departments of an organization to concentrate solely on their own areas of interest. Cooperative, positive interaction and communication with other departments is likely to be perceived as an added burden. Yet positive interface activity is so vital to the competitive success of the company. In this era of international competition, it is essential that team spirit be established across all barriers within both formal and informal organizational structures.

In Japan, successful implementation of the principles of marketing, design, and manufacturing hinges upon corporate policies that produce flexible coordination between different functional areas. Key policies designed to meet this objective include: (1) broader responsibilities for employees; (2) lower barriers between departments (this objective is critical for successful interface); (3) more job training for employees; and (4) greater job rotation.[20] Employees in more successful firms typically work in small teams that have broad responsibilities relating to the design of an entire product line or a large part of the order management process. Japanese employees are usually rotated through many jobs. College graduates are rotated within and between functions, while noncollege graduates receive increased exposure only within their primary functional areas. The highly effective use of multifunctional design teams enhances manufacturing processes, service requirements, and make-or-buy strategies in a parallel fashion.[21]

THE CRITICAL ROLE OF COMMUNICATION

Independence and lack of communication among components of an organization is not uncommon. This is particularly prevalent where a profit center concept has been established. While the motivation and incentive that flow from a profit center structure are desirable, cooperation and communication throughout the organization are essential to competitive success. Such objectives and connections have a profound effect on the skills needed by those managers at the cutting edge of both formal and informal areas of communications networks. As was previously stated, skilled diplomacy is a necessity in intercorporate relations.[22] Communication-sensitive management must often transform factors such as strategic agreements into solid information links. Acceptable courses of action

require a sensitivity to different corporate cultures and excellent negoti-
ating skills. Protocol involved in such areas concerns human relations
more than technical aspects.

MERGERS AND ACQUISITIONS

There are generally three types of mergers: the horizontal merger, in
which two or more direct competitors operating in the same market are
linked; the vertical merger, where firms that operate different stages of
production within a particular market are joined; and the conglomerate
merger, in which there is a union of firms that are neither direct rivals
nor operate in the same area of productive activity.

The ultimate test of the interface process is the integration of one autonomous organization into or within another. By any measures, economic
or behavioral, this process is seldom accomplished with the degree of
skill one would expect from a professional management team. The successful integration of economic activities is an unexpected area of difficulty, but the problem of cultural integration of autonomous organizations
is seldom addressed as much as it should be by acquisition analysis.
Detailed records of such problems are not available, so only by general
consideration of data concerning acquisitions and divestitures can the
magnitude of this problem be estimated.

In the 1970s, 40 divestiture transactions were recorded for every 100
acquisitions.[23] It is, therefore, a most probable conclusion that of this
reported 40 percent divestiture rate, a significant amount, if not a majority,
of the cases were the result of failed structural, behavioral, and other
interface activities.

Why do such a significant number of mergers fail? Considering the
billions of dollars in fees paid to banks, brokerage houses, and attorneys
for their expert advice, analysts of this failure are considering only economic factors, which is not enough. The complexity of the interface process and the time required to fully evaluate and plan for the integration
of independent organizations is the culprit leading to such a high degree
of merger failure.

The terms *merger* (the merging of one company with another), *acquisition* (the acquiring of company by another or by a group of investors
inside or outside the company), and *takeover* (the taking over of one
company by another or by interested investors) are often used synony-
mously.

A majority of mergers are undertaken with incumbent management
approval, but the stockholders must agree to any merger action. While
the required majority of agreeing shareholders varies by state, a two-third
majority is common. Thus, mergers are typically friendly unions between
the management and stockholders of the two firms. Although some man-

agement and stockholders are friendly to the merger, a significant number of employees and managers will be very guarded toward any merger.

Power plays a significant role in the integrative process. The acquiring organization anticipates a profit from the transaction. In most cases a high, if not excessive, price is paid for the acquired organization. Ego is often involved, which further complicates the issue. A case in point is the 1987 acquisition of SCI Television by the partnership of George Gillett and Henry Kravis. Gillett, the owner of Vail and Beaver Valley ski resorts in Colorado, had engineered a series of turnarounds, starting with the Harlem Globetrotters. In spite of his seemingly high level of acquisition expertise, Gillett is cited as making a $1.3 billion deal following an afternoon on the ski slopes with Kravis.[24] Trouble followed almost immediately when junk bonds financing the acquisition were offered to the general public through an open market offering three days following the 1987 market crash. Gillett did improve ratings and profits in his new stations, however; revenues in 1989 were $220 million while interest and principal due equaled $250 million.[25]

The Gillett/Kravis acquisition is a classic example of the fact that mergers and acquisitions are often the most expensive way to do business. In the purchase of an existing firm, the buyer typically knows a great deal less about the future earning prospects of the target firm than does the seller. In the case of SCI Television, Gillett overpaid in terms of both price and interest. To date, this lesson has cost him some $100 million of his initial investment. Not only is it difficult for a buyer to make a bargain considering the information available, but evidence suggests that prices paid to former owners typically exceed the book value of the purchased firm's assets plus market value of the stock holdings. Such premiums are estimated to range between 10 and 50 percent, in part reflecting the difference in information available to buyer and seller.[26]

In the case of hostile takeover actions, the justification of raiders such as Carl Icahn is that current management is not acting in the best interest of the shareholders and that a takeover will enhance the performance of a target firm. Since the negotiation process is basically between a bidder and the shareholders, the raider who gains control feels free to replace incumbent managers. Even if the acquired operations are streamlined, a significant number of deposed managers must be replaced. Replacement management typically comes from the ranks of the acquiring organization. These individuals have little knowledge of the culture of the acquired group, plus they are under pressure to operate in an atmosphere of short-run expedient actions to increase profits and cash flow. These objectives, coupled with a lack of knowledge of the acquired organization, leave replacement management with few tools and little probability of attaining desirable interface between the acquired and parent organizations. Adding to the tension and distrust of those remaining in the acquired organization is that corporate raiders, such as Icahn and Lorenzo, often rationalize the price paid to shareholders in the takeover through wage losses extracted from union labor.[27]

THE "UNPLEASANT SURPRISE" FACTOR

Few issues are a greater impediment to effective integration than inadequate information gathered prior to acquisition. It is impossible for potential buyers to learn everything about a new acquisition, and, once the purchase is made, some unpleasant surprises are quite likely. One of the most publicized examples of the difficulties of prepurchase inspection was the 1986 takeover of Kidder Peabody, a top U.S. investment bank, by General Electric. In the first year of this takeover, a former Kidder Peabody director was charged with criminal insider trading activity. For General Electric, which was attempting to keep a hands-off posture and not disrupt the culture of the Kidder Peabody organization, this totally changed its interfacing strategy. Jack Welch, CEO of General Electric, set the tone of the problem remarking, "We would not have touched Kidder Peabody with a ten-foot pole if we had known there was a skunk in the place. Unfortunately, we did and now we've got to live with it."[28] As a direct result of the Securities and Exchange Commission (SEC) disclosure of improprieties, GE's hands-off strategy was changed. Senior executives at Kidder Peabody were retired or dismissed, and a GE team was installed. Corporate style differences between Kidder Peabody's investment bankers and GE's manufacturing-oriented management team were enormous. Integration of the two corporate cultures became nearly impossible. A former Kidder Peabody manager asserted, "The G.E. people were clods; they broke two-thirds of the china in the shop."[29]

The necessity for ethical controls in an organization where each individual sets his or her own standards represents a worst-case scenario in terms of effective interface. A new corporate culture must be constructed piece by piece. For many of the acquired managers, resentment and resistance to change is such that leaving the acquired organization is the only alternative. One of the truly difficult decisions facing an organization such as G.E. in the Kidder Peabody acquisition is how best to deal with the presumption that managers of the acquiring company are totally out of their element of expertise within the acquired company's culture.

Critical to the integration of two corporate cultures is a plan that deals with behavioral as well as financial considerations. So much effort is expended on financial analysis that little energy is left for the other area. In the Kidder Peabody example, the original strategy was turned around 180 degrees when the fraud of senior officials surfaced. Expectations of the acquiring organization need to be clearly delineated. At the same time the fears and concerns of the acquired organization's members need to be inventoried. An understanding of the differences in management styles of the acquiring and acquired segments is useful, if not essential. Finally, a forward-looking, adequately staffed structure should be developed to support the merged organizations' expected style of operation. These steps are demanding both in terms of the skill of those charged with information gathering and analysis and in terms of time. Corporate expectations of time required to integrate corporate cultures range from the sublime to the ridiculous. A major problem is that senior management is bottom-line oriented. Factors of human behavior are a secondary concern in the game of acquisitions. The assumption remains that if the numbers are right, the people problems can be solved.

COMPANY EVALUATION

Organizational interface directs attention to one of the most neglected areas in the art and science of management. The need to integrate the specialized functions of management has been recognized since the turn of the twentieth century. Beyond giving a profound nod of the head to this stated objective, relatively little is done in terms of management interface, either between functional areas within an individual firm, between divisions of multidivisional firms, or with other firms that have been or are being acquired, merged, or taken over by a parent company. Table 11.1 can assist in the identification of key areas of interface strengths and weaknesses found within a typical organization.

NOTES

1. *Webster's New World Dictionary* (New York: Simon and Schuster, 1984), p. 734.
2. Leonard R. Sayles, *Leadership* (New York: McGraw-Hill, 1979), p. 8.
3. Robert C. Christopher, *The Japanese Mind: The Goliath Explained* (New York: Linden Press, 1983), p. 53.
4. Joseph A. Litterer, *The Analysis of Organizations*, 2d ed. (New York: John Wiley and Sons, 1973), pp. 455–473.
5. Osamu Sato and Mesahiro Horiuchi, "Information Resource Management as a Coordinating Mechanism: A Study in Large Japanese Firms," *Information & Management* (Netherlands) 15, no. 2 (September 1988): 93–103.
6. Kenichi Ohmae, *The Mind of the Strategist* (New York: McGraw-Hill, 1982), pp. 222–223.
7. Ibid.
8. Dean Tjosvold, "Cooperative and Competitive Dynamics Within and Between Organizations Units," *Human Relations* 41, no. 6 (June 1988): 425–436.
9. James C. Dekle, "The Corporate Integration of Data Processing," *Business* 36, no. 2 (April-June 1986): 9–14.
10. Ibid.

11. John Dix, "No Easy Way Seen to Integrate DP, Communications," *Computer World* 18, no. 29 (July 16, 1984): 12, 23–25.

12. Ibid.

13. John Gantz, "Will the Growth of Networks Mean Migration to MIS Control?" *InfoWorld* 9, no. 14 (April 6, 1987): 30.

14. Julia King, "Voice/Data Integration: Dual Departmenting," *Network World* 3, no. 28 (September 15, 1986): 35–36.

15. Ibid.

16. Jeffrey C. Hardy, "Patient Administration: One-Stop Patient Processing," *Healthcare Financial Management* 40, no. 12 (December 1986): 27–32.

17. Robert Dickey and Kevin Murray, "Making the Merger Work: A Commercial Lending View," *Commercial Lending Review* 1, no. 4 (Fall 1986): 3–11.

18. Dean Tjosvold, "Cooperative and Competitive Interdependence: Collaboration Between Departments to Serve Customers," *Group and Organization Studies* 13, no. 3 (September 1988): 274–289.

19. T. Janz and Dean Tjosvold, "Cost Effective versus Ineffective Work Relationships: A Method and a First Look," *Canadian Journal of Administrative Science* 2 (1985): 43–51.

20. Jeffrey L. Funk, "How Does Japan Do It?" *Production* 100, no. 8 (August 1988): 57–62.

21. Ibid.

22. Eric Schmall, "Becoming a Manager/Diplomat," *Network World* 5, no. 11 (March 14, 1988): 23–34.

23. Cited in F. Scherer, "Mergers, Sell-offs, and Managerial Behavior," in Lacy Thomas, ed., *The Economics of Strategic Planning* (Washington, D.C.: Brookings Institute, 1986), pp. 143–170.

24. "A Bad Stumble on the Slopes," *Newsweek*, March 5, 1990, p. 39.

25. Ibid.

26. J. F. Weston, "Determination of Share Exchange Ratios in Mergers," in W. Albert and J. Segal, eds., *The Corporate Merger* (Chicago: University of Chicago Press, 1974), pp. 131–138.

27. M. Jensen, "Takeovers: Their Causes and Consequences," *Journal of Economic Perspective*, Winter 1988, pp. 21–48.

28. Jack Welch, "G.E.'s Costly Lesson on Wall Street," *Fortune* 117, no. 11 (May 9, 1988): 72.

29. Ibid., p. 78.

Table 11.1
Typical Strengths and Weaknesses in Planning, Organizing, Directing, and Controlling Organizational Interface, Takeovers, Mergers, and Acquisitions

	Strengths	Weaknesses
PLANNING	Top management is committed to strong interface throughout the organization. Areas of weak, provincial communication and coordination are known, identified, and subject to correction.	The driving force in merger and takeover analysis is financial. Time lines are relatively short range. Interface problems tend to be simplified. In-depth consideration of potential problem areas again is focused upon financial issues.
	Candidates for mergers and acquisitions are identified and considered as a regular part of management action and concern.	Few activities are planned based upon joint organizational activities. Such planning is limited due to a lack of understanding of the potential for mutual reinforcement of overall goals and objectives.
	Those firms and principals that could logically be considering this organization as a candidate for takeover or acquisition are identified and considered in terms of level of threat on a regular basis.	A basic objective of tight, quantitative outcomes in planned organization activities reduces the potential of interface operations in the broad sense. It is far more difficult to predict with precision the time or magnitude of joint activity, thus broader latitude is required in the setting of initial objectives.
	Planning includes joint activities with provisions for coordination of individual units in areas of strength and unique abilities.	Planning for the integration of technical aspects inherent in the tasks of telecommunications and data processing does not exist. These two departments operate autonomously and fail to move toward essential interface in many technical areas of operation.
	A balanced approach to planning activities includes consideration of corporate culture in areas of interface and merger, acquisition, and takeover actions.	
ORGANIZING	A critical consideration in the design of the structure of this organization is the smooth coordination of activities. In the interest of effective interface activity the number of scalar levels is limited to six. Span of control, while greater than desired in some cases, is still limited in all cases to no more than nine reporting subordinates.	Organization design is based upon insurance of clear reporting channels, precise accountability, and small spans of control. This results in a highly peaked structure of some fourteen scalar levels.
	Artificial boundaries between line organizations are not tolerated. Special efforts by top management are taken to review reporting relationships and insure the greatest degree of open interaction. Information processing is considered a critical interface	The tightly focused assignment of responsibilities results in a closed organizational focus and a lack of consideration of those areas of weakness that make the organization an attractive candidate for raiding or takeover activity.
		Artificial boundaries between like functions are allowed to develop. Upper level management does not assign

Table 11.1 (Continued)

Strengths	Weaknesses
activity. Priority considerations including financial and material resources are provided to insure greatest effectiveness.	priority to the identification and elimination of such problem areas.
	Reporting channels are basically vertical and top down in nearly all cases. Horizontal channels are essentially informal and officially discouraged.
DIRECTING	
The chief executive officer directs all management levels to assume personal responsibility for monitoring the effective interaction with both internal subsystems and external units. Quality of such interface is considered. Measures are taken for the improvement of interface relationships when and where required.	Actions by senior management which tend to restrict communication to clearly defined vertical and horizontal channels has significant impact upon free-flowing interaction and positive interface between units and divisions.
A key factor in the determination of promotion and salary is the reputation of a unit or division as a body that readily cooperates and assists other units within the organization.	Perception by subordinate managers relating to the desire of senior management for close adherance to formal structure results in development and maintenance of artificial boundaries between like functions and the significant reduction of desirable interface.
Lateral communication is encouraged and facilitated through ad hoc committees and groups. Feedback from such lateral interaction to the top levels of the organization is encouraged, with the CEO and members of the executive committee often directly contacting managers at lower scalar levels to solicit their opinions on a variety of subjects.	Organizational culture is basically an "I" form rather than "we." Emphasis is placed upon the reward of individual accomplishments, and little recognition is given to team accomplishments, even though many highly successful actions could be credited to special groups and task force teams.
Any takeover or merger action, either acquisition of another firm or a hostile movement toward their own firm, is treated at the earliest possible date as information of concern to the entire organization. All members are encouraged to search out useful information and to provide upper management with any possibly relevant data on an expedited basis.	Overlapping functions between units or divisions are strongly discouraged. Even where possible "linking pin" benefits may be realized, management policy is to assign like or similar functions only to one body.
	Information on takeover actions, hostile or friendly, and possible merger candidates is treated as classified information for senior executives only. Even upper level middle managers are not involved in the decision process; not even their knowledge and information is solicited.
	In cases where new firms are acquired and integrated, no tone is set by senior management that would encourage the integration of acquired personnel into the culture or the primary organization

176

As a result, barriers are established almost immediately, which serve to block effective integration and interface objectives.

CONTROLLING

Flexibility is built into standards and policies basic to the control process. Goals and objectives are maintained and enforced, but freedom for some choice as to how these goals are attained allows for significant interface actions between groups and units.

A key objective of the design of the control system is insurance that the specific goals and objectives are no more complex than necessary. Methods for compliance are tailored to fit the people involved. Task requirements are stated in understandable terms.

Consistent with the organizational structure and objectives, the control system is designed to get data into the decision-making structure at points where authority exists to act. This is often critical in questions of merger and acquisition where time is often a key factor.

Exceptions to trends and deviations that may have critical long-term impacts are identified and reported by the control procedures. The system is designed to report exceptions quickly enough that critical trends can be corrected before much harm is done, thus balancing the need for flexibility and individual creative motivation vs. the cost to the organization of standard deviation.

To the greatest degree possible, control is identified as each person's individual responsibility. Standards are not a factor to be reported to another staff body but rather are tools to be used by each person in their individual and collective efforts for meeting overall organizational objectives.

Control is a prime objective in this organization. Standards, procedures, and policies are clearly stated and highly inflexible. As a result, managers are reluctant to engage in joint actions whereby they may be held accountable for the actions or lack of action by others.

Control standards are far more complex than necessary. The system is tailored to fit the organization, not its people. As structured, this system raises the prospect of adverse human reactions.

Self-control is not an objective of the control process. It does not, in its highly restrictive form, encourage good communication, mutual trust, and especially inter-participation between the parties involved.

The system, as stated, is basically negative in its nature. It stresses penalty and reprimand with dismissal as an ever-present option. Very limited attention is given to using the process as a tool for development and individual growth.

The control policies are not likely to be viewed as fair and objective. Standards are highly subjective and are a tool for punishment for those who deviate.

Although the control system stresses data as a key variable for analysis of any significant deviation, the MIS system is not fully utilized to reduce demands upon the individual units. Allocation of funds for software development in many possible areas of use is highly limited. Centralization of such authority reduces the opportunity for creative interface between individuals and the data system.

12

Social Responsibility and the Corporation

A company's social responsibility program has three major areas: complying with laws, setting—and abiding by—moral and ethical standards, and philanthropic giving. How can firms evaluate their performance in each of these areas?

INTRODUCTION

Social responsibility is a major subject of concern and action for all but the smallest or least aware of companies. Today it is generally accepted that business firms have social responsibilities that extend well beyond what in the past was commonly referred to simply as the "business economic function." In earlier times managers, in most cases, had only to concern themselves with the economic results of their decisions. Today managers must also consider and weigh the legal, ethical, moral, and social impact and repercussions of each of their decisions.

In many company organizations, however, this area of social responsibility is often not identified as a major or separate functional area. Quite often the responsibility for actions in this area is vested in an individual or small staff, frequently within the human resources management area. Personnel assigned to this area, then, have responsibility for social issues in three major areas:

1. Total compliance with international, federal, state and local legislative laws and acts;

2. Moral and ethical standards and procedures under which the firm will operate; and

3. Philanthropic giving.

Most companies find it no simple matter to formulate and implement socially responsible actions and programs. However, all companies must become concerned and involved in this area. To operate without major disruptions, a company must at all times be in compliance with legal requirements—international, federal, state, and local. It must develop, establish, implement, and police a code of ethical and moral conduct for all members of its organization. In the area of philanthropic activity, where there is considerably more latitude of operations in how, when, where, and even *if* the company or division wants to contribute money or other resources to "worthy causes," the firm must deliberate about and resolve many questions prior to establishing fair and workable guidelines.

Gone are the "public-be-damned" attitudes once held by some companies. With a more active government and populace, company social responsibility in reach of the three major areas has continued to gain greater concern and prominence over the past several decades. Social responsibility will continue to take more time, money, consideration, and concern in all future management decisions and actions. Diverse managerial skills, ranging from simple to highly complex, are required in all of these areas of social responsibility.

UNIQUE PROBLEMS AND CONFLICTING DEMANDS

Social responsibility is complex because decisions must be made in a wide variety of areas.[1] Among the factors that must be considered are:

—Unique laws and codes of ethics in each country;
—Taxes, price fixing, and bribery;
—Joint ventures as differentiated from full ownership of foreign operations;
—The training of foreign nationals;
—Control of air, water, solid waste, radiation, noise, land, and chemical pollution;
—Safety standards;
—Health care;
—Education;
—Equal opportunity regardless of race, sex, age, handicap, religion, or creed;
—Unemployment;
—Inadequate transportation;
—Product safety, packaging, and quality;
—Pricing;

—Support of the arts; and

—Other areas of community enrichment.

When evaluating these conflicting demands and their impact upon the revenue and profitability of the company, management must maintain a degree of detachment. Professional decisions must be relatively free of hypocrisy or self-deception. This is no easy task, as reflected by the pragmatic view of one observer:

Few corporations engage in philanthropy because others need money, as though a corporation were a well-heeled uncle who should spread his good fortune around the family. For the most part, corporations give because it serves their own interests—or appears to.[2]

Each of the three major decision areas of legal compliance, moral and ethical standards, and philanthropic giving—represents unique problems as well as some overlapping points of concern.

LEGAL COMPLIANCE

Corporate policy should state clearly, "illegal actions in any form will not be condoned or tolerated by the company". Stringent enforcement of such a policy must develop at the highest levels and be supported all the way down the organization. Internal enforcement action should be immediate, not simply a reaction to external discovery and prosecution.

Even though such policies are found in most firms, they are not uniformly enforced. *Fortune* listed 117 companies that were prosecuted by the federal government during the 1970s for violation of a major U.S. law or statute.[3] The federal government is now going after defense procurement frauds, bank scams, money laundering, and insider trading.[4]

MORAL AND ETHICAL STANDARDS

Closely related to legal compliance are moral and ethical standards. Political contributions, bribery, and other acts of conduct illegal in this country may not be illegal in other parts of the world. They fall into this category, as do areas such as proprietary information, product misrepresentation, disparagement, premature disclosures, acquiring or divulging confidential information, certain gifts and entertainment, and conflicts of interest. One example of the border between legal and ethical-moral boundaries is Steven Jobs' leaving Apple Computer with some other employees to found another company.[5] By taking these key people with him and starting a new computer company in competition with his old company, he might be legally liable if the old company failed for pirating key information and employees from another company or simple because he deprived his old company of some of the expertise it needed to remain competitive. Legal cases have been decided in either direction in cases similar to this. Although Steve Jobs was not found legally guilty in this particular case, many people feel that what he did was certainly unethical.

To deal with areas that may be considered technically legal but, in the eyes of American management, improper or unethical, companies must develop and disseminate explicit policies, which are rigidly and expeditiously enforced if broken. A typical set of the clearly delineated policies generated by large companies is a small booklet handed out to IBM employees.[6]

Developing a code of morals and ethics is not always simple. The frame of reference is large and sometimes complex. Consideration must be given to existing and proposed laws, Judeo-Christian values, family norms, society and industry as a whole, the firm, and the background and desires of owners, managers, and other employees.

In spite of these complexities, a recent survey (condensed in Table 12.1) shows that most large and many smaller firms have codes of conduct that are distributed to offices and employees, who periodically must sign a statement that they have read the code. Further, these firms have specific procedures for enforcing the code and handling violations.

PHILANTHROPIC GIVING

Under the changes in the 1982 federal tax laws, a company may allocate up to 10 percent of taxable income to philanthropic causes. Prior to the tax changes, the upper limit had been set at 5 percent. Quite a few companies give 5 percent of their income. However, in recent years company contributions have averaged only little more than 1 percent.[7]

One of the basic problems in philanthropic giving is to first determine whether the company wants to give any money at all to social causes and, if so, how much. After a decision to give has been made, questions remain. Which internal and external agencies should receive money, and how much? Should the money be distributed equally between all contributing subsidiaries, or should it be spent primarily in a few selected high-payoff areas? Should other companies be pushed to give the maximum allowable amount? What strings, if any, should be attached to the funds? Who should be involved in determining the answer to these questions?

The answer to these questions must take into account the views and reactions of the company owners, the stockholders, the potential recipients, the competition, and society as a whole. In making decisions on giving, emotions and feelings sometimes run high. They may vary from

Table 12.1

Percentage of Companies (overall and by size) Reporting Various Practices Related to Corporate Codes of Conduct

Question	Overall Response	Size Categories*									
		1	2	3	4	5	6	7	8	9	10
Does your company have a code of conduct?	(N = 611)										
Yes	77%	40	57	74	75	72	90	85	87	92	97
Who receives a copy?	(N = 486)										
Officers/key employees	97%	83	97	94	98	100	100	98	96	100	100
Other employees	55%	46	60	35	54	58	42	60	46	70	68
Who signs it periodically?	(N = 481)										
Officers/key employees	85%	75	62	80	87	80	85	91	86	91	90
Other employees	(N = 451) 27%	23	27	12	17	30	25	23	31	47	39
Are procedures specified for handling violations of the code's provisions?	(N = 478)										
Yes	63%	41	46	38	54	58	55	66	75	85	83
Have procedures been enforced in the last several years?	(N = 463)										
Yes	62%	42	43	30	48	48	64	63	77	83	91

Source: Bernard J. White and B. Ruth Montgomery, "Corporate Codes of Conduct," *California Management Review* 23 (Winter 1980): 82.
*The overall sample of 673 was broken into deciles by size. Category 1 is $0-60 million; category 2 is $60-132 million; category 3 is $132-207 million; category 4 is $201-300 million; category 5 is $300-467 million; category 6 is $467-717 million; category 7 is $717-1,150 million; category 8 is $1,150-1,900 million; category 9 is $1,900-4,000 million; category 10 is $4,000 million and above. The overlap in categories 3 and 4 exists in the original table.

an absolute "No", to a "Yes, under certain conditions", to a very emphatic "Yes."

On the "No" side of giving, Howard Johnson, when interviewed by management consultant Chester Burger, said, "My job is to make a profit. I give my taxes to Uncle Sam, and he spends it to improve social conditions."[8]

Milton Friedman basically agrees with this philosophy. He states, "Corporations have no money to give to anyone. It belongs to their workers, their employees, or their shareholders."[9]

Moving slightly away from the "Absolutely No" position, Friedman does, however, makes two exceptions. First, he feels that closely held corporations, in which the managers are the owners, should be permitted to contribute directly to charity to decrease the tax bite. Secondly, he approves of contributions to local institutions and arts (such as hospitals, universities, parks, and museums) when they provide marginal returns to the company greater than the marginal costs. Friedman does not consider this second category true philanthropy, however. He considers it a business expense.

Friedman is opposed to real philanthropy: "Real philanthropy is that which will cost the company more than it will add to its value in the short term or in the future."[10]

Some individual stockholders do not believe that companies should contribute their income to charitable, educational, or similar organizations that do not further the business interest of the corporation. They feel that this money could better help society by improving or expanding facilities and creating more jobs.

One such person is Evelyn Y. Davis, who has twice submitted a proposal (in 1972 and again in 1979) to the board of directors of the Procter & Gamble Company, asking that stockholders vote on her proposal at the annual meeting. The proposal would have the company give no corporate funds to any charitable, educational, or other organizations, except for the purposes of directly furthering the business interests of the corporation. In 1972, more than 97 percent of the shares voted against Mrs. Davis's proposal. At the 1979 shareholders' meeting, the proposal received only 1.2 percent of the vote.[11]

Today, more and more companies and their chief executive officers believe very strongly in corporate charitable giving and sit on the "Yes" side of the fence. Dayton-Hudson Corporation has given 5 percent of its taxable income to philanthropic agencies since 1945 and pushes other corporations to do so as well.[12]

At one annual meeting when an angry stockholder assailed the company's hefty donation to charity, Xerox's C. Peter McColough replied, "You can sell your stock or try to throw us out, but we aren't going to change."[13]

The Berkshire Hathaway Company has tried to solve some of these problems by letting the shareholders designate, on the basis of shares owned, to what recognized charities they want to send money.[14] With proper precautions, people can make charitable donations without subjecting the money to double taxation: once as company profits, and a second time as taxpayer dividends, which would occur if the company first sent the stockholders the money in the form of dividends and then the stockholders sent the money to their favorite charities. In essence, the Berkshire Hathaway plan permits the stockholders to have a choice in where the money goes and the ability to contribute up to twice as much tax-free money through the company as they would on an individual contributor basis. This idea has not been widely accepted by most major companies, who think it would be too costly. The IRS has serious reservations about this and other similar procedures.[15]

ESTABLISHING AND IMPLEMENTING A SOCIAL RESPONSIBILITY PROGRAM

The choices of avenues in which to participate are quite limited in the legal arena. They are a little broader in the moral and ethical area, and there is considerable latitude in the philanthropic area.

Alternatives should be chosen in light of the personal values and support of the manager and retention of the inner coherence and health of the organization. The depth and breadth of involvement in any area will depend on the company's available resources. Once involvement is determined, it must have the complete backing and support of all levels of management if it is to be satisfactorily implemented and enforced. This need for continuous top management and other levels of management participation and support in such programs is reinforced by four separate studies on establishing and implementing social responsibility programs. The four studies indicate that establishing and implementing a program is not a simple process and requires continued top management involvement. Although these studies looked at only a small number of companies, they pointed out several areas that must be considered in establishing and implementing social responsibility programs within a company.

According to two studies, by Robert W. Ackerman, successful implementation of these programs takes place in three overlapping phases and can take up to eight years from inception to completion.[16]

Phase I is the *commitment phase.* Top management acknowledges the corporation's responsibility in a certain area or on a certain issue, and a policy statement is generated.

Phase II is the *learning phase.* Pertinent data are collected, analyzed, and evaluated by top and middle management.

Phase III is the *institutionalization phase*. Responsibility for the program is transferred from the staff to the line organization. Resources are committed, performance and expectations are communicated, and evaluation is instituted.

Edwin A. Murray's study identified the same three-phase responses as did the Ackerman studies but defined two sub-phases within Phase II: technical learning and administrative learning, with administrative learning the more time-consuming of the two.[17]

The principal purpose of the study by John W. Collins and Christ G. Ganotis was to determine if there was any gap between the attitudes of top, middle, and lower management in implementing corporate social involvement. The study indicated a definite difference in the attitudes toward social issues and the perceived ability to influence the implementation and corporate response to such issues.[18]

As these four studies demonstrate, for the proper implementation and participation in the areas of social responsibility, top management must continuously be active in all phases of the program.

After the broad objectives of social responsibility have been determined, then the more detailed objectives in the three areas of legal, moral and ethical, and philanthropic giving must be established.

Legal

In the legal area the objective should be simply to obey the law. If the company considers the law unfair, then it should make efforts to get the law modified or repealed, or it should attempt to get relief from certain sections of the law. If none of these options are available and the law is too restrictive, then the company must evaluate the possibility of changing its way of doing business, or of moving to a new location where the law does not exist.

Moral and Ethical Standards

Because many people perceive right and wrong from different angles, the objective of the company in the area of ethical and moral standards must be to establish what it will and will not tolerate. Once the level of integrity has been established, then the areas of vulnerability must be examined and limits established in each of these areas. Since not detecting or overlooking violations weakens the fear of punishment, a system of inspection must be implemented and strict levels of punishment enforced for violation of the code. Great care must be exercised in all of these areas. Expenses for implementation and control cannot get out of hand, and policing and enforcement cannot be done in a way that adversely affects the attitudes or the creativity of the employees.

Philanthropic Giving

The objectives of the company in the area of philanthropic giving should be as clearly defined and explicit as are those in economic policy and strategy. The company should be as firm about what it intends to be and do in this area as it is about the business in which it wants to be involved and the type of people it wants to attract to its organization.

COMPANY EVALUATION

Complying or not complying with a law is fairly straightforward; however, a great care must be exercised in assessing and evaluating the correctness or incorrectness of moral and ethical codes and philanthropic giving. Extensive value judgments and the personal desires of top management enter into these decisions.

To help evaluate how well a company is doing in the areas of social responsibility, Table 12.2 has been developed as a preliminary guide. This table can assist in determining the strengths of the company in the various social responsibility areas. Based on the results of this basic evaluation, the company can then see what and where improvements can be implemented.

NOTES

1. Dan R. Dalton and Richard A. Cosier, "The Four Faces of Social Responsibility," *Business Horizons* 25, no. 3 (May–June 1982): 19–27.

2. Lee Smith, "The Unsentimental Corporate Giver," *Fortune* 104, no. 6 (September 21, 1981): 121.

3. Irwin Ross, "How Lawless Are Big Companies?" *Fortune* 102, no. 11 (December 1, 1980): 56.

4. Carol J. Loomis, "The Limited War on White-Collar Crimes," *Fortune* 112, no. 2 (July 22, 1985): 91.

5. "When a Key Worker Leaves with Secrets," *U.S. News & World Report* 99, no. 15 (October 7, 1985): 67; and Bro Uttal, "The Adventures of Steve Jobs," *Fortune* 112, no. 8 (October 14, 1985): 119.

6. IBM Corporation, *Business Conduct Guidelines* (Armonk, NY: IBM Corporation, 1983).

7. Smith, "The Unsentimental Corporate Giver," p. 122.

8. Chester Burger, "What It Takes to Run a Business Today—An Expert's Advice," *U.S. News & World Report* 75, no. 2 (July 10, 1978): 81.

9. Smith, "The Unsentimental Corporate Giver," p. 123.

10. Ibid., p. 124.

11. See the Procter & Gamble Company Notice of Annual Meeting and Proxy Statement, Annual Meeting of Shareholders, September 4, 1979, Cincinnati, OH, p. 10; and Report to the Shareholders of the Procter & Gamble Company Annual Meeting of Shareholders, October 19, 1972, p. 11.

12. C. Roland Christensen et al., *Business Policy: Text and Cases*, 5th ed. (Homewood, IL: Irwin, 1982), p. 510.

13. Richard A. Shaffer, "Xerox Faces Problems in Trying to Duplicate Its Own Past Success," *Wall Street Journal*, February 16, 1978, p. 1.

14. Lee Smith, "Shareholders Get to Vote on Charity," *Fortune* 110, no. 10 (November 30, 1984): 169.

15. Ibid., p. 170.

16. Robert W. Ackerman, *The Social Challenge to Business* (Cambridge, MA: Harvard University Press, 1975); and Ackerman, "How Companies Respond to Social Demands," *Harvard Business Review* 51, no. 4 (July–August 1973): 88–98.

17. Edwin A. Murray, "The Social Response Process in Commercial Banks: An Empirical Investigation," *Academy of Management Review* 1, no. 3 (July 1976): 5–15.

18. John W. Collins and Christ G. Ganotis, "Is Social Responsibility Sabotaged by the Rank and File?" *Business and Society Review/Innovation* (Autumn 1973): 82–88.

Table 12.2
Typical Strengths and Weaknesses in Planning, Organizing, Directing, and Controlling Social Responsibility

	Strengths	Weaknesses
PLANNING	A committee or organization studies, evaluates, and prepares legal interpretations, practices, and codes of moral and ethical conduct to be adhered to by company employees.	No formal legal, moral, or ethical standards planning exists within the company.
	A committee studies, evaluates, and recommends: • Recipients of company philanthropic aid, and • Company people and money amounts to be allocated to such endeavors.	The only remedial action taken against legal, moral, or ethical problems is a reaction to a serious problem that has arisen in one or more of these areas. There is no consistent plan for philanthropic giving.
ORGANIZING	There is a clearly defined, firm written policy against any illegal acts.	There is no written policy about moral or ethical standards, or it is poorly or loosely worded.
	There is a clearly defined written policy on moral and ethical conduct.	Unwritten or loosely worded, vague standards are poorly communicated.
	A social responsibility committee within the company ensures a consistent policy of giving and screens potential recipients.	There is little or no consistent or organized policy of charitable giving with respect to quantity, organization, or location.
DIRECTING	The president and all management levels firmly support direct adherence to legal, moral, and ethical standards.	Little or no direction or suupprt is given with respect to conduct, penalties, or punishments to be taken by management and/or employees in the areas of legal, moral, or ethical standards.
	All charitable giving is reviewed by the president and key management personnel to make certain that it is distributed where it will be of the most help to the company and to society.	Little or no direction, guidance, or support is given with respect to what the company will do about choosing and giving to charitable organizations.
CONTROLLING	All company personnel are required periodically to read, agree to, and sign a code of legal, moral, and ethical practices.	There is poor, little, or no control over legal, moral, or ethical conduct.
	Immediate remedial action is taken against violation of legal, moral, and ethical standards.	Each person performs according to his or her understanding and standard legal, moral, and ethical conduct.
	Monitoring, feedback, and evaluation are required on results achieved as a result of each area of charitable giving.	Money is given and/or people are loaned to charitable organizations without regard to efficiency, standards, or quality of work undertaken by the organization. Little or no control exists over the consistency of giving.

13

Multinational Business

Multinational business includes all business transactions that involve two or more countries. These business relationships may be private or governmental in nature. The private firm enters into these transactions for a profit, whereas the government activity may or may not be profit-oriented.

UNIQUE PROBLEMS AND CONFLICTING DEMANDS

Most companies wishing to become involved in multinational trade are motivated by a desire for expansion of sales, acquisition of resources, or diversification. The means for accomplishing these objectives are both operational and functional in nature. In the area of operations, the corporation must look at many variables, such as the field or fields of business in which it wants to be involved: service or product exports or imports; travel, tourism, and transportation; management turn-key operations; franchises, licensing agreements, and royalties; or joint ventures. In the functional area the company must consider the aspects of production, marketing, R&D, accounting, finance, personnel, distribution, and social responsibility.

Not only must a corporation interested in multinational business be concerned with its own objectives and operational and functional considerations, but it must also examine the multinational external legal, ethical/moral, historical, geographic, economic, cultural, and political climate. It must also examine and evaluate characteristics of the competitive environment: the number and types of customers; quantity purchases by each customer; customer homogeneity; local and international competitors; capabilities and characteristics of competitors; cost of transportation; rapidity of product changes; and optimum production size.

Entering into and competing in the multinational arena requires much preparation and serious consideration of many factors. The remainder of this chapter will briefly examine and expand on some of these areas.

MULTINATIONAL OPERATIONS

Early Growth

Although the terms "multinational" and "globalization" are relatively new in business vocabulary, international trade and business has been conducted for centuries. It has followed the concept of *comparative advantage*, which in principle means that a country tends to export goods that use its abundant and low-cost resources while importing goods that use scarce or high-priced resources. Tariffs and trade restrictions, of course, alter this mix of imports and exports. Japan, for example, has had fairly free reign in exporting a multitude of goods into the United States with few, if any, restrictions, while it, in turn, has imposed stiffer import restrictions on abundant and low-priced goods from the United States and other countries.

Perhaps one of the first multinational moves involving the United States was made by the German chemical producer Bayer when it purchased an interest in an aniline plant in Albany, New York, in 1865.[1] It might be more correct to assign the title of true multinational to Singer, whose sewing machine plant, built in Glasgow, Scotland, in 1867, manufactured, shipped, and mass marketed a single product throughout the world.[2] As Singer grew, it developed manufacturing and marketing capabilities in each of the areas where it sold sewing machines.

In spite of the problems and difficulties involved, multinational companies have spread and grown rapidly since the time of the initial plunge into this area by Bayer and Singer. England was the leading nation in direct foreign investment in the early twentieth century. These investments were primarily in the area of development of mineral and other resources and in the investment and development of processing, packaging, and distribution of goods in a host country for export back to England.

Direct foreign investment by the United States started to exceed those of England in the early 1900s. It started in Mexico in 1919, followed by Canada in 1922, and other parts of Latin America in 1929.[3] U.S. multinational expansion grew rapidly. In 1914, only nineteen major companies fell into this category, whereas, by 1929, the list boasted fifty such companies.[4] Prior to the 1920s, mining was the major area of U.S. foreign investment.[5] By 1929, manufacturing had surpassed mining as the leading sector of direct U.S. foreign investment. With the emergence of oil companies, petroleum became the second major area of direct foreign investment by U.S. companies.

Recent Multinational Growth of Multinationals in the United States

Direct investment by the United States in foreign lands has continued to grow throughout the years, with little apparent concern for foreign direct investments in the United States. As late as 1980, U.S. foreign investments and holdings exceeded by $100 billion the value of foreign-owned assets in the United States.[6] Since that time, however, the positions have been reversed.

Foreign-owned companies are shaking the foundation of the U.S. construction industry, chipping away at domestic semiconductor manufacturers, and colliding with U.S. car producers. U.S. children are riding to school in buses operated by a Canadian company. American firemen depend on hydrants made by an Arab company in Illinois. Foreigners have bought land in practically every state, a piece of virtually every industry, and one-seventh of the federal debt.[7]

In total, foreigners took over 260 American corporations in 1986. The total assets held by foreigners in the United States by the end of 1986 was $1.3 billion; this is up from $2.6 million at the end of 1976 and $1.0 billion in 1985.[8] By the end of 1988 annual foreign acquisitions in the United States had reached 646, almost double that of 1985, and overseas companies controlled 13 percent of U.S. manufacturing assets—many of them in key industries.[9] In dollar amounts in 1985, England led the list of direct investors in the United States, followed by the Netherlands, Japan, Canada, West Germany, Switzerland, Netherlands Antilles, France, Sweden, and Belgium.[10]

The United States not only welcomes foreign investment but actively courts it. City mayors and state governors collide with one another as they tour Europe and Asia attempting to induce foreign governments, usually through tax incentives or free land, to invest in their cities or states. The examples are endless. Nestlé recently purchased Carnation for $3.0 billion; Celanese was purchased by a West German company, as was Doubleday and RCA Records. Japanese landlords now own and operate the Maui Marriott in Hawaii, the Exxon Building and the Tiffany Building in New York City, and Columbia Pictures Entertainment. American Express sold a part interest in its Shearson Lehman Brothers subsidy to Nippon Life Insurance Company, Japan's largest insurance company; Campeau of Canada bought out Allied Stores for

$3.2 million in 1986 and paid over $6.5 million in 1988 for Federated Department Stores, the fifth largest retailer in the United States; "golden parachute" clauses for top Federated executives, legal and investment banking fees, a deferred compensation program, and other assorted costs brought the total cost to $8.8 billion (in early 1990, the Campeau operation went bankrupt). Land purchases have also been extensive in some states. In Connecticut and Rhode island, foreigners own less than 0.1 percent of the farmland; in Maine, New Hampshire, Vermont, Florida, Arizona, Washington, Oregon, and Hawaii they own 2 to 10 percent of the farmland; while in all of the remaining states they own between 0.1 to 1.9 percent of the farmland.[11]

This foreign investment and ownership of businesses and farmland in the United States is applauded by some while others take a dim view of it. Those in favor of it argue that it enriches the U.S. economy by bringing in new industries, it increases employment and increases local and national purchasing power, and it bolsters the GNP and balance of payments. Jobs and increased purchasing power are the two strongest reasons given for support of foreign investments.

Those who object to foreign ownership of American assets pose interesting arguments and questions about "the selling off of America." Some people do not want foreigners taking over the country's banks, businesses, and farmland. Some people express the fear that foreigners are retaliating economically for what they could not do militarily in past wars. Other concerns are: whether or not foreign investments are actually as beneficial as they seem to be; whether or not the United States is giving up its technology edge and relying too much on foreign technology; how foreign investments influence U.S. competitiveness in world markets; and, most important, whether or not foreign investments jeopardize U.S. national security. This last concern was brought into the limelight when Commerce Secretary Malcolm Baldridge and Defense Department officials opposed the $200-million bid by Fujitsu Ltd. of Japan to buy 80 percent of the Fairchild Semiconductor Corporation, one of the United States' major producers of computer chips in California's Silicon Valley. As a result of this opposition, Fujitsu withdrew its offer. Another argument voiced by some businesspeople is that much of the foreign competition starts off in the United States with a 10 to 15 percent cost advantage over U.S. companies. They attribute this advantage to the special land, buildings, and tax concessions given to foreign businesses, along with the facts that they have lower retirement and health costs due to younger employees, and they have negligible liability costs because their products have only been on the U.S. market a short time compared to many American products.

U.S. Multinational Corporation Growth

Growth of and investment by U.S. companies overseas continues at a rapid pace. In early 1990, for example, McDonalds opened its newest and largest fast-food establishment in Moscow. Also, Procter & Gamble in late 1989 opened a multiple office building structure in Tokyo.

Even though it is difficult to purchase companies in Japan, and it has to be accomplished slowly over time, a number of U.S. companies have recently done just this. In 1983, Merck bought just over half of Banyu drugs; Corning Glass gained majority stakes in Ashi Medical and Nasco unit of Tokina Optical; Data General gained majority stakes in Nippon Mini Computer; Emerson Electric took over controlling interest of Ueshima Seisakusho; and Eastman Kodak acquired three units of Kusuda Business Machines.

Expansion in Europe and other Asiatic countries by American companies has been growing at an even greater pace. Procter & Gamble's chairman and CEO, Edwin L. Ortz, was for the last several years located in Europe and was in charge of multinational operations for the company. During the 1980s, Procter & Gamble started operations in 23 additional countries, with opportunities for growth in some 45 different businesses in more than 150 countries. In 1989 overseas operations accounted for about one-third of Procter & Gamble's business, and it could shortly account for 50 percent of its total business. This is truly a global enterprise.

Joint Ventures

American companies have begun to realize that to increase market share globally, simply exporting goods and services does not suffice. More and more countries require that any foreign company seeking market share can do so only by improving the host country's economic and technological base. As American companies come to realize and understand this, it also becomes apparent to them that several advantages exist in this form of market share growth potential, such as lower labor costs, combined sales forces, the ability to minimize research and development costs, and the additional competitive advantage of being a global company in the U.S. domestic market as well as overseas. Many companies are realizing that they can produce something of high quality for less cost in another country and compete more effectively in both foreign and domestic markets. Global partnerships, however, are difficult and call for management controls that are new and different from those by which they currently operate. Companies, therefore, must be very careful to form alliances with foreign companies whose corporate strategies align closely with those of their own. Failure of a global alliance can be a financial disaster to those involved and, as a result, can give a huge advantage to a competitor.

A company engaged in global competition can gain a competitive advantage through a coordinated strategy that includes all the countries in which it operates. A global corporation might have a product designed partly in the United States and partly in Europe or Asia, have components manufactured in Mexico or Taiwan, assemble the final unit in Korea, and sell it all over the world.

The following example shows how a global company can possess the ability and flexibility to maximize its earning potential by producing a quality product abroad at a lower cost than it could if the product were produced domestically. The company can select a location and management approach for each element in the value chain that gives it strategic advantage. For example:

- Raw material may be purchased in business environments that support just-in-time inventory replenishment techniques.
- Computer-integrated manufacturing can be used where a skill base exists.
- Labor-intensive manufacturing can be located in low-labor-cost countries, and capital-intensive manufacturing can be established in locations with low financing costs.
- Transportation to the assembly plants or distribution warehouses can be planned in low-cost ways.
- A common sales force can be used to serve a number of countries, and proprietary techniques can realize more scale cost reductions.
- Other advantages of lower costs due to scale may be achieved by centralized and vertically integrated manufacturing, centralizing purchasing, and spreading R&D and market research costs over larger product volumes.[12]

The strategy of optimizing corporate business worldwide can devastate the nonglobal competitor. Choosing an effective and efficient strategy—never mind implementing one—in order to maximize the scenario outlined above is not an easy task. It must be emphasized again that it is absolutely crucial that common strategies be identified in order to maximize achievement of success; failure of an alliance can give the competitive advantage to a domestic or international rival. According to John J. Dymet, a corporation that wants to compete globally must

first agree on its mission, define its vision of what it wants ultimately to become, its product or service scope, and the territory in which it wants to operate. The mission must be based on the beliefs and values of the operating executive responsible for implementation of the strategy, otherwise implementation will not be achieved. With the heavy involvement of the operating executives, the organization next needs to analyze systematically:

The environment. What opportunities and risks will result from emerging trends, by segment of the market? What likely technological changes may take place? What is happening to the economy that will likely affect the company's strategies?

The competition. Who are they, how big are they, and what are the strategic excellence positions of each?

The organization's own capabilities. What does the company do particularly well that has a value to an important segment of the market? What resources can the company use to improve each element of its value chain (from design to manufacturing, to distribution, to after-sales service)?[13]

Even after all of the above questions have been answered and analyzed and a global strategy has been formulated and implemented, a partnership will still not succeed unless it is often reinvigorated by both parties. Both parties must have an ongoing, active interest in the operations and make decisions that jointly benefit the partnership. What happens in such a partnership is rather ironic in that one of the emerging strategies of multinational competition is to team up with a foreign company in order to meet or beat a more dangerous domestic threat. For example, General Electric joined with Japanese and European firms in order to strengthen its position against Westinghouse, and AT&T allied itself with Olivetti and Philips in Europe and Toshiba in Japan.[14] More recently AT&T joined with Mitsubishi Electric Corporation of Japan to share technology and worldwide marketing and manufacturing of static random access memory (SRAM) microchips, a type of computer memory chip used in computer workstations, advanced personal computers, supermicrocomputers, and telecommunications equipment.[15]

As multinational trade continues to become more truly globalized, there will be more and more firms entering into multinational joint ventures. As very aptly expressed by Marjorie A. Lyles, there are both advantages and risks involved in these types of joint ventures.

One reason that firms form joint ventures centers on reducing risks and minimizing the chances of making mistakes in uncertain environments. By sharing resources and information, firms attempt to eliminate the risk of making a mistake in achieving their strategic goals. However, forming a joint venture creates a risk in itself, namely, that of managing an entity jointly. Misunderstandings of the role of each partner and false concepts of the relatedness of the firms may exist. Difficulties arising from difference in size force partners to confront power issues. Unclear performance expectations create stress.[16]

There are several critical areas in which partnerships can fail. First and foremost is in the area of integration. If the companies do not have the same objectives, goals, and strategies, along with full commitment to these by top management, the venture is doomed to failure. A lack of full commitment on the part of Rolls Royce was said to be the main ingredient in the failure of the General Electric and Rolls Royce jet engine partnership several years ago. Another area where failure can take place is in the transfer of technology. This could be extremely damaging to a company; another competitor that may have initially lacked the technology to compete could easily bounce back. This company might then steal the market because it is able to manufacture a product easier and cheaper. The human resources area can also present problems. Whereas turnover and career paths in American companies move quite rapidly, in many foreign companies turnover is low, and people stay in their current jobs for long periods of time. Sometimes ambiguous language is used in a contract to give each company an "out" in case of a changing situation; these ambiguous clauses often cost each company more time, effort, and money than if they had been specific on the issues at the beginning. Partnership rapport, faith, and trust in each other are also necessary ingredients; without these, the partnership is doomed to failure from the beginning.

The global market is here to stay and cannot be ignored.

In the 1990's global corporations will have to develop strategies which take account of a wide variety of possible environments. They will also have to pay attention to appropriate management styles and control systems which can generate acceptable profits in a highly competitive environment while remaining flexible to shifts in the environment which are of significance to its operations. The global corporation is an impressive invention for accomplishing things and this will be a highly valued asset in a world poised for sustained growth. In a world of conflict and confusion, the adaptive corporation is a remarkable system for corporate survival.[17]

Global Markets

As the term implies, global markets exist everywhere today. Some of these markets involve individual nations while others can be grouped into market areas.

The area that is sometimes referred to as the Pacific Rim includes the United States, Canada, Mexico, Japan, Australia, New Zealand, China, Hong Kong, Singapore, South Korea, Taiwan, Brunei, Indonesia, Malaysia, the Philippines, and Thailand. In 1988, total trans-Pacific trade amounted to about 40 percent of the record $2.7 trillion in goods traded; this region produced 44 percent of the world's total output and is considered one of the world's richest markets.[18]

The second largest market area exists in Europe. Through the Treaty of Rome in March 1957, the European Economic Community (EEC) was formed. It originally consisted of West Germany, Belgium, the Netherlands, Luxembourg, France, and Italy. The membership of the EEC has since been expanded to include the United Kingdom, Ireland, Denmark,

Greece, Spain, and Portugal. In May of 1960, as a result of the Stockholm Convention, the European Free Trade Association (EFTA) was formed by seven European countries that were not members of the EEC: Austria, Norway, Sweden, Portugal, Denmark, Switzerland, and the United Kingdom. The composition of the EFTA has since changed; it now includes Austria, Finland, Iceland, Norway, Sweden, and Switzerland. To ease the movement of goods, services, capital, and people between the two groups, the EFTA forged a pact with the EEC to establish a larger free-trade zone and a special relationship between the eighteen European nations of the EFTA and the EEC. This has been termed the "European economic space" and will insure favored trading between all eighteen countries when the EEC establishes a single barrier-free market by 1992.

With German reunification, freedom in the east European countries, and possibly improved trade relationships with the Soviet Union, a new block of countries may form or may operate economically as individual countries. A unified Germany could result in a new German economic zone, speculatively consisting of West and East Germany, Estonia, Latvia, Lithuania, Poland, Czechoslovakia, Austria, Hungary, Rumania, Yugoslavia, Bulgaria, Greece, and Turkey. If this were to take place, it would be one of the most powerful trading blocks in the world. Regardless of whether or not the eastern European countries unite under a German economic zone or stay independent, they and the Soviet Union present a tremendous market potential yet to be fully tapped.

A third major trading area, what might be called the Latin American cooperation, is made up of four semi-integrated trade associations including Mexico, some of the Caribbean islands, and Central and South America; this organization is classified as semi-integrated because some of the countries belong to more than one group, with each group emphasizing slightly different privileges for its members. A study by the Inter-American Development Bank (IDB) identifies three types of integration in Latin America: a free trade area, a common market, and a partial economic preference model.[19] Of these integration types there are four groups of countries. The first group is the Latin American Free Trade Association (LAFTA), which is composed of Argentina, Bolivia, Brazil, Chile, Colombia, Ecuador, Mexico, Paraguay, Peru, Uruguay, and Venezuela. The second group is the Cartagena Andean Group, made up of Bolivia, Chile, Colombia, Ecuador, Peru, and Venezuela. The third group is known as the Central American Common Market (CACM). Costa Rica, El Salvador, Guatemala, and Nicaragua are members of this group; Honduras was a member but withdrew in 1971. The fourth and final group is the Caribbean Community and Common Market (CARICOM), which includes Antigua, Barbados, the Bahamas, Belize, Dominica, Grenada, Guyana, Jamaica, Montserrat, St. Christopher and Nevis, St. Lucia, St. Vincent, and Trinidad and Tobago.

Another major trading area is the Association of South East Asian Nations (ASEAN), which was organized in 1977 and tries to cooperate in many areas, including industry and trade. This association is made up of Brunei, Indonesia, Malaysia, the Philippines, Singapore, and Thailand.

On the continent of Africa, several forms of integrated and semi-integrated affiliations exist. The major African groups are the West African Economic Community (Ivory Coast, Mali, Mauritania, Niger, and Senegal), the Entente Council (Benin, Ivory Coast, Niger, and Togo), the Economic Community of West African States (ECOWAS) (Benin, Bukina, Cape Verde, Gambia, Guinea, Guinea-Bissau, Ivory Coast, Liberia, Mali, Mauritania, Niger, Nigeria, Senegal, Sierra Leone, and Togo), the Organisation Commune Africaine et Mauricienne (Benin, Central Africa Republic, Ivory Coast, Mauritania, Niger, Rwanda, Senegal, and Togo), the Organization of African Unity (nearly every country in Africa), and the Southern African Development Coordination Conference (Angola, Bostswana, Lesotho, Malawi, Mozambique, Swaziland, Tanzania, Zambia, and Zimbabwe).

Even though arguments abound for forming integrated economic associations among neighboring nations, there are still many problems with this concept. Strong nationalism might remain within the countries or territories. There may be difficulty in reducing nontariff barriers within a country. Other problems with integrating are the extensive economic divergence among the countries, the cost of implementation and control, language and social custom barriers, and possible expansion of membership.

In spite of these problems, they are forces that must be dealt with by any firm involved in multinational trade. Not only must the company desiring to do international business concern itself with the laws and customs of the country or countries with which it is dealing, but it must also be aware of what impact multinational affiliations might have on such an undertaking.

MULTINATIONAL ENVIRONMENT

The United States has diverse complexities in and differences among local, state, and national laws. For example, educational systems and requirements vary between school systems; tax laws and other business requirements differ from state to state and from locality to locality; and attitudes, climate, resources, transportation, and history all vary within the 50 states. Obviously, such factors affect the way firms do business in various parts of the country.

Thus, when a business moves across international boundaries, the cultural, educational, economic, political, legal, ethical, moral, and social differences are compounded manyfold. The chances for mistakes or misunderstanding are multiplied many times. What might be considered a commission in one locale could very well be considered a bribe somewhere else; what might be considered by the business as being helpful to the host government might be considered by the host government as a hostile attempt to take advantage of and dominate the local or national economy. The role of women, the number of U.S. workers used versus number of local workers, pay levels, work schedules, and type of business permitted can vary from place to place. The international arena can serve as a place of great conflict and controversy as well as growth and profit.

In order for firms to take advantage of the opportunities and minimize the risks and threats of multinational business, they must understand how to respond to factors of the multinational environment, some of which have already been discussed and some of which will be discussed below.

Cultural Environment

In every society there are specific, learned norms based on certain beliefs, attitudes, and values. These norms determine the culture of the people in a society. Anyone involved in multinational operations must have at least a basic understanding of what influences the culture of different countries and how it might differ from that of the United States.

Group Affiliations. In the United States, people are accepted for jobs and promotions based primarily on their performance and capabilities. This, however, is not the prime requisite in many countries where some criterion other than performance is considered just as valid.

For example, in many countries there are still strong differences between men and women in the workplace. This is particularly true in Saudi Arabia, many South American countries, and even in Japan where men are the mainstay of the workplace.

In some societies in the Latin American and Mediterranean countries, the family is the most important group and the source of power and advancement. Family members show a great trust in one another and often distrust outsiders.

Some cultures have adopted the attitude that age and wisdom are correlated, and thus promotion and seniority are based on this belief. In a similar vein, some countries base acceptability into society and the workplace on social status or respectability of the individual's family.

Religion. Religion influences the cultural behavior of a nation in two important ways. First, it establishes social codes and value priorities that are learned in childhood and carried into adulthood. These values motivate people to follow these codes and priorities in their actions. Second, religion has an impact on both production and consumption patterns. Each religion has its own holy days which range from a few to many per year. The *World Christian Encyclopedia* lists Christian, Moslem, Hindu, and

Buddhist as the four major religions of the world, which constitute approximately 70 percent of the world population.[20] When workers from different countries work side by side, these religious differences can create problems.

Language. Most Americans speak and write only one language while many foreigners speak more than one language. Even within the same general language groups there are many dialects or different meanings for the same words. It is true that most countries have a national language; however, many countries have more than one national language. For instance, English, French, and Spanish are each a national language in over twenty countries, and Switzerland has four official languages. For the United States to be successful in the multinational market, language and cultural skills must be emphasized, as well as technical and business skills.

Political Systems. In theory, political systems range from pure democracy (all citizens should be equal politically and legally and should enjoy widespread freedom) on the one hand to totalitarianism (a single party, individual, or group of individuals monopolizes the power structure and does not recognize or permit opposition) on the other. Because of many factors, most countries that are considered democratic in nature are not pure democracies but representative democracies. Totalitarian governments also appear in many forms: communism as practiced in the Soviet Union, China, Cuba, and many other countries; the sheikdoms of the Middle East; and the vacillation from military rule to representative democracies in several Central and South American countries. The multinational company must learn how to operate in all of these changing political environments.

Education. The education system of a country is culturally specific. Even when similar subject matter is taught in different countries, it is taught within the cultural orientation of that country. If ecological, economic, and technological requirements differ between countries, this also influences the direction of education and educational requirements. The educational system must be compatible and in tune with the cultural orientation of the country because it affects human behavior, it influences the relationships between the people and the environment, and it influences the relationship between the people and their religion. Therefore, countries with similar educational systems may vary dramatically in their cultural focus. Again, unless this is understood and taken into consideration, it can cause confusion and misunderstanding in multinational operations.

Economic Environment. Most economic systems can be loosely classified as capitalist, socialist, or mixed. The ownership and factors of production and control can be viewed on a continuum from complete private ownership to complete public or state ownership. The United States, which is one of the best examples of private enterprise, has some factors of production owned and operated by the government. Some Communist countries, on the other hand, have some parts of their economy operated in a free-enterprise, capitalist manner. Each of these levels of systems has an impact on how multinational business can be conducted within the various parts of the world. How this influences and impacts multinational operations will be shown below in a specific area.

Marketing. Marketing systems in different countries vary considerably. They range in complexity from a simple marketplace in emerging countries to complex systems that include processing of goods from basic materials, through manufacturing, wholesalers, distributors, and retailers. In some countries, such as India, a middleman supplies basic materials and equipment to a family operation or a local factory installation, the people manufacture the goods at home or in the local factories, and the middleman pays them for their work and takes the goods to market or sells them directly to a wholesaler or retailer. In Sweden and Finland many people work and sell their products or services through cooperative groups. Other countries such as China and the Soviet Union control almost all levels of distribution. A number of East Asian countries operate independently of each other in making foreign purchases. In centrally planned economies (CPEs), such as those found in some Second World countries (such as Poland, Hungary, Rumania, and China) and Communist-controlled countries, foreign trade organizations (FTOs) operate autonomously. Any company or organization wanting to do business in a country that has FTOs must contact and work through these organizations. Many FTOs are set up for a specific product line (for example, the Soviet Union has over fifty of these groups spread over different product lines). Therefore, when operating through an FTO, care must be exercised that the correct organization for the particular product line is contacted.

These are only a few of the complexities of marketing in a global environment. For a more detailed examination of the complexities of various marketing channels, refer to Chapter 6.

Financial Considerations. A company must consider a number of financial factors before proceeding with any global excursion. Two of the more prevalent factors are inflation and exchange rates.

Inflation is a very important aspect of the economic environment because it has an impact on interest rates, exchange rates, the cost of living, the confidence of a country's political and economic system, and the profitability of a company operating in a particular country. For example, during 1980–1985, inflation increased by 342.8 percent in Argentina, 147.7 percent in Brazil, 569.1 percent in Bolivia, and 196.3 percent in Israel.[21] In Brazil, by the end of 1985, inflation was at 225 percent, but by February 1986, it was running at a rate of between 400 and 500 percent. These types of inflation rates can be devastating to anyone trying to trade or operate with one of these countries.

An exchange rate can be defined as the number of units of one currency that must be given to acquire one unit of a currency of another country.

If a country can keep its currency value so that it buys less of foreign currency than it might in a free-market determination, its products will have a relative cost advantage. When banks and other people or institutions become involved in the exchange of money of one country for that of another, there is a difference between the value of the money in the home country and what an outsider has to pay for that currency; in essence, the money exchanger must make a profit on its transactions. To help protect themselves, some companies become involved (usually through brokers) in arbitrage or "money baskets." This is where several currencies are involved, and one currency is exchanged for another to take advantage of the currency fluctuations in a given set of markets. The idea is to take advantage of money rate fluctuations from one country to another in the hope of salvaging profits gained in one of these countries, especially during inflationary times. This is an extremely risky business, and anyone interested in becoming involved in it should engage a knowledgeable individual or institution to help.

Technology. Technology is more than just technical knowledge. It involves the natural resources of a nation, the means and methods of appropriating these natural resources, and transferring them into useful and needed end products. Technology differs from country to country, depending on what and where that country places emphasis. This difference can be the result of a communication problem or it can be a culture and value system difference. Regardless of why a difference might exist, it is imperative that any company desiring to enter into multinational business transactions be aware of and understand these conditions. Just because a given product sells well in the United States does not necessarily mean it will sell well in another country; or the fact that a given country has certain natural resources that another country would like to have does not mean that that country places much or the greatest emphasis in this area.

COMPANY EVALUATION

This discussion merely scratches the surface of the complexities of multinational operations. It does, however, present a few critical areas for thought and shows that it is an area that should not be jumped into without considerable thought, groundwork, and evaluation. Table 13.1 presents a method for preliminary evaluation in this area in order to determine where a company stands on this subject.

NOTES

1. Christopher Tugendhat, *The Multinationals* (New York: Random House, 1972), p. 12.

2. Ibid., p. 13.

3. Mira Wilkins, *The Emergence of Multinational Enterprise: American Business Abroad from the Colonial Era to 1914* (Cambridge, MA: Harvard University Press, 1970), p. 155.

4. Mira Wilkins, *The Maturing Multinational Enterprise: American Business Abroad, 1914–1970* (Cambridge, MA: Harvard University Press, 1974), p. 142.

5. Neil A. Jacoby, "The Multinational Corporations," *Center Magazine*, no. 3 (1970): 39.

6. Jaclyn Fierman, "The Selling Off of America," *Fortune* 114, no. 14 (December 20, 1986): 44–45.

7. Ibid., p. 45.

8. America on the Auction Block," *U.S. News & World Report* 102, no. 12 (March 30, 1987): 56–57.

9. "Overseas Operators," *U.S. News & World Report* 108, no. 2 (January 15, 1990): 43.

10. "America on the Auction Block," p. 57.

11. Fierman, "The Selling Off of America," p. 45.

12. John J. Dymet, "Strategies and Management Controls for Global Corporations," *The Journal of Business Strategy* 7, no. 4 (Spring 1987): 22.

13. Ibid., p. 23.

14. Kenichi Ohmae, "The Triad World View," *The Journal of Business Strategy* 7, no. 4 (Spring 1987): 16.

15. "AT&T Joins Venture to Make Chips—Mitsubishi Shares SRAM Design," *The Cincinnati Enquirer*, February 18, 1990, p. H–12.

16. Marjorie A. Lyles, "Common Mistakes of Joint Venture Experience Firms," *The Columbia Journal of World Business* 22, no. 2 (Summer 1987): 80.

17. Peter Schwartz and Jerry Saville, "Multinational Business in the 1990's—A Scenario," *Long Range Planning*, December 1986, p. 37.

18. "Pacific Overtures: The Merits of Cooperation in One of the World's Richest Markets," *U.S. News & World Report* 107, no. 20 (November 20, 1989): 65–70.

19. "Inter-American Development Bank Predicts Renewed Push for Economic Integration in Latin America," *IMF Survey*, December 10, 1984, pp. 369, 374–376.

20. Rev. Dr. David B. Barrett, *World Christian Encyclopedia* (Oxford: Oxford University Press, 1983).

21. *World Development Report, 1987* (New York: Oxford University Press, 1987), pp. 202–203.

Table 13.1
Typical Strengths and Weaknesses in Planning, Organizing, Directing, and Controlling Multinational Operations

	Strengths	Weaknesses
PLANNING	Top management participates in and is committed to a strong multinational operation.	Any multinational efforts are done on a haphazard basis.
	All company plans and strategy consider multinational involvement in the total operation.	Few or no plans are made for product extension into multinational areas.
	Joint ventures and multinational partners are planned for when it will benefit the company.	Little or no effort is expended on plans to work on joint ventures or multinational partners on company products.
	Long-range, medium-range, and short-range plans exist for multinational operations.	No plans exist for involvement in multinational operations.
	Experts and special committees exist for planning and formulating strategy for the complex and often confusing arena of multinational operations.	No committees or experts exist in the area of multinational operations.
ORGANIZING	Experts and special committees work with the president and board of directors in formulating strategy for multinational operations.	No committees or experts exist within the company for company involvement in multinational operations.
	Multinational strategy is a corporate or company-wide integrated operation.	No company-wide involvement exists in the area of multinational operations.
	The experts and special committees only advise the president, board of directors, and division managers and review, recommend, and help formulate multinational strategy but do not direct or implement it.	No experts or special committees exist in the area of multinational operations. At best, individual program managers attempt to get involved in multinational operations.
	The president and responsible vice president and directors implement and direct all multinational operations.	If any multinational involvement exists, it is carried out in an inept manner by a particular product manager.
	Responsibility for multinational operations is vested in a vice president or executive vice president whose prime responsibility is multinational operations.	No one person or group of people are given specific multinational responsibility.

DIRECTING	Multinational planning, strategy formulation, implementation, and directing is undertaken by a vice president or executive vice president whose prime responsibility is multinational operations.	If any multinational involvement exists it is carried out and directed by a particular product manager.
		No MIS is involved in any area of multinational operations.
	MIS is used to help implement and direct multinational operations.	
		Inadequate interface, integration, and coordination exist in multinational operations.
	Excellent interface, integration, and coordination exist between all company divisions and multinational partners and/or operations.	
CONTROLLING	Strategy, tactics, budgets, policies, and procedures are constantly reviewed and updated by all involved personnel to make certain that multinational operations are proceeding as planned.	No special effort or emphasis is placed on adequately controlling multinational operations, if indeed they exist at all.
		MIS is not used to track or provide feedback on any multinational operation.
	MIS is used to track and provide feedback on the status of all operations.	
		Where multinational operations exist only "seat of the pants" guidelines are used to evaluate and control program progress and performance.
	Both quantitative and qualitative techniques and standards are used as guidelines to evaluate and control multinational progress and performance.	

III

The Procedure and Its
Application and Use

14

The Corporate Operational Analysis Procedure

Few actions require greater skill from an operating manager than the evaluation of strategy and resulting policies, procedures, or standards. This area of analysis embraces core factors that are the determinants of organizational efficiency and effectiveness. In this broad and uncharted triangle of interrelationships between corporate functions, resources, and operating plans, determining the basic "problem" is often an equal or more demanding task than finding a feasible solution.

Ideally, problem finding is accomplished by managers with adequate knowledge of their organization and theoretical foundations in finance, marketing, human resource management, and all other functional areas. A blend of experience and breadth of management knowledge, which is rarely available, is needed. Faced with such realities, many firms substitute a committee for the individual effort in areas of complex analysis. In committees, personal intuition and differences of opinion come into play as each individual evaluates the inputs of others. Suggested problem areas too far removed from traditional wisdom are quite often rejected, as are creative approaches that often challenge the status quo.

For operating managers, finding and solving problems for strategy formulation and implementation can theoretically be simple, especially if one assumes, or the organization enjoys, adequate resources in terms of people, money, and material. This, however, is a situation that for most companies does not exist. Finding and solving multiple problems is more difficult, as is the prioritizing of assets as it becomes apparent that resources adequate to solve all known problems are not available.

Next, the problem solver must address a new series of problems that arise from an uneven application of assets to areas of apparent need. As shortages in people, money, and needed material continue, structural changes may be required, which create additional stress on the total system. The relative impact of such stress must be considered, which raises more questions about the true needs and the real problems facing the firm—questions which are related to actual survival. In other words, after weeks or possibly months have passed during which key resources have been allocated in a suboptimal manner, a question is asked that should have been asked in the beginning: What is the real problem facing this organization? To answer this question and to properly formulate strategy, structure, and policies as core problem areas, there is a critical need for comprehensive tools for analysis and a system for effective application.

One major problem-solving tool that has been developed, tested, and implemented with great success by the authors in recent years, both in industry and for classroom case study analysis, is the *corporate operational analysis procedure* (hereafter referred to as "the procedure"). The framework around which this procedure is structured is shown in Table 14.1 and discussed below.

TOOLS FOR ANALYSIS

The essence of a problem-finding approach lies in the consideration of the total breadth of the basic functions of management—planning, organizing, directing, and controlling—as they relate to significant functional areas of importance such as marketing, manufacturing, personnel, and so on. It is a diagnostic approach that tries to find the cause of an illness rather than dealing only with the symptoms. The problem-finding procedure is also future oriented. Survival of the firm needs to remain uppermost in the mind of the problem solver. Some of the greatest financial disasters have resulted from a failure to find fault with current operations that were returning a high rate of profit while making little or no investment in future products, plants, or the training of personnel.

THE PROCEDURE IN COMPOSITE

The procedure, as shown in Table 14.1, is designed to examine and evaluate an organization in detail. Phase I is diagnostic in nature and reviews the *marco* aspects of a firm or organization. Phase II continues this diagnostic process but looks in depth at the *micro* aspects of an organization. Phase III is concerned with *prescriptive* and remedial results from analysis and evaluation. A brief overview of each phase is presented as follows.

Table 14.1
The Corporate Operational Analysis Procedure

PHASE I (Macro Analysis)

(A) COMPANY BACKGROUND

- Initiate Reading
- Review of Exhibits
- Consideration of financial statements
- Note key statements/ incidents/issues

(B) DETERMINE

1. Life Cycle of Industry and Firm
2. Basic Strategy

(C) SIGNIFICANT FUNCTIONAL AREAS OF IMPORTANCE

CONSIDER:
  Marketing
  Manufacturing
  Financial
  Human Resources
  Interface Areas
  Other Areas

(D) FUNCTIONS OF MANAGEMENT APPLICATIONS

	EXCELLENT	SATISFACTY	POOR
Marketing	Planning	Organizing	Directing
		Controlling	
Manufacturing	N/A	N/A	N/A
Human Resources	Planning	Organizing	Directing
			Controlling
Interface Areas	--	Planning	Organizing
		Controlling	Directing

PHASE II (Micro Analysis) Diagnostic

(E) COMPANY NARRATIVE

- Reading for specific answers to (C) and (D)
- Extrapolation/Extension of Data for filling of gaps (Detailed discussion)
- Financial/Balance sheet analysis and generation and presentation
- Expansion of basic strategy statements

(F) FUNCTIONS OF MGT/FUNCTIONAL AREA ANALYSIS

	STRENGTHS	WEAKNESSES
Marketing	Planning	Planning
	a-	a-
	b-	b-
Manufacturing	Organizing	Organizing
	a-	a-
	b-	b-
Financial	Directing	Directing
	a-	a-
	b-	b-
Human Resources	Controlling	Controlling
	a-	a-
	b-	b-
Interface Areas	a-	a-
	b-	b

(G) "FORCE FIELD" (Summary of most frequently cited strengths)

STRENGTHS	WEAKNESSES
Planning	Planning
a-	a-
b-	b-
Organizing	Organizing
a-	a-
b-	b-
Directing	Directing
a-	a-
b-	b-
Controlling	Controlling
a-	a-
b-	b-

PHASE III (Prescriptive)

(H) COMPANY NARRATIVE

- Review of key areas of strength and weaknesses-- looking for interface relationships, ruptured linkages and overall fit

(I) PRESCRIPTIVE ACTIONS

Identification of prescriptive formulas to correct weak functions and build on strong functions identified in (G) (CORRECTIVE ACTIONS)

(J) IMPACT OF PRESCRIPTIVE ACTIONS

Analysis and evaluation of the impact of each prescriptive action upon the company as a whole

(K) SUMMARY

Summary of final justified action

IN RANK ORDER OF IMPORTANCE

Phase I (Macro Analysis): Diagnostic

A healthy concern for the future survival of an organization sets an appropriate and solid foundation for analysis. Such a foundation requires a general understanding of the industry, environment, and operations. Steps A through D in Phase I of the procedure outline needed areas of investigation.

Step A. Basic information for later decisions flows from the work expended during this first phase. Initial effort is directed toward the gathering of financial statements, annual reports, 10-K forms, industry publications, and appropriate articles from current news journals.

Step B. Data gathered in Step A yields information on a number of key statements, incidents, and issues necessary in Step B, which determines the lifecycle and basic strategy positions of the organization, its industry and target environment. How the subject of this analysis and competing entities fit into an overall pattern of interaction is important information.

At this point, a highly focused definition of basic strategy followed by the organization under analysis is determined. This information involves both short- and long-term goals. The resulting determination of strategy should be limited to those actions necessary for survival and should not include secondary tactical considerations.

Step C. Significant functional areas critical to the predetermined strategy are isolated and listed in rank order of importance with the most critical area placed first. This step in the procedure is important for determining where to focus attention and expend effort on functions vital to goal attainment.

Step D. It is appropriate to invest time in an overview analysis of how well the key processes of planning, organizing (with emphasis on staffing and structure), directing (including development and communication), and controlling are discharged in each of the key functional areas ranked in order of importance in the prior step. A relatively simple three-level ranking, such as excellent, satisfactory, or poor, is adequate at this stage of analysis.

Phase II (Micro Analysis): Diagnostic

Phase II builds upon Phase I data with significantly greater depth of analysis. The objective here is a detailed operational look at the subject organization, leading to the isolation of key strengths and weaknesses.

All available material should again be reviewed in great detail. The objective is to use three steps to sort out basic details, discovered in Phase I, on how the organization operates.

Step E. This step involves:

- Searching for specific answers to initial evaluations of quality in key functional performance. Data and opinions must be examined in detail for verification or modification. This is an excellent time to scrutinize this information for specific strengths, weaknesses, or other problems.

- Extrapolation and extension of data to fill information gaps. Examples of such action would be extension of sales forecasts; comparison of sales, manufacturing, and advertising budgets against actual costs; generation of demographic data; comparison of data for different plant location options (using both quantitative and qualitative data); and a multitude of other areas of interest that would normally be extracted from gathered information.

- Financial/balance sheet generation and analysis. Computation of financial ratios, especially ROI, ROE, inventory turns, and other important information available for extraction from several financial data sheets.

- Expansion of the basic strategy statement prepared in Phase I. An in-depth examination of material prepared and compiled to date now permits expansion and/or modification of the basic statement of strategy.

Step F. Detailed analysis of key functional areas of marketing, manufacturing, finance, and so on is performed in respect to the functions of planning, organizing, directing, and controlling. The process should focus on only one functional area at a time. All identified strengths and weaknesses in planning, organizing, directing, and controlling are identified. A brief discussion follows, which explains or elaborates on the positions taken. This process should be repeated, one functional area at a time, for all the areas identified.

Step G. The "force field," an executive summary of the most frequently cited strengths and weaknesses, is a key document. The process of summarizing the factors that have great positive or negative impact on the organization represents the apex of prior analysis. Inability to identify objectively all critical areas of organizational strengths and weaknesses will result in a suboptimal listing of corrective action areas. A solid listing of key strengths is necessary for evaluating the impact of corrective actions, especially from the diversion of vital resources.

Phase III (Prescriptive)

While the prescriptive process is demanding and often time consuming, careful discharge of the suggested actions in the procedure should provide a logical and fruitful end result from the efforts. It is within this final section of analysis and evaluation that carefully thought through and weighted solutions to organizational problems occur. Organizational strengths should be enhanced and weaknesses corrected or eliminated. All such actions must be accomplished within organizational constraints of time availability and resources in terms of personnel, money, and materials.

Step H. A review of the interrelationships of strengths and weaknesses is an important action at this point immediately prior to identifying prescriptive actions. Some key factors of consideration are ruptured linkages and related interface problems among functional areas, critical divisions, and vital task forces.

Step I. Prescriptive actions for the most effective and efficient correction of key areas of organizational weaknesses should now be clearly and precisely delineated. This is the critical end objective of the entire procedure. In most cases, prescriptive solutions encompass secondary level areas of weakness and are ideally limited to six to eight basic areas of action.

Step J. Impact of the actions taken in Step I must be carefully reviewed. Each action must be considered in light of impact upon interfacing areas of organization strength, impact of corrective actions on each other, and, overall impact on the total organization. Financial impact and ability of the organization to accept such an impact are very important. Political concerns and market costs must be also considered.

In these areas of final impact analysis, the organization is viewed as an integrated unit. It should no longer be examined only from a limited perspective. Short-run, intermediate, and long-run impacts of possible solutions must be considered and a total evaluation of all consolidated data and research must be made.

Step K. In light of the final impact analysis, the list of final recommended solutions is presented in order of importance. This establishes a priority for application and an order of demand upon necessary resources. To insure that these recommended corrective actions are incorporated in an orderly manner, a time activity chart should be included as an integrated segment of the corrective action document. Exhibits such as a PERT, CPM, or bar charts help establish the orderly sequence of change, along with cost variables, personnel requirements, and capital equipment loading data.

CONCLUSIONS

This procedure is not a quick or simple answer to the process of problem finding and solving as the foundation for strategy formulation and implementation. There is no guarantee that if followed with diligence and a degree of precision, this procedure will lead all organizations to an in-depth understanding of where it stands. However, with this information, necessary and critical actions to progress and profitably grow efficiently and effectively in today's competitive world will be apparent. This is a procedure that is now in use and has been proven effective in the class-room, in large and small companies including several Fortune 500 com-panies, and in government agencies. In addition, it serves as an excellent development tool in executive development programs.

15

The Case for Analysis: Midwest Chemical Products Company, Inc.

This chapter presents a case study of a rapidly growing hypothetical company in the specialized chemical products industry that has set its sights on growing even faster in the future. The goals and objectives that it has set for itself over the next several years require a performance that is superior to any that has been experienced in the past and considerably in excess of what is projected for the specialized chemical products industry in general. The case presents the past and present history of the company so that the reader, through the use of the corporate operational analysis procedure discussed in Chapter 14 and the assessment discussions of the key internal and external functional areas discussed in Chapters 2 through 13, can analyze and evaluate the company in an attempt to determine whether or not the company can achieve the required growth rate that is needed to reach specified goals and objectives.

For several specific reasons, the setting of this case takes place in 1983. The company had just had a phenomenal sales growth year in 1981, followed by a disappointing year in 1982. Based on its 1981 growth rate and the fact the company would celebrate its one-hundredth birthday in 1987, the company projected sales growth and other financial goals far in excess of anything it had previously achieved. Although the economy was down in 1983 and competition was increasing, there was the potential for expanded growth in western Europe and Asia and possible entry into eastern Europe, and it was a period when numerous growth, expansion, and structural changes were taking place within the company and the specialized chemical products industry. This time setting for the company, therefore, presents a situation that requires extensive analysis and skillful interpretation of data in order to determine what steps and what actions the company should take either to achieve its projected goals and objectives or to revise its projected goals and objectives to something more realistic.

The case analysis presented in the next chapter thus follows this same format. It is presented as if the person conducting the case analysis is doing it in 1983 and only has data available for the analysis through early 1983. Based on this available data, the analyst is trying to project where the company can be and will be in the important future year of 1987. This is typical of what is done in most companies, and this presentation is standard case writing and analysis procedure used in most business schools throughout the United States.

COMPANY BACKGROUND

The Midwest Chemical Products Company, Inc. was founded in 1887 as a family-owned business that manufactured and sold wallpaper paste. It operated as such for about thirty years. Then they franchised their operations in Ohio, Georgia, and Minnesota. In the late 1920s, Edward Andrews, an accountant at Midwest, bought the Cincinnati, Ohio, franchise. He diversified the product line over the next twenty years and by 1940 had bought all the other franchises. The company has been publicly owned since 1968. Insiders control 30 percent of the common stock voting power. In addition, Andrews owns 100 percent of the preferred stock. Holders of preferred stock are entitled to eighty votes per share, and holders of common stock are entitled to one vote per share. Both classes of stock vote as a single class in election of directors and in all matters submitted to shareholders.

Midwest is now a compounder and marketer of specialized chemical products for customers who desire and need formulated products and technical services. Its primary products include adhesives, sealants, costings paints, industrial waxes, floor maintenance equipment and materials, and other specialty chemicals. Table 15.1 gives a summary of Midwest's products as a percentage of consolidated sales and revenues, by class of product.

The company operates from plants and technical service centers in forty cities in the United States. It has manufacturing facilities in Canada, Latin America, Europe, the Caribbean, and the Pacific. The strength and diversity of its markets sustain its long-term growth, even during times of economic uncertainty.

Midwest places great emphasis on securing and maintaining technological leadership, both in the introduction of new products and in finding new and better ways of serving customers with existing products. High

Table 15.1
Midwest Chemical Products Company, Inc. Class of Products Summary (as a percentage of consolidated sales and revenues)

Sales and Other Revenues	1982	1981	1979	1977	1975
Adhesives, Sealants and Coatings	77%	75%	73%	75%	69%
Paints	6	8	8	9	10
Specialty waxes	5	7	8	6	7
Floor Maintenance Equipment					
and Sanitation Chemicals	8	7	7	7	9
Other	4	3	4	3	5

priority is given to expanded and improved laboratory facilities and a pilot plant in Blue Ash, Ohio. This new facility, which is approximately twelve miles north of Cincinnati, will also include administrative and marketing headquarters. This plant, the first phase of the company's new $10 million corporate headquarters, is scheduled to be finished by 1987. Located on this 150-acre plot of land is a large lake area that will be preserved as a wetland and wildlife habitat.

Midwest promotes itself as a "people" company, dedicated to the proposition that a company grows by helping its employees to grow and by serving the customer and community well. At Thanksgiving, each employee receives a large turkey, and at Easter each receives a smoked ham—symbols of management's recognition and appreciation of each employee's individual contributions to corporate success. At the close of the fiscal year in November, each of the approximately 4,000 employees worldwide receives a pro rata share of that year's profit in the form of a bonus check.

Midwest's corporate philosophy is to share the benefits of growth with all constituencies: customers, stockholders, employees, and the community. Top management believes that if the communities in which the employees live and work are strong, viable, and responsive to society, everyone prospers. Therefore, there is a strong commitment among Midwest employees to be responsible, active, and socially responsive corporate citizens. Active support and participation in the community affairs councils in thirty-two locations around the United States encourage individual involvement in the local community accompanied by corporate contributions. Like many other corporations around the country, Midwest devotes 5 percent of its pretax profits to these councils. Nationally, Midwest is focusing on the problems of battered women and abused children. Staff time and contributions are helping with this critical social issue.

Midwest has had continuous growth due to both domestic and international acquisitions. Some of these are listed below:

Reliable Powder Products

Midwest Chemical Industries, S.A.

Midwest Germany, ARC

Midwest France SARL

Smith Products Division

New York Adhesives

Detroit Paraffine Company

Adhesives Division of Best Brands

Midwest Industries, Ltd. Canada

Prestige Products

Exceptional growth occurred in the company's international operations in 1981. This came about as a result of a strategic decision made several years ago to identify and develop growth opportunities in Europe, Latin America, and other major world markets. Since as far back as the 1960s, Midwest's international expansion strategy has been to identify unique products, services, or market segments that allow success and then to commit money and people to their operation in those areas. For example, the Pacific area operations in Japan were complemented in 1978 by an acquisition in New Zealand. Midwest also has operations in eleven Latin American countries. Future growth will come from the strength and diversity of these rapidly developing economies. The three adhesives manufacturing plants established in Australia in 1979 likewise were established at considerable cost, but a foothold was established and operations there are now flourishing. In 1979 Midwest's manufacturing facilities in Nicaragua were badly damaged during a civil uprising. After a brief interruption, business was resumed using paints imported from other Midwest plants in Central America. Facilities that were minimally damaged were replaced. These steps were all taken in accordance with the overall long-term growth objectives of the company.

Midwest's strategy for entering new markets is to establish a sales base, add manufacturing facilities as needed, and build up to a position of profitability as quickly as possible. Short-term losses are quite often experienced initially, but this philosophy works well in developing future markets.

Another key element of Midwest's expansion (both domestic and international) is through acquisition and licensing arrangements. In either case, it is essential to have a good fit in terms of products, markets, and geographic matrix.

Most of Midwest's overseas operations have developed since the mid–1970s. International expansion continued in 1982. On July 1, 1982, Midwest acquired the assets and certain operating units of Asp-Rundall Chemie (ARC), a subsidiary of Schmidlap AG of West Germany, for about $27 million (including $13 million of assumed liabilities). Midwest was able to pursue ARC because ARC fit into Midwest's program of long-term growth objectives.

According to Adam Andrews, president and chief executive officer, the strategic implications of this acquisition were threefold:

First, we want to expand the volume of our European Operations. Second, we want European markets to become the primary focus of our international business. And third, we want to shift the current emphasis of our European business toward industrial adhesives.

Andrews went on to say:

ARC holds a solid position in the European adhesives market. Its 1981 sales volume of about $75 million more than doubles our European sales last year of about $35 million. Moreover, ARC's 1981 sales volume equaled about 22 percent of Midwest's consolidated total last year. If the company had been with us in 1981, its sales would have amounted to nearly one-third of our U.S. sales. In addition, the majority of our overseas assets are now concentrated in the politically stable economies of western Europe.

The assets we acquired include property, manufacturing facilities and equipment, product formulas, trade information and worldwide licensing agreements. Employing more than 800 skilled people in six Western European countries, ARC has sales offices and first class manufacturing plants in West Germany, Austria, Spain, Belgium, and the Netherlands. Sales offices, alone, were acquired in the United Kingdom.

I should also note that ARC's facilities in Austria transact business with nations of Eastern Europe. Consequently, ARC will permit Midwest to begin penetrating the vast Eastern block market.

The synergism between our domestic and European adhesives operations will also have solid, ongoing impact on Midwest. ARC is strongest in the wood adhesives and footwear markets—precisely where we are weak. In 1981, ARC had 45 percent of the European footwear market and 40 percent of the wood adhesives market. We'll now have the opportunity to import these important products and technologies to the U.S. as well as other non-European markets.

But there will definitely be a two-way street between ARC and the U.S. For instance, ARC sales have not been strong in paper and packaging adhesives, markets that happen to be Midwest's greatest strengths. So now we'll have a vehicle for introducing some key U.S. products and technologies into Europe.

ARC made sense from still another strategic standpoint. We can now shift the

Figure 15.1
Percentage of 1982 Sales by Major Product Line and by Geographic Location

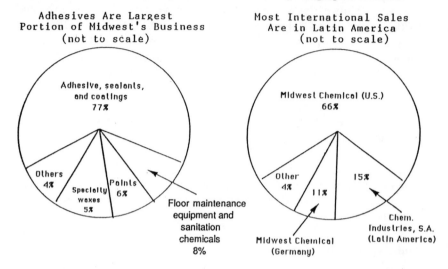

primary focus of our international business away from politically unstable Latin America. As you know, our Latin American—and particularly our Central American—operations have historically accounted for the majority of our overseas sales and earnings. But political instability and currency devaluation have placed the profitability of these operations under some pressures.

Figure 15.1 shows the percentage of 1982 sales in each product area and the percentage of sales in each geographical location where Midwest plants are located.

An interesting feature of the ARC acquisition was the concern the upper management of Asp-Rundall Chemie expressed for their personnel and the effect of the acquisition on them. Their concerns were relieved by assurance that Midwest was a "people-oriented" company and its philosophy that corporate growth can be achieved only through the individual growth of its employees. Midwest was not permitted to terminate any ARC employees but was required to achieve reduction in forces over a period of time through attrition.

Growth is a primary goal at Midwest. Growth since 1941 has been steady, resulting in sales approximately doubling every five years. There is great excitement over the corporate goal of becoming a billion-dollar company (in sales) and increasing net earnings to 5 percent (as a percent of net sales) in 1987 when it celebrates its 100th anniversary. Other long-term performance goals communicated to ARC were 10 percent return on assets, 15 percent return on invested capital, and 20 percent return on shareholders equity.

A consultant group from the American Management Association has been retained by Midwest to guide and provide expertise to middle management in developing strategic plans and objectives to achieve corporate goals.

Marketing services recently introduced a program designed to stimulate interest and support from all employees in attaining the $1 billion goal. The "Plug It" program encourages employees to submit ideas for new products for which they may win a variety of large appliances. Hence, "plug it" applies to a color television, microwave oven, or a stereo. A trip to Hawaii and anywhere in the territorial United States will also be awarded.

A continuous stream of new products and technology have likewise resulted in sales growth. Many products sold by Midwest today did not exist five years ago. New products and new product applications, such as the protection sealant introduced by the Smith Products Division in 1980, is an example of new technology. This sealant encapsulates spray-applied asbestos installed in many schools and industrial and commercial buildings during the 1950s and 1960s. This is characteristic of the product and market diversification that tempers the effects of recessionary periods.

Midwest is recognized throughout this highly fragmented, steadily growing industry as one of the largest independent specialized adhesives manufacturers (i.e., a company that is not a subsidiary of a large corporate giant) involved only in the manufacture of adhesives. In general, the market is fragmented into regional companies that supply only a particular geographic area. Some companies target specific industries; others may provide only one or two products. Among the eight to ten companies that do have a variety of products, in many areas Midwest is the leader. Some companies that obtain 90 percent or more of their sales in the specialized chemical area include Himont, International Flavors and Fragrances, Nalco Chemical, Great Lakes Chemical, Vista Chemical, Loctite, Witco, H. B. Fuller, and Midwest Chemical Products Company. National Adhesives Company (a division of National Starch and Chemical Company), Borden Chemical Company, Swift and Findley are key diversified competitors. None of these has a product line of the breadth or depth of Midwest's. Each has similar adhesive products: rubber based, thermoplastic, thermosetting, two polymer and vegetable, protein based, hot melt, anaerobic, and elastomeric sealants. None provides all of these products in as many locations as Midwest. In the packaging adhesives market, Midwest and National Adhesives have dominant market shares, with approximately 25 percent each.

The early strategy of entering areas where the competition does not exist holds true today.

MIDWEST PRODUCT GROUPS AND MARKETS

Adhesives

Today's economic environment has created a need for improved productivity in manufacturing plants. Therefore, Midwest's technical expertise and process knowledge has enabled it to improve efficiency in the adhesive systems of its plants. Adhesives that permit increased line speed, better quality control, and less down time come from the joint cooperation of Midwest and its customers. The demand for increased performance and energy conservation has led to expansion of the packaging adhesives line.

The largest part of Midwest's business—packaging adhesives—supplies customers such as food and beverage processors. Midwest products are used to seal and label virtually all types of food packaging. This business does not significantly decrease during slow economic periods. Consequently, this business, like the food industry, is less vulnerable to swings in the economic cycle and holds up well during recessionary periods. One of the stronger segments of this industry is the beverage industry. Significant gains were made in sales of labelling adhesives for bottlers of soft drinks, beer, wine, and liquor in 1981. Gains should be achieved in 1982 and thereafter in paper and packaging adhesives with the acquisition of ARC.

The customer base is continually expanding as new applications for Midwest products are found. New, more efficient products replace older adhesives that may be costlier and less efficient. An important achievement in 1978 was the development and introduction of adhesives and sealant application equipment to manufacturers of insulated glass and refrigeration appliances. Since these high technology adhesives and sealants involve changing the customer's manufacturing process, a systems approach of selling both the product and its application equipment was very effective.

Midwest's strong position in the U.S. packaging market has been retained primarily through better penetration of new and existing markets. This was achieved by significant product and process innovations. In most market segments served, market share was increased through new product introductions and a strong commitment to customer service. In numerous instances, Midwest established laboratories and supplied research personnel at the plant locations of companies having sealant problems. This usually resulted in rapid and successful solutions to most problems.

Specialty markets in the packaging area that have become increasingly successful include hot-melt, pressure-sensitive adhesives for tapes and labels and wax emulsion coatings for corrugated containers. Also, a water-resistant coating for corrugated boxes is successful.

Midwest has maintained a leading position in the hot-melt segment of the packaging adhesives market through product innovation and customer service. This fast, efficient way of bonding various materials is making rapid progress in areas such as labelling for plastic soft drink bottles, disposable diapers, and pressure-sensitive tapes and labels. Technical superiority has won a strong market position with good growth prospects.

Sealants and Coatings

Growth, particularly in the international market, has resulted from new business opportunities that complement the product market and geographical matrix.

As the construction industry begins to recover, sealant sales to the window industry are expected to increase as more manufacturers convert from manual to automated systems. The line of energy-related products is being broadened with products such as Quick Seal thermal barrier, a urethane material that prevents heat transfer in metal windows and doors. This fast-curing sealant allows inline fabrication of the metal frames and, thus, improved productivity for the manufacturer. Also, Midwest's sales of waterbase contact adhesives have increased because OSHA regulations in furniture manufacturing require reduction or discontinuation of solvent adhesives.

New and innovative products for the automotive industry resulted in strong sales during 1981. Midwest produces fabrithane, which is used to bond structural plastics in automobiles. To further the service and commitment of Midwest to the automotive industry, a technical center was established in Detroit. It is anticipated that an increasingly significant share of this market will be captured in the future.

Softness in the economy in 1981 and subsequent lowered production by several major customers did not adversely affect the sales of another line of Midwest products—powder coatings for thin film decorative finishes. A new generation of industrial finishes, powder coatings are quickly replacing solvent-based paints because of their nonpolluting characteristics and superior performance. At the end of 1980 Midwest formed its Industrial Coatings Division. This new product group has gradually grown enough in size to be a separate, viable business organization. To complement internal product development, the assets and business of Reliable Powder Products was purchased from Reliable International. This increased Midwest's powder coatings capabilities and its ability to service customers.

Midwest's new applications of its products and broadening of its customer base should insure future sales growth.

Consumer Market

Midwest's entry into the consumer market in 1977 and the introduction of "EXTRA" bond panel and construction adhesive was well timed. The consumer products market is actually countercyclical because "do-it-yourself" activity tends to increase during economic down cycles. Promoting the wide range of consumer products among home centers and building supply distributors through the use of modular "Room to Grow" displays have increased sales rapidly. Other products include carpeting and ceramic tile adhesives, roof and window caulks, and bathtub sealants. "Extra Beauty" decorative brick, a lightweight inorganic brick replica, is sold along with the adhesive/mortar to install it.

In 1978 reorganization of Midwest's Construction and Consumer Products Division allowed better focus on the two distinct market segments— the retail or "do-it-yourself" market and the ceramic tile and floor covering market served primarily by contractors.

Other promising areas are urethane coatings for gasoline and chemical storage tanks, hot-melt coated string systems for plywood bonding, and Unithane (one-component urethane adhesives for bonding metal and plastic). These products represent a big breakthrough for the customer in application and performance properties.

Even though the consumer and construction markets were off considerably in 1981 and 1982, sales to those markets were down only slightly. Gross margins were substantially improved through controlling operating and production expenses.

Specialty Chemical Products

Midwest's specialty chemical products include paints, specialty waxes, floor maintenance equipment and sanitation chemicals, and specialized polymers.

Paints. Midwest Chemical Industries, S.A., with headquarters in Costa Rica, is Midwest's principal international subsidiary (80 percent owned by Midwest). They produce paints and lacquers that are sold in Mexico, Panama, and other countries in Central America. The majority of its business is residential and commercial paints marketed through company-owned (retail) paint stores and some distributors. These stores also market adhesives and decorating products.

Midwest holds a leading position in the Central American industrial and consumer paint market. Because of high inflation rates, instability, and other problems, management has tried to minimize its exposure and its risks in politically troubled areas of Central and South America.

Midwest industrial finishes have had continuous strong growth. These powder coatings and water-based finishes are mainly used for coating of lawn and garden maintenance equipment, appliances, tools, and recreational equipment. They are well accepted as nonpolluting alternatives to solvent-based finishes.

Specialty Waxes. Midwest is the leading supplier of specialty waxes to the packaging, food, rubber, dairy, and cosmetic industries throughout Europe. These waxes are produced in West Germany and France. Recently, there have been large sales increases in cheese and cable waxes along with those used for protective and hot-melt coatings. This was a result of concentrated marketing efforts in those countries. Midwest has long been recognized as a technological leader in the western European specialty wax market.

Floor Maintenance Equipment and Sanitation Chemicals. Sales of Multifold-Klean floor maintenance equipment and chemicals have increased, as has their profitability. Cost control programs, improved inventory control, and better market focus have all contributed to these sales increases.

In 1978 Multifold-Klean introduced a patented automatic rug scrubber to round out its line of cleaning systems. It offers "one pass" shampooing of carpeted floors, thus reducing labor costs for building maintenance. The customer group in this market includes industrial plants, schools, hospitals, shopping centers, supermarkets, hotels, restaurants, and office buildings.

Midwest's competitive position has improved in the dairy, food, and beverage industries through technical improvements in the product line. The range of customer services is being widened by developing programs around chemical and equipment systems. Midwest personnel promote the recycling of cleaning chemicals, a situation that new government clean water standards underscore.

Polymers. Polymers are made through the process of polymerization. Chemically this involves a process of changing the molecular arrangement of a compound so as to form new compounds having the same percentage composition as the original but of greater molecular weight and different properties. Acetylene and benzene are two examples of the polymerization process.

Midwest will be expanding work in this area with the centralization of its R&D facilities. Old compounds will be examined and reevaluated, and new compounds will be developed in light of new needs in all of the major industries (automotive, construction, etc.) and new local, state, and federal laws governing the use of chemical compounds. This area is expected to be a growing segment of Midwest's business, both sales and profitwise.

All Product Groups

In all product groups, inefficient manufacturing facilities have been replaced with warehouses. New manufacturing techniques have been introduced to improve overall productivity and other operating efficiencies.

Figure 15.2
Midwest Chemical Products Company, Inc. Organizational Chart (1982)

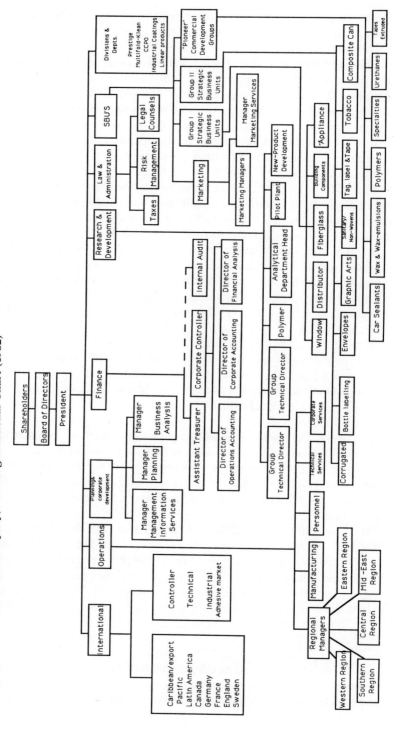

All plants are staffed by nonunion personnel. In some areas high wages are paid for low-quality work. This, of course, affects efficiency and profit. But for the most part, production personnel are capable and have considerable experience. Nevertheless, Midwest's policy of promotion from within has, in some instances, resulted in supervisory personnel who lack both management experience and skills.

FUNCTIONAL OPERATIONAL AREAS

Operations and Organization

Midwest has grown through acquisition, occasional divestures, and new product development within each of its divisions, which operate as independent businesses and profit centers. Each division is divided into geographical regions, which are further divided into districts. The managers of these areas report to a division manager, who in most instances is a vice president.

The district managers operate as general managers and are responsible for profit. District managers hire, train, and coach sales representatives. In some divisions, there is national coordination of initial sales training and also subsequent updating at sales meetings. The district units have access to corporate research and development, data processing, human resource services, and marketing services (advertising, public relations, conventions, and meetings). Management philosophy in the company encourages decisions to be made and situations to be dealt with at all levels. This decentralized structure fosters the development of managers with good decision-making ability.

The success of any organization depends entirely on the individual and collective success of its people. Midwest's management integrates decentralized operating management with strong centralized planning and control. This structure allows all employees to work together to execute a demanding long-range corporate strategy. It allows Midwest to assess immediate opportunities in light of future growth goals and strategies. Figure 15.2 illustrates Midwest's organizational chart.

Finance

The financial objective of Midwest in simplified terms is to operate a financially sound company that generates a return on equity sufficient for continued growth. The specific financial goals are reiterated here:

—$1 billion in sales by 1987
—a doubling of sales every five years
—5 percent net earnings as a percent of sales by 1987

—10 percent return on assets by 1987
—15 percent return on invested capital by 1987
—20 percent return on shareholders equity by 1987

As shown in Figures 15.3 and 15.4 and Tables 15.2 through 15.7, there was an increase in sales every year from 1972 to 1982. Net earnings and net earnings per share were down in 1975 when the acquisition of Prestige Products and the decrease in availability of raw materials resulted in increased costs and a consequent decrease in profitability. Net earnings and net earnings per share were down again in 1982.

Unprecedented success was achieved in 1981 with the largest net earnings increases since 1974. This was reflected in a strong financial position in areas such as return on sales, ROE, ROI, and ROA. During that year, return on assets and return on invested capital reached their highest levels in ten years. Return on shareholder's equity was 19 percent in 1981, up

Figure 15.3
Financial Highlights

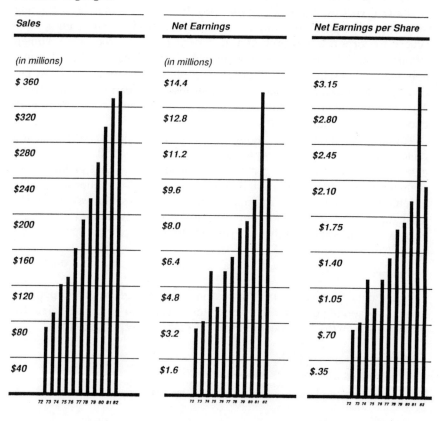

Figure 15.4
Results of Operations

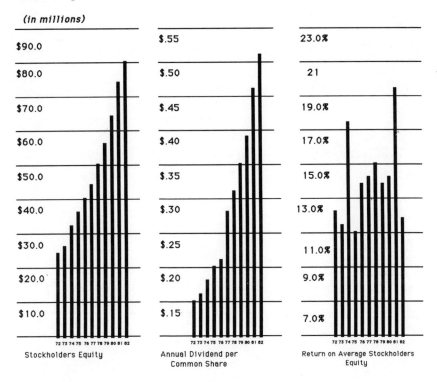

(in millions)

Stockholders Equity

Annual Dividend per
Common Share

Return on Average Stockholders
Equity

Table 15.2
Financial Highlights

Years Ended November 30				%Change	
(Dollars in thousands, except per share amounts)	1982	1981	1980	1982	1981
For the Year:					
Net sales	$ 331,800	328,682	296,860	1.0	10.7
Net earnings	9,493 (a)	13,587	8,921	(30.1)	52.3
Net earnings per common share	2.06 (a)	2.97	1.98	(30.6)	50.0
Dividends per common share	.51	.46	.39	10.9	17.9
At Year End:					
Stockholders' equity per common share	17.70	16.44	14.50	7.7	13.4
Return on average stockholders' equity	12.1%	19.3%	14.5%	(37.3)	33.1
Number of common stockholders	3,463	3,621	3,720	(4.4)	(2.7)
Number of employees	4,000	3,300	3,400	21.2	(3.0)

(a) Includes an extraordinary gain of $897,000 ($.19 per common share).

Table 15.3
1972–1982 in Review and Selected Financial Data

(Dollars in thousands, except per share amounts)	1982	1981	1980	1979
Income Statement Data				
Net Sales	$331,800	328,682	296,860	259,367
Operating Earnings	25,285	31,249	24,680	21,550
Earnings Before Extraordinary Items	8,596	13,587	8,921	7,999
Net Earnings	9,493	13,587	8,921	7,527
Depreciation	5,082	4,592	4,507	3,986
Interest Expense	5,486	5,107	6,020	4,107
Income Taxes	8,290	12,410	8,304	8,162
Balance Sheet Data				
Total Assets	207,196	157,997	147,557	139,739
Working Capital	53,447	47,344	44,113	35,838
Current Ratio	1.9	2.0	2.0	1.7
Net Property, Plant and Equipment	73,409	47,227	47,504	42,481
Long-Term Debt	44,083	23,072	26,049	23,375
Stockholders' Equity	81,645	75,842	64,951	57,867
Stockholder Data				
Earnings Before Extraordinary Items				
Percent to Net Sales	2.6	4.1	3.0	3.1
Per Common Share	1.87	2.97	1.98	1.7
Net Earnings				
Percent to Net Sales	2.9	4.1	3.0	2.9
Per Common Share	2.06	2.97	1.98	1.67
Dividends · Per Common Share	.51	.46	.39	.35
Equity · Per Common Share	17.70	16.44	14.50	12.91
Return on Average Equity	12.1	19.3	14.5	13.7
Common Stock Bid Price				
High	25.50	26.13	13.38	12.87
Low	14.25	11.75	8.75	9.75
Average Common Shares				
Outstanding (Thousands)	4,595	4,568	4,493	4,491
Number of Employees	4,000	3,300	3,400	3,400

* Effective December 1, 1973 the Company changed its
inventory valuation basis to last-in, first-out (LIFO) from first-in,
first-out (FIFO) for U.S. inventories.

from 15 percent in 1980. Net earnings were a record $13.6 million ($2.97/share—a gain of 52 percent). Returns for 1982 were not nearly as impressive. Sales gains in all U.S. operations and improvements overseas, along with the "Trim It" program contributed to 1981 being a successful year. (The "Trim It" program was initiated in 1980 to generate cost reductions by asking for suggestions from every part of the company.) Improvement of profit by reducing operating expenses was something in which all Midwest employees participated.

Fiscal 1982 was considered a year of transition by Midwest. It successfully completed the restructuring of much of its U.S. business into fifteen strategic business units (SBUs), which allowed Midwest to capitalize on their technological leadership and market knowledge. Midwest also completed a major, strategic acquisition in Europe, thereby strengthening its position in the worldwide adhesives market.

Midwest feels that its long-term optimism is justified in spite of a shadow cast in 1982. Year-end results show the effects of worldwide economic recession and the instability of foreign currencies. New sales totaled

Table 15.3 (Continued)

1978	1977	1976	1975	1974*	1973	1972
219,962	192,848	167,892	129,426	121,839	91,572	78,257
18,681	15,504	13,571	9,060	12,745	8,657	7,394
7,122	6,181	5,382	3,785	5,323	3,274	3,112
7,122	6,181	5,382	3,785	5,323	3,274	3,112
3,319	2,897	2,383	2,000	1,705	1,518	1,464
3,161	2,524	2,369	1,900	2,098	1,370	1,173
7,355	6,584	5,322	3,290	5,023	3,470	3,080
116,222	100,847	90,670	78,643	70,830	61,021	51,194
32,575	32,135	29,194	28,410	20,244	17,087	14,599
1.9	2.1	2.1	2.5	1.9	2.0	2.1
35,478	30,154	28,110	24,446	20,739	18,676	16,498
22,235	20,977	21,247	21,368	12,537	13,108	10,336
50,698	45,016	40,075	35,666	32,787	28,259	25,603
3.2	3.2	3.2	2.9	4.4	3.6	4.0
1.58	1.38	1.20	.85	1.19	.73	.69
3.2	3.2	3.2	2.9	4.4	3.6	4.0
1.58	1.38	1.20	.85	1.19	.73	.69
.32	.275	.215	.20	.175	.1625	.15
11.31	10.04	8.93	7.94	7.29	6.28	5.71
15.0	14.5	14.2	11.1	17.4	12.2	12.8
14.25	10.62	9.12	6.87	5.62	13.00	11.12
8.37	7.37	5.25	3.00	3.12	3.25	4.00
4,491	4,454	4,454	4,454	4,454	4,457	4,473
3,300	3,000	2,800	2,600	2,300	2,100	1,800

Table 15.4
Consolidated Statements of Earnings

Years Ended November 30	1982	1981	1980
(Dollars in Thousands, except per share amounts)			
Net sales	$ 331,800	328,682	296,860
Cost of sales	228,019	226,117	205,338
Gross profit	103,781	102,565	91,522
Selling, administrative and other expenses	78,496	71,316	66,842
Operating earnings	25,285	31,249	24,680
Interest expense	(5,486)	(5,107)	(6,020)
Other income (deductions), net	(2,610)	594	(748)
Earnings before income taxes, minority interests and extraordinary item	17,189	26,736	17,912
Income taxes	(8,290)	(12,410)	(8,304)
Net earnings of consolidated subsidiaries applicable to minority interests	(303)	(739)	(687)
Earnings before extraordinary item	8,596	13,587	8,921
Extraordinary item	897	—	—
Net earnings	$ 9,493	13,587	8,921
Earnings per common share			
Earnings before extraordinary item	$ 1.87	2.97	1.98
Extraordinary item	.19	—	—
Net earnings	$ 2.06	2.97	1.98

$331.8 million, up 1 percent from $328.7 million in 1981. Net earnings declined 30 percent to $9.5 million, or $2.06 per share, as compared with 1981's record $13.6 million, or $2.97 per share. Included in 1982 earnings is an extraordinary gain of $897,000, or $.19 per share, as a result of the sale of land in the first quarter.

Table 15.5

Consolidated Statements of Retained Earnings

Years Ended November 30, (Dollars in Thousands, except per share amounts)	1982	1981	1980
Retained earnings at beginning of year	$ 59,787	48,315	41,149
Net earnings	9,493	13,587	8,921
Cash dividends paid:			
Preferred: $1.00 per share	(15)	(15)	(15)
Common: $.51, $.46 and $.39 per share, respectively	(2,343)	(2,100)	(1,740)
Retained earnings at end of year	$ 66,922	59,787	48,315

Research and Development

Midwest's research and development department is called upon for the development of new products or to test new applications of existing products if it is beyond the scope of the chemist in the manufacturing plant. Both manufacturing chemists and R&D people work with plant personnel in implementing new processes or in trouble-shooting problem situations. In this way, they complement the efforts of the field sales force who generally have a technical background and are given technical training. This approach has been very successful for Midwest and its customers; however, in some instances it has resulted in nearly reinventing a product previously developed for another account.

Even though the cost of the Midwest product used in the manufacture of other products is usually the smallest portion of the total cost, it often determines the difference between the success or failure of those items. The products may be used in vast amounts, as when laminating vinyl to particle-board, or by the drop, such as in intricate electronic circuitry.

Because of the highly technical nature of the product line, there is great emphasis in the area of R&D. There are approximately 250 research and technical personnel employed by Midwest around the world (more than 7 percent of the 3,200 employees). An orientation toward application involves anticipating future adhesive and specialty chemical needs as well as solving present problems. Technical efforts are concentrated in five basic areas:

Analytical and central testing: Raw materials, existing products, and new products chemically analyzed and tested for performance.

Formulators: Compound new adhesives or specialty chemicals; emphasis on long-range customer problems.

Technical service chemists: Operating out of plants worldwide and assisting salespeople in solving immediate customer problems.

Polymer chemists: Responsible for developing raw materials for adhesives, binders, sealants, paints, coatings, and floor waxes.

Table 15.6
Consolidated Balance Sheets, November 30, 1982 and 1981

Assets (Dollars in Thousands)	1982	1981
Current assets:		
Cash and cash equivalents	$ 14,240	12,699
Trade receivables and other, less allowance for		
doubtful accounts of $2,266 in 1982 and		
$1,602 in 1981	49,686	40,656
Receivables due from		
unconsolidated subsidiaries and others	6,462	4,742
Inventories	42,394	34,873
Prepaid income taxes and other current assets	3,439	1,880
Total current assets	116,221	94,850
Property, plant and equipment, at cost:		
Land	15,818	9,589
Buildings and improvements	35,095	25,525
Machinery and equipment	46,729	38,801
Construction in progress	9,565	3,402
Total property, plant and equipment	107,207	77,317
Less accumulated depreciation	33,798	30,090
Net property, plant and equipment	73,409	47,227
Other assets:		
Investments in and advances to		
unconsolidated subsidiaries	6,808	5,284
Deposits, deferred charges and other assets	9,059	8,785
Excess of cost over net assets of consolidated		
subsidiaries, less amortization	1,699	1,851
Total other assets	17,566	15,920
	$ 207,196	157,997

Liabilities and Stockholders' Equity (Dollars in Thousands)	1982	1981
Current liabilities:		
Notes payable to banks	$ 8,239	8,720
Notes payable to others	1,355	678
Current installments of long-term debt	2,681	2,252
Accounts payable—suppliers	25,354	19,362
Accounts payable—others	10,486	2,109
Accrued payroll	4,726	5,305
Other accrued expenses	8,003	3,818
Income taxes payable	1,930	5,262
Total current liabilities	62,774	47,506
Other liabilities:		
Long-term debt, excluding		
current installments	44,083	23,072
Deferred income taxes	3,551	3,168
Accrued pension costs and other deferred credits	10,194	3,435
Total other liabilities	57,828	29,675
Minority interests in consolidated subsidiaries	4,949	4,974
Stockholders' equity:		
Preferred stock of $20 par value. Authorized		
and issued, 15,300 shares	306	306
Common stock of $1 par value. Authorized		
6,000,000 shares; issued 4,594,388 shares	4,594	4,594
Additional paid-in capital	11,304	11,304
Retained earnings	66,922	59,787
Equity adjustment from foreign currency translation	(1,481)	(149)
Total stockholders' equity	81,645	75,842
	$ 207,196	157,997

Table 15.7
Consolidated Statements of Changes in Financial Position

Years ended November 30, (Dollars in Thousands)	1982	1981	1980
Working capital provided (used) by:			
Earnings before extraordinary item	$ 8,596	13,587	8,921
Items which do not use working capital:			
Depreciation of plant and equipment and assets under capital leases	5,082	4,592	4,507
Other amortization	780	776	652
Minority interests in net earnings of consolidated subsidiaries	303	739	687
Equity in net losses of unconsolidated subsidiaries	1,699	773	1,171
Deferred income taxes and other items	1,333	913	721
Working capital provided by operations before extraordinary item	17,793	21,380	16,659
Extraordinary item	897	—	—
Proceeds from long-term debt	14,804	15,470	14,248
Long-term debt and other deferred credits of businesses acquired	17,557	—	—
Proceeds from building construction fund	1,568	—	—
Proceeds from issuance of common stock	—	1,184	—
Effect of currency exchange rate changes on non-current assets and liabilities	720	559	428
Other	167	(34)	630
	$ 53,506	38,559	31,965
Working capital applied to:			
Property, plant and equipment, deposits and deferred charges of businesses acquired	$ 17,726	—	—
Additions to property, plant and equipment, net	16,788	7,011	9,209
Reduction of long-term debt	4,578	18,161	11,574
Cash dividends	2,358	2,115	1,755
Increase investments in and advances to unconsolidated subsidiaries	3,481	1,172	812
Increase deposits, deferred charges and other assets:			
Certificate of deposit	—	2,576	—
Building construction fund	—	1,568	—
Miscellaneous	1,140	960	258
Change in equity adjustment from foreign currency translation	1,332	1,765	82
Increase in working capital	6,103	3,231	8,275
	$ 53,506	38,559	31,965
Changes in working capital:			
Cash and cash equivalents	$ 1,541	5,525	2,557
Receivables	10,750	2,213	3,180
Inventories	7,521	(1,917)	(1,578)
Prepaid income taxes and other current assets	1,559	(734)	539
Notes payable to banks and others	(196)	1,751	894
Current installments of long-term debt	(429)	646	27
Accounts payable and accrued expenses	(17,975)	(1,395)	3,149
Income taxes payable	3,332	(2,858)	(493)
Increase in working capital	$ 6,103	3,231	8,275

Product development: New raw materials, products, and production processes are developed and tested in equipment similar to that used for regular production.

In addition to service labs in every Midwest plant, there are complete laboratories in Cincinnati, Ohio; Montreal, Quebec; and Toronto, Ontario. There are also large modern laboratories in West Germany and Costa Rica.

In 1982, R&D started to become more centralized. The increased sophistication of the adhesives industry necessitates greater concentration of technical resources. Centralization is now underway and will be accomplished by mid–1983 when a 90,000-square-foot, $12-million research and development facility will open in Blue Ash, Ohio. Beyond simply consolidating research and development efforts, the centralization creates a synergism and a rapid increase in new product development. It reduces the duplication of product development efforts inherent in a decentralized organization and focuses efforts on specific industrywide needs.

One of Midwest's priorities is increasing the product development emphasis of the technical group by expanding the number of Ph.D's on the staff and encouraging individual creativity by all members of the technical group.

The network of technical service chemists at plants across the United States has been strengthened by an improved communications link. This network provides the local technical assistance that is essential to customers and plays a key role in the successful marketing of products.

A "Special Opportunities" group has been organized to lead the company in state-of-the-art, cutting-edge technological advancements. This group includes not only scientists but marketing and production experts. It identifies projects that likely have the greatest impact on the company's future stream of sales and earnings and ultimately enhances Midwest's position as a technologically superior specialty chemical and adhesives company.

Management Information Systems

MIS is the complete responsibility of the data processing department, which in 1981 had a staff of six people. Recently, a centralized computer was installed that speeds up the turnaround time and increases the services that are offered. This computer compiles data for financial and sales reports and does invoicing for some plant locations. The centralized computer system is designed to provide the sales staff with properties and uses of Midwest's formulas, which effects an increase in sales of existing products.

Human Resources

With the strong emphasis on people orientation and the career and personal development of its individual employees, Midwest's human resources department plays an important role. In all areas, promotion from within creates a need for continuous upgrading of skills and evaluation of personnel. At present, the weakest link in the chain is the lack of any structured formal strategy or program for the development of management personnel. The company philosophy of promotion from within, except in critical areas where new expertise is required, makes that factor vital to future corporate growth.

The well-developed staff in the human resources department administers a variety of programs for employees. The Thrift Plan is a matched savings program available to all Midwest employees. If needed, there are clinical dependency and employee counselling programs available at no cost to the individual.

Marketing

The success of Midwest in the past has been accomplished in an atmosphere of limited emphasis on marketing. Past success is attributed to technical expertise, high quality products, and customer service. Marketing services provide advertising and public relations support, primarily at the corporate level. They are active in the promotion of Midwest at trade shows and conventions.

Some divisions operate without any marketing staff at all. Others, such as the packaging and adhesives groups, have marketing personnel whose background is sales. The construction group has a marketing manager whose background and experience are in marketing. Due to both scarcity of experienced marketing personnel and the projected corporate growth, this is an area that must be addressed immediately.

According to John May, general manager of marketing, this is one of the areas that will be addressed during the 1980s. He states:

The steady growth experienced by the company during the past 40 years has required many changes in Midwest's structure. During the '40's and '50's we developed a network of regional plants to serve our growing number of customers on a local basis. In the '60's, we began specializing by product groups, with international growth and divisionalization during the '70's. For the '80's, we are integrating our product and marketing strategies to focus on more important growth markets.

We have identified a number of strategic business units and assigned industry specialists to these areas. Additional such units will be named in future years.

Carefully focused marketing efforts will allow the company to improve its penetration in both new and existing market areas.

Sales

Early in 1980, it was recognized that the recession in the United States would have an impact on sales of construction and consumer products. Consequently, Midwest focused its efforts on improving profitability. Although unit sales to these markets were lower, profits increased due to improved operating efficiencies and cost reductions.

The economy had the same effect on sales of adhesives, sealants, and coatings to the traditional product assembly markets. However, by focusing efforts on market segments where market share could be gained through product innovation, better service, or added value, again profitability improved.

Strong direction came from sales management in dealing with this situation. A salespersons' compensation (commission) plan was designed to encourage emphasis on the more profitable products. The only complication to this plan was the "time sharing" of some representatives by two or three product groups. This occasionally left the salesperson in a quandary.

While the recession and downturn in new housing starts affected the company's sales of specialty caulks and adhesives to residential construction and "do-it-yourself" markets, a new subfloor adhesive, Certain-Bond, is expected to play an important role in the company's future success in the construction industry.

In all areas of the company, a reputation for product excellence and performance, customer-oriented technical expertise, and localized service are recognized strengths.

Manufacturing

Midwest's manufacturing is done in many small, nonunion plants worldwide. Most manufacturing processes are neither labor intensive nor capital intensive (in regard to the sophistication and cost of the equipment needed). The majority of products require no more than three or four days lead time and are not manufactured until there is an order for them. This enables Midwest to maintain a very low inventory of finished products. The need to quickly assemble products does, however, require a sizable raw materials inventory. The plant manager and the district manager work together to schedule production of both finished goods and products that can be sold as raw materials to another division.

The finished products are shipped to consumers in either metal or paper drums. By having plants in many locations, shipping costs are minimized. Midwest owns a fleet of tank trucks and other delivery vehicles. This allows prompt delivery of products at a lower cost than if outside services were used.

Corporate Planning and Development

In 1977 Midwest began implementing a strategic planning process using a market growth/market share matrix system to analyze the company's business. The new process complements the annual budget system used in the past and gives managers a more specific framework to use in making long-range operating decisions. It also provides a mechanism to respond to change and a systematic process to monitor performance.

In 1980, CEO Adam Andrews announced the development and implementation of a systems-oriented strategic planning process to seek out new opportunities, analyze them against corporate goals, and set priorities and checkpoints. This is part of Midwest's SWOTI technique where they examine and evaluate the strengths (S), weaknesses (W), opportunities (O), threats (T), and possible innovations (or incentives) (I) of each situation. The use of systematic strategic planning combined with the long-established company attitude of flexibility toward current events is a good balance for decisions made for the long-term development and management of the company.

During 1981, Midwest's six divisions were separated into fifteen strategic business units (SBUs), which were organized along product lines. General managers supervise these operations and have responsibility for profit. They oversee marketing, sales, and production. Some SBUs have salespeople who sell that particular product line exclusively. Others use the general sales force on a part-time basis.

Each of the SBU managers, along with the managers in R&D, finance, and human resources, has developed long-range strategic plans that will be implemented in late November of 1982. Guidelines for preparing these plans are originated by the director of planning and a strategic planning consultant from the American Management Association.

Andrews described the SBUs and their use as follows:

All of our 15 SBUs are focusing on the opportunities presented by one industry or market. Each SBU manager has either a sales or technical background, and is responsible for gaining an in-depth knowledge of that particular industry. Because of this high degree of specialization, the SBU manager is an authority on the current and future production and technical needs of that industry. In addition, people in the SBU sales force have a specific person to contact for product and technical information.

The creation of a specialized sales force will have particularly important ramifications for us. In the past, a typical sales representative would cover customers and prospects in many different industries . . . for example, tobacco, box, bag, laminating, envelopes, and graphic arts. Each of these industries has its own set of production and technical problems, and our sales people were generalists rather than specialists in any one of these areas. As a result, we were unable to fully capitalize on all available market opportunities.

Our SBU structure represents a solution to this problem. By its nature, the SBU will weave together targeted marketing industry specialization and technical service. More than ever, our technological capabilities will be guided . . . or driven . . . by needs of our markets and industries. Our research and product development will be given a new sense of direction as we cast ourselves in the role of technologically competent problem-solvers for given industries. There will be considerably more stress on tackling industry problems and working to develop sophisticated solutions.

Specifically, these objectives will be accomplished in several ways.

First, if Midwest does not have a product that will meet the particular requirements of a customer, this fact will be communicated to the SBU manager. The SBU manager will then coordinate an R&D effort to come up with the right formulation. In this way, R&D will be guided and directed by concrete market considerations.

The SBU managers will also work closely with another newly formed group . . . the Special Opportunities Group. This group deals with research projects that generally require high levels of expenditures. It is responsible for directing Midwest's R&D efforts which are on the leading edge of technological advancement and that could have future impact on the company sales and earnings.

Coordination between marketing and research is being bolstered by one other entity . . . the Pioneer Group. Composed of people with lab and sales backgrounds this group has primary responsibility for bringing new products to market. Under this new system, the Pioneer Group again . . . in conjunction with input from the SBUs . . . will help speed up the process by which new products are introduced.

PROBLEM

CEO Adam Andrews has been reviewing all of the information on his company for an upcoming meeting with his top management people. He is particularly concerned with the six financial goals and objectives that he and his top management team have set for the company to achieve by the end of 1987. Previous discussions with his top management revealed that they feel very strongly that all goals and objectives could be met or beat by the end of 1987; however, based on 1982 financial data, and some expressed doubts by middle and lower management about meeting these goals and objectives, Andrews has some pangs of concern. In examining all of the information in his possession, he has decided that all internal and external areas in which the company is involved and by which the company is influenced must be reexamined and reevaluated. Andrews formulated the following questions to present to his staff that he feels must as a minimum be answered in order to determine what course of action the company should take between now and the end of 1987.

1. Are all of the company goals and objectives as stated compatible and achievable?

2. If the answer to question 1 is yes, how are they compatible and how can the results be achieved?

3. If the answer to question 1 is no, why are they not compatible and why can't the results be achieved? What changes do you recommend in the goals and objectives and overall company operation?

4. In answering questions 2 and 3, construct a time activity chart (bar graph, PERT, or CPM) for the entire time period involved in your recommendations.

5. In analyzing, evaluating, and answering questions 1, 2, and 3, thoroughly examine and evaluate all the company functional areas: marketing, manufacturing, engineering, R&D, accounting, finance, corporate planning, management and organization, human resources, MIS, interface, and so on. Also take into consideration cash flow, financial ratios, domestic and foreign inflation rates, interest rates, world currency rates, political unrest, market penetration, and other political and economic factors. As part of this company self-analysis, evaluation, and improvement, examine and comment on the possibility and desirability of:

   a. possible additional acquisitions (who, what, when, where, how, and why);

   b. takeovers of someone else by Midwest, or of Midwest by someone else (who, what, when, where, how, and why);

   c. spinoffs (who, what, when, where, how, and why);

   d. mergers (who, what, when, where, how, and why);

   e. joint ventures and/or desirability and applicability of using certain other companies as suppliers (who, what, when, where, how, and why); and

   f. any other areas of use or applicability in achieving company goals and objectives.

   That is, thoroughly examine, analyze, and evaluate all internal and external areas and factors that affect the company and justify your solutions and recommendations.

Andrews felt that although the task he was about to assign to his top managers was extensive, it was necessary and the answers could be generated within thirty days on the basis that all of the information needed to answer his questions was obtainable from existing internal and readily available external sources and documents.

CONCLUSION

Andrews has very aptly and candidly set forth the problems that Midwest Chemical Products Co., Inc. faces. At first glance it might appear to present a difficult and complex task from which many people would shy away. Although the workload is considerable, Chapter 16 will help, through the use of the corporate operational analysis procedure, analyze and evaluate the Midwest case in a step-by-step, systematic manner and supply answers and recommendations to all Andrews' questions and concerns.

16

Application of the Corporate Operational Analysis Procedure to the Case

As explained in chapter 15, the time setting of the case to be analyzed and evaluated takes place in early 1983, a crossroads year for Midwest in which numerous critical decisions must be made on which road or roads to follow in attempting to determine whether or not the company can meet all of its old and new goals and objectives, or if it should modify some of these very ambitious goals and objectives. The case is now analyzed and evaluated in strict accordance with the procedure presented in chapter 13 and will be presented as if this analysis and evaluation is taking place in early 1983. Therefore, only case data and public domain data external to the company available through early 1983 are used in the analysis and evaluation. (This is all common and standard practice in case analysis and evaluation—the "you are there" approach.)

Additionally, for the purpose of proper and complete use and compliance with all sections of the procedure, some of the data included in the case is of necessity repeated as part of the analysis and evaluation that takes place in this chapter. The reason for this is because the procedure is designed to be used internally by a "real world" company to analyze and evaluate itself, by a consultant to analyze and evaluate a company, or by a seminar group or college class to analyze and evaluate a company case such as Midwest. In the first two instances, the data presented in the case would not be visible (at least in a detail written form) to the recipients of the analysis and evaluation report; therefore, any data in the report would be seen by the reader of the report for the first time. In the third instance, the case and the analysis and evaluation of the case do not normally appear side by side in the same book, as is the case in this book. The standard and commonly accepted practice in case analysis is to assume the two documents (the case and the analysis and evaluation of the case) are separate entities, and the case analysis report must stand on its own merits and be in complete compliance with the procedure. This is the approach that is taken in this chapter. It is only by this complete approach that the use and application of the procedure in the decision-making process can be clearly demonstrated. That is the central purpose of this book.

INTRODUCTION

The primary objective of Midwest Chemical Products Company, Inc., presented in chapter 15, is to operate a socially responsible, financially sound company that will generate a return on equity sufficient for continued stable growth. To celebrate its centennial birthday, and meet its primary objective, Midwest has established a number of new specific financial goals to be met by 1987, along with its long-standing, equally important broader company goals and objectives. The new financial goals to be achieved by 1987 are:

- $1 billion in sales;
- a doubling of sales every five years;
- 5 percent return on sales;
- 10 percent return on assets;
- 15 percent return on invested capital; and
- 20 percent return on shareholders' equity.

The more general goals include securing and maintaining technical leadership; continued introduction of new products and finding new and better ways of serving customers with existing products; being a people-oriented company; sharing the company's good fortunes with the employees, stockholders, and society as a whole; and continuing an orderly expansion through internal growth and acquisitions.

Midwest's objectives are in keeping with its past strategy and desire to maintain continued growth through reinvested earnings. Although it would give Midwest tremendous publicity to reach its goal of $1 billion in sales, along with its other proposed financial goals, these financial achievements may not be mutually compatible, easily attained, or in the best long-run interest of the company. For example, to achieve $1 billion in sales by 1987 will require a compounded annual sales growth of 24.7 percent for the next five years; net earnings as a percent of sales must grow at a compounded annual rate of 39.2 percent for this same time period in order to reach the 5 percent rate of $1 billion in sales by 1987. At no time in the history of Midwest has this rate of growth been achieved; neither have any of the other newly proposed financial goals been met at any time by Midwest.

Can Midwest attain these financial heights through acquisitions without overloading itself with debt? Will a lending institution even lend Midwest any more money in light of its present high debt load? An alternative might be to raise cash through a stock offering, but Midwest might then lose control of the company by diluting its share of ownership in the company. Was Midwest too hasty in establishing these new financial goals, hoping for success based on 1981 performance and prospects of publicity forthcoming on its one-hundredth birthday? Because 1982 was not such a great year, a number of middle-level and lower-level managers have expressed doubts about reaching the proposed goals by 1987. Therefore, should Midwest revise some of these financial goals downward or at least push them a little further into the future?

It should come as no surprise, as the case ends in chapter 15, that Andrews is concerned about whether or not Midwest can truly reach any or all of its lofty 1987 financial goals and objectives and that if they are attained, these goals might hurt the long-range prospects of the company.

The remainder of this chapter will show how, through the use of the corporate operational analysis procedure, defined in chapter 14, and the functional area background information supplied in chapters 2 through 13, the Midwest case (or that of any company) can be examined, analyzed, and evaluated to determine the feasibility and desirability of achieving any or all of the company's specified financial goals and objectives. The procedure will also help determine the compatibility of both new and old goals and objectives with one another. After this has been accomplished, the procedure will be used to propose, evaluate, and recommend solutions, in chronological order, to all problem areas uncovered. In other words, the remainder of this chapter will, with the use of the procedure, thoroughly analyze the Midwest case, answer all of Andrews' questions, and make recommendations to Andrews. By doing this, the format, the procedure, and its practical application will be presented in a practical and useful manner. This analysis and evaluation takes place in the spring of 1983, shortly after the 1982 annual report was released.

PHASE I (MACRO ANALYSIS): DIAGNOSTIC

Lifecycle of the Industry

Midwest is a part of the chemical industry and, more specifically, a part of the specialty chemical industry. This industry is highly competitive. Several large international firms as well as numerous smaller regional or local companies compete in one or several of Midwest's targeted markets. These companies, however, do not carry the large, varied product line that Midwest does and are not in the same broad geographical markets that Midwest serves. Therefore, the company does not recognize a specific number of competitors as major competition; Midwest does, however, meet competition from one or more companies in all of its business areas.

The industries that Midwest competes in are the adhesive, sealant, paint, specialty waxes, and floor maintenance equipment industries. The adhesive and sealant industries have the largest impact on Midwest because those products constitute over 75 percent of Midwest's sales.

The adhesive industry is broken down into seven market areas: construction, transportation, rigid bonding, packaging, nonrigid bonding, consumer, and tapes. The market in general is fragmented into regional companies that supply only a particular geographic area. The *construction* adhesive market consists of installation of ceiling panels, floor tiles, and wall coverings. This market has been hurt by the recession, but with new products eliminating old methods it is expected to grow at a faster rate than the GNP. The *transportation* adhesives, which consist of installation of interior and exterior trim parts to all transportation equipment, is expected to have the most attractive growth rate of all adhesive markets. The automotive industry is reducing the weight of vehicles because of energy costs and will be using more adhesives. Bonding operations in facilities are also more efficient than mechanical fasteners. The *rigid bonding* market consists of products that prevent the loosening of mechanical fasteners in metal and wood products. The *packaging* area consists of adhesives that assist in the manufacturing of cartons, packages, and containers. It is expected to grow at the same rate as the GNP. This market is reaching saturation level; however, it holds up well in recessionary periods. The *nonrigid bonding* area consists of shoe, filter, carpet, and book manufacturers. Hot-melt adhesives are replacing solvent adhesives in this market. The *consumer* market consists of do-it-yourself products. This area is countercyclical because it tends to increase during economic down cycles. As the recession ends, this area is expected to stabilize. The final area in the adhesive industry is the *tape* area, which consists of adhesives that are used on packaging, industrial, surgical, and masking tapes. This area is growing rapidly in the pressure-sensitive industry, and many competitors are entering this area.

The global markets, especially the European market, need to be addressed. The European adhesive market is approximately the same size as the U.S. market. The global market areas are divided differently, with the construction and rigid bonding areas being greater in Europe and the consumer, tapes, and packaging areas being much larger in the United States.

The sealant industry is split up into four market areas: consumer, industrial, transportation, and construction. The European sealant market is approximately half the size of the U.S. market. Construction makes up 70 percent of the European market while it is only 55 percent of the entire sealant industry in the United States. Opportunities for growth are the development of sealants for the window industry and water-based adhesives for the furniture market. Water-based adhesives will replace solvent adhesives due to OSHA's antipollution regulations.

The paint industry has been declining. This trend is expected to continue as powder coatings replace solvent-based paints because of their non-polluting characteristics and superior performance. The paint market in Latin America is unstable, and the devaluation of currency is now making that area unprofitable.

The specialty wax industry has grown in Europe because of increases in cheese and cable waxes. This market is expected to have moderate growth consistent with Europe's economic trends.

The floor maintenance industry is growing moderately because of technical improvements in the products and improvements that meet government clean water standards.

Lifecycle of the Firm

Midwest was founded in 1887 to manufacture and distribute wallpaper paste. The company was family-owned and, in the first thirty years of business, had franchised operations in Ohio, Georgia, and Minnesota. A Midwest accountant, Edward Andrews, purchased the Cincinnati, Ohio, franchise in the late 1920s. Over the next twenty years, he expanded and diversified his product lines. By 1940 he had purchased all the other franchises. The company went public in 1968 and is presently traded over the counter.

Today, Midwest is a full-fledged specialty chemical company whose primary product lines include adhesives, sealants, coatings, paints, industrial waxes, floor maintenance equipment and materials, as well as other specialty chemicals. Its products are generally characterized by the customer's desire for formulated products and technical services. Over 75 percent of the company's sales are generated from adhesives, sealants, and coatings. The remainder of Midwest's business is roughly equally divided among paints, specialty waxes, floor maintenance equipment, and sanitation chemicals, as well as other products.

The company operates from forty cities within the United States, as well as other facilities in Canada, Latin America, Europe, and Asia. This has been accomplished through internal growth and by acquisition in both the domestic and international arenas. This growth has been capped by the 1981 acquisition of ARC in West Germany for $27 million. This company was acquired as an attempt to get a firmer grasp on the European adhesives market. The long-term growth objectives of the company and the stability of the European and American markets is also important to consider. Midwest has also expressed an interest in pulling out of its operations in Latin America where political and economic instability have created problems.

The company's management believes that it has a social responsibility to its employees and the communities in which they live. Management believes that if the communities in which the employees live and work are strong, viable, and responsive to society, everyone benefits. On a national level, Midwest is focusing on the problems of battered women and abused children; staff time and contributions are helping in these areas. On the corporate level, the company distributes turkeys at Thanksgiving and hams at Easter to all employees in appreciation of their service. Employees also share in the preceding year's profits in the form of a bonus check at Christmas.

Midwest has recently undertaken a strategic planning process to identify the future direction of the company. The company has used a variety of planning tools and has used outside consultants from the American Management Association to assist in the process. One major result in this process is the separation of the company into fifteen strategic business units from its previous six-division format. It is from this point that the company desires to view its long-term strategy and decide which direction it should move.

Basic Strategy

Midwest's basic strategy is to sustain orderly long-term growth, even during times of economic uncertainty, by securing and maintaining technological leadership in the introduction of new and innovative products and in finding new and better ways of serving customers with existing products. Midwest has had continuous growth due to domestic and international acquisitions and because of new product development within each of its divisions, which operate as independent business and profit centers.

Since as far back as the 1960s, Midwest's international expansion strategy has been to identify unique products, services, or market segments that will allow success and then commit money and people to its operations. A strategic decision was also made several years ago to identify and develop growth opportunities in Europe, which was partially implemented with the acquisition of Midwest GmbH in Germany. The strategic implications of this acquisition were threefold: first, Midwest wanted to expand its volume of European operations; second, European markets were to become the primary focus of international operations; and third, the company wanted to shift its current emphasis of European business toward industrial adhesives. It obviously wanted to be the leader in its field.

The strategy in entering new markets is to go where the competition isn't, establish a sales base, add manufacturing facilities as needed, and build to a position of profitability as quickly as possible. The company is willing to experience short-term losses that may arise during this process.

Another part of Midwest's strategy that bears repeating is to be a socially responsible, people-oriented company. Midwest feels that by helping its employees to grow it will also grow, and Midwest will therefore share the benefits of growth with its customers, stockholders, and the community.

Midwest's focus for the 1980s is to concentrate on the integration of products and marketing strategies in national and multinational growth markets. SBUs and aggressive financial goals, listed at the beginning of this chapter, have been established to help achieve this.

Significant Functional Areas

The significant functional areas of importance to Midwest are listed below in rank order of importance. Several of them are very close to one another in rank so that switching their positions in this list would not matter, but they will be discussed and evaluated, including their strengths and weaknesses, in the following order:

- Corporate planning
- Research and development (R&D)/engineering
- Manufacturing
- Finance/accounting
- Marketing/sales
- Human resources
- Interface
- Management information systems (MIS)

Corporate planning is the most significant functional area because Midwest has shown steady, profitable growth both domestically and multinationally since its inception; it is adept at finding proper market niches and developing them; it manufactures and distributes products competitively; and it is a people-oriented, socially responsible company. Effectively and efficiently performing these tasks as a coordinated effort requires dedicated corporate planning.

R&D and engineering are combined into the second most significant functional area because of their ability to develop innovative and practical application products. They have repeatedly demonstrated their technological leadership in both new products and application of existing products to new areas.

Manufacturing comes close to R&D and engineering in importance. R&D, engineering, and manufacturing have very close ties and operate with one another in timely development, production, and delivery of high quality, innovative products.

Finance/accounting is listed fourth because all of the goals set forth by the CEO are stated in financially related constructs. It is in this functional area, and its interfaces with the other areas, that a determination will be made of whether the goals set forth by Andrews are realistic.

Marketing/sales is listed fifth because of the historically insignificant role marketing has played in the success of Midwest. Midwest has relied on its technical relationships with customers to develop new products. The salesforce has often been shared among divisions. This functional area has not received proper attention from senior management, but managers are aware that this area requires immediate attention.

Human resources is listed sixth because, on the positive side, the firm emphasizes the growth of the individual as part of the growth of the firm. Many of Midwest's past programs reflect the correlation between corporate growth and rewards to the employees, customers, stockholders, and the community. The role that human resources plays within the firm has a great impact on Midwest's ability to achieve its goals. The ethical stance of Midwest is encompassed in this functional area. There are also several negative factors that require more attention. These include extensive promotion from within without regard for total qualification, high wages for work that does not require or justify these wages, and inadequate managerial training in some areas.

Management and organization are included under the human resources umbrella and help lower human resources to sixth place on the list. This is due to many factors: Management and organization changes are now taking place; some of the uncertainties associated with the implementation and control of fifteen newly installed SBUs are just starting to receive serious consideration, as is marketing; and MIS is not organized at all.

At this point in the evaluation, the interface between functional areas does not appear to be a major concern for Midwest. Its organizational structure, information system, and history of duplicate efforts in new product development all point to a problem in this area. Andrews is attempting to interface the various areas during the assessment of the goals he has set before the current management; but after the planning stage, there appears to be a lack of emphasis on interface.

MIS is listed last for several reasons. Midwest has grown to over 4,000 employees, and management boasts of fifteen separate SBUs. Yet Andrews has no way to readily obtain vital information from this complex organization in a format that could answer some of his questions about

Table 16.1
Rating of Significant Functions of Management Applications

Functional Area	Excellent	Overall Rating Satisfactory	Poor
Corporate Planning	Directing	Planning Organizing Controlling	
R&D	Directing	Planning Organizing	Controlling
Manufacturing		Planning Organizing Directing Controlling	
Finance/Accounting		Planning Organizing Directing Controlling	
Marketing/Sales		Planning Organizing	Directing Controlling
Human Resources	Directing	Planning Organizing	Controlling
Interface		Planning Organizing Directing Controlling	
MIS			Planning Organizing Directing Controlling

the goals he has set, other than canvassing the opinions of his subordinates. Midwest now devotes only six people to the task of bringing the new computer system online. Clearly, this area is of extreme significance, but it has received little if any priority or resources.

Functions of Management Application

Midwest has steadily grown over the years largely because of its philosophy toward growth and its employees. The operating objectives of Midwest were developed under the general corporate goal of building a leading, worldwide specialty chemical company with emphasis on superior service to the customer. These things can be best accomplished when all functional areas within the company are performing well in the functions of planning, organizing (with emphasis on staffing and structure), directing (including development and communication), and controlling. Table 16.1 provides an insight into the effectiveness of Midwest's operations in each of its functional areas.

PHASE II (MICRO ANALYSIS): DIAGNOSTIC

Case Narrative

The material reviewed in Phase I is again reviewed in Phase II, but to a much greater depth. This section will build on the knowledge developed in Phase I and sort out basic details on how the organization operates.

Expansion of Basic Strategy Statement. Midwest is a diversified specialty chemical company with 1982 sales reaching $331.8 million.

Concerns for customers, employees, shareholders, and the community—the philosophy on which Midwest is built—has directed the company's growth and expansion over the past forty years. Midwest has gone from a regional adhesive supplier to a multinational specialty chemical company. It has accomplished this through a commitment to creative product development and technical service, close customer relations and focused marketing efforts in specific product areas, continued expansion through internal growth and external acquisitions, and being a socially responsible, people-oriented company.

In 1981, Midwest achieved its largest net earnings increase since 1974. It had a strong financial position in the areas of return on sales, return on equity, return on invested capital, and return on assets. Although 1982 was a successful year, Midwest's financial position was not quite as strong as in 1981.

During fiscal year 1982, Midwest saw a number of transitions, internally and externally:

- It completed the restructure of much of its U.S. business into strategic business units.
- It completed a major strategic acquisition in Europe, strengthening its position in the worldwide adhesives market.
- It felt the effects of worldwide economic recession and the instability of foreign currency.
- It continued to experience the effects of political instability and currency devaluation in Latin America, including the civil uprisings in Nicaragua.

With the current domestic and international economic and political climate, Andrews must consider very important internal and external factors for the future success of Midwest, such as: (1) the financial situation of Midwest as it relates to the six proposed financial goals and corporate strategy; (2) international concerns, specifically economic and political instability in Latin America and the German and the European economic climate; (3) the current product-market structure of Midwest and potential for mergers, acquisitions, or takeovers; and (4) the current organizational structure and associated personnel problems.

Extrapolation/Extension of Data and Analysis of Financial/Balance Sheet Data. Based on the financial and balance sheet data, shown in the figures and tables in Chapter 15, a considerable amount of extrapolation and extension of this data can be done. This work can show how well the company has done in the past and how well it will have to perform in the future in order to achieve its financial goals and objectives.

When a least squares trend line analysis is performed on the financial data, as Figure 16.1 shows, actual earnings as a percent of sales have actually trended downward from 1972 to 1982. If 5 percent earnings as a percent of sales is to be reached, this trend must be reversed and earnings as a percent of sales must increase at the rate of 12 percent per year from 1982 to 1987. This 12 percent rate increase holds regardless of whether or not it applies to the doubling of sales in that five-year period or to the 1987 $1-billion sales goal. Tables 16.2 and 16.3 verify this statement. Figure 16.2 shows that if future earnings keep pace with past earnings, sales will not even double by 1987. For sales to double by 1987, they must increase at a rate of 14.9 percent each year between the end of 1982 and 1987. For sales to reach the $1-billion level by 1987, the rate of sales increase must jump to 24.7 percent per year.

Returning to earnings again for a moment, Tables 16.2 and 16.3 and Figure 16.3 show that for earnings to reach 5 percent of sales, for a doubling of sales by 1987, the earnings must grow at a rate of 28.5 percent per year from 1982 to 1987. For earnings to reach 5 percent of sales, for $1 billion in sales by 1987, the earnings must grow at a rate of 39.5 percent per year from 1982 through 1987.

Figure 16.4 shows that the past trend on average return on equity has been increasing at a slow rate but not rapidly enough to reach the desired 20 percent level by 1987. At no time in its recent history has average return on equity reached 20 percent. A one-time high level of 19.3 percent was reached in 1981; however, the average return on equity for the ten years prior to and including 1982 was 14.25 percent. In order to reach a level of 20 percent by 1987, a compound rate of growth of 10.6 percent on average return on equity must be achieved each year through 1987.

Midwest has expressed a 10 percent return on assets as one of its goals. Figure 16.5 shows that if future trends parallel past trends, this goal cannot be reached. In fact, return on assets averaged only 5.6 percent from 1972 to 1982, with a slightly positive slope to the least squares linear regression

Figure 16.1
**Past Actual Earnings as a Percent of Sales and Projected Growth Rate Required
in Earnings as a Percent of Sales (if earnings as a percent of sales are to reach
the 5 percent level by 1987)**

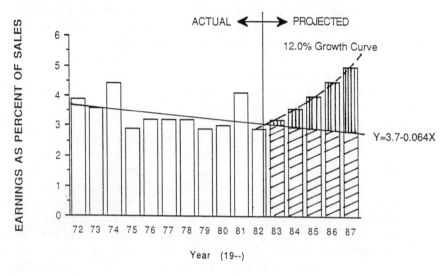

KEY:

☐ Actual earnings as a percent of sales

▨ Projected earnings as a percent of sales
   (based on past trend)

▥ Projected earnings as a percent of sales
   (Growth rate required with either doubling
   of sales or $1 billion sales by 1987)

analysis curve. In order to achieve 10 percent return on assets by 1987, there must be a compound growth rate of 16.9 percent in this area for the years 1983 through 1987.

Table 16.4 shows some historical key financial data and financial ratios for the ten-year period of 1973 through 1982 for trend and comparison purposes. Table 16.5 presents, in a different format, some key financial ratios for 1981 and 1982, shows the change in these ratios with the 1982 industry averages, as given by Dun & Bradstreet Credit Services. Tables 16.6 and 16.7 respectively compare Midwest's 1982 and 1981 operating performance with four of Midwest's competitors. Table 16.8 compares several key financial ratios of Midwest with those of five of its competitors and the adhesive and sealants averages. All of this data will be examined in greater depth in the next section of this chapter when a detailed analysis

Table 16.2
Doubling of Sales by 1987

Year	Sales[1] Needed	Earnings[2] Needed	Net Earnings to Sales (%)
1982	331,800	9,493	2.9
1983	381,238	12,199	3.2
1984	438,043	15,675	3.6
1985	503,311	20,142	4.0
1986	578,304	25,883	4.5
1987	664,471	33,260	5.0

[1] Sales growth at 14.9% per year
[2] Earnings growth at 28.5% per year

Table 16.3
Reaching $1 Billion in Sales by 1987

Year	Sales[1] Needed	Earnings[2] Needed	Net Earnings to Sales (%)
1982	331,800	9,493	2.9
1983	413,755	13,243	3.2
1984	515,952	18,474	3.6
1985	643,392	25,771	4.0
1986	802,310	35,950	4.5
1987	1,000,480	50,150	5.0

[1] Sales growth at 24.7% per year
[2] Earnings growth at 39.5% per year

and evaluation is performed on the finance/accounting area of the company.

Table 16.9 lists the average yearly consumer price index, from which inflation rates can be derived, for several industrial countries with whom or where Midwest does business. During this period, inflation rate increases ranged from an average of 4 percent per year in Japan to about

Figure 16.2
Past Actual Sales and Future Projected Sales Under Various Conditions

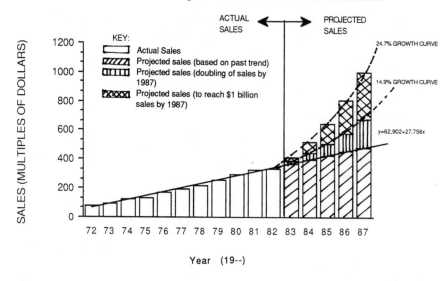

Year   (19--)

7.5 percent per year in the United States (6.13 percent in 1982) and to almost 14.5 percent per year in Italy. These inflation rates were, however, relatively calm compared with the magnitude of the inflation rates in some developing countries where Midwest does business. During the period of 1980 to 1985, inflation increased on the average each year in Argentina by 342.8 percent, in Brazil by 147.7 percent, and in Bolivia by 569.1 percent.[1] In 1984 alone, Argentina suffered an inflation rate of between 600 and 700 percent, and Brazil suffered an inflation rate of over 200 percent.[2] Inflation is projected to reach 400 percent in 1988 in Brazil where Midwest supplies adhesives for application in the manufacture of Brazil's large shoe industry.

High inflation rates have an important impact on the business environment. As discussed earlier, they influence interest rates, exchange rates, the cost of living, and the general confidence in a country's political and economic system. In highly inflationary environments, it is difficult for firms to plan and schedule for the future and to run profitable operations. Prices change almost daily in order to produce a sufficient cash flow to replace inventory and keep the firm operating. This becomes a delicate balancing act; underpricing the product will result in a cash flow shortage, while overpricing the product can result in loss of market share. Midwest can at least try to partially offset this problem by centrally sourcing funds (to be discussed in greater detail later in this chapter) and/or by using the LONI (last out, next in) concept of accounting, where an outgoing product

Figure 16.3
Past Actual Earnings and Future Projected Earnings Under Various Conditions

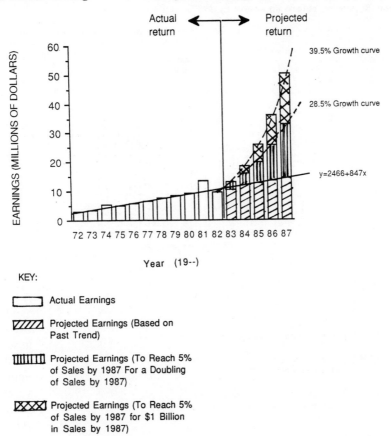

Year   (19--)

KEY:

☐ Actual Earnings

▨ Projected Earnings (Based on
    Past Trend)

▥ Projected Earnings (To Reach 5%
    of Sales by 1987 For a Doubling
    of Sales by 1987)

▧ Projected Earnings (To Reach 5%
    of Sales by 1987 for $1 Billion
    in Sales by 1987)

is sold at the price of the next material items coming in (of course, with appropriate markup for profit).

Annual industrial production is shown in Table 16.10 for the same seven countries for which inflation rates were given in Table 16.9. By comparing both tables, it is noted that while inflation rates increased substantially in each of the seven countries in 1982, industrial production levels rose only in minuscule amounts in Japan and the United Kingdom and fell in the other five nations. In other words, 1982 was not a good business year worldwide.

Money exchange rates against the U.S. dollar vary considerably around the world. Just as different inflation rates in different countries can cause severe multinational problems, different money exchange rates can produce many headaches for a multinational firm. Table 16.11 lists exchange rates for 1975, 1981, and 1984 (projected) for many of the countries in and with which Midwest does business.

Figure 16.4
Past Average Return on Equity and Projected Increase in Growth (needed to reach 20 percent return on equity by 1987)

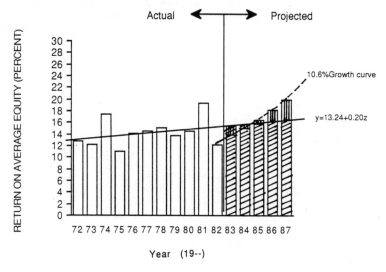

KEY:

☐ Actual Return on Average Equity

▨ Projected Return on Average Equity (Based on Past Trend)

▥ Projected Return on Average Equity (Growth Rate Required to Reach 20% by 1987)

Overseas markets have been besieged by continued U.S. recession and inflation, which have caused the chemical industry to stagnate worldwide. In 1979, the U.S. dollar started to strengthen against most countries and continued to do so, as is shown in Table 16.11. A strong dollar, a fairly stable U.S. inflation rate, relatively high interest rates (compared with some other countries), a strong U.S. stock market, a perception of the United States as a safe haven from world crisis, and a demand for dollars by multinational companies helped continue to strengthen the dollar. Strong dollars have given foreign exports cheaper access to U.S. markets and have helped them compete with U.S. companies abroad. This also resulted in the United States purchasing more of the cheaper foreign goods and helped increase the U.S. trade deficit by increasing foreign imports relative to domestic exports.

Domestic exports have been much lower than imports in every major

Figure 16.5
Past Return on Assets and Projected Increase in Growth (needed to reach 10 percent return on assets by 1987)

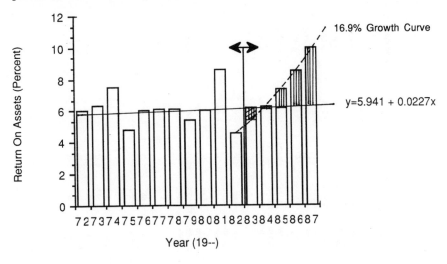

KEY:

▭ Actual Return on Assets

▨ Projected Return on Assets
(Based on Past Trend)

▥ Projected Return on Assets
(Growth Rate Required to Reach 10% by 1987)

industry except for chemicals. The balance of trade in the chemical industry is shown in Table 16.12. It is important to note that not only have imports of chemicals been increasing since 1966, but the ratio of imports to exports has also been increasing, thus making competition for market share in the United States even rougher.

The largest competitors (by rank order) in the world chemical trade include: (1) United States; (2) Canada; (3) the European Economic Community (EEC); (4) France; (5) Italy; (6) the Netherlands; (7) the United Kingdom; (8) West Germany; (9) Switzerland; and (10) Japan. A major trend in the industry is for foreign firms to acquire existing American chemical businesses. Many large foreign chemical concerns view the United States as the biggest and most promising chemicals market, offering key consumer and industrial end markets much larger than their own home markets.[3]

Competition is also intense within the United States itself. Some of the major players in the domestic specialty chemical industry in 1982, listed

Table 16.4
Midwest Historical Key Financial Ratios (dollars × 1,000)

	1982	1981	1980	1979	1978	1977	1976	1975	1974	1973	Average
Growth											
Net Sales	331,800	328,682	296,860	259,367	219,962	192,848	167,892	129,426	121,839	91,572	
% of Inc-Dec	0.9%	10.7%	14.5%	17.9%	14.1%	14.9%	29.7%	6.2%	33.1%	17.0%	15.90%
Net Earnings	9,493	13,587	8,921	7,527	7,122	6,181	5,382	3,785	5,323	3,274	
% Inc-Dec	-30.1%	52.3%	18.5%	5.7%	15.2%	14.8%	42.2%	-28.9%	62.6%	5.2%	15.75%
Earnings/Sales	2.86%	4.13%	3.01%	2.90%	3.24%	3.21%	3.21%	2.92%	4.37%	3.58%	3.34%
Dividends/Share	0.510	0.460	0.390	0.350	0.320	0.275	0.215	0.200	0.175	0.162	
% Inc-Dec	10.9%	17.9%	11.4%	9.4%	16.4%	27.9%	7.5%	14.3%	7.9%	8.2%	13.17%
P.E. Ratio	9.65	6.37	5.58	6.77	7.16	6.52	5.99	5.81	3.67	11.12	6.86
Total Assets	207,196	157,997	147,557	139,739	116,222	100,847	90,670	78,643	70,830	61,021	
% Inc-Dec	31.1%	7.1%	5.6%	20.2%	15.2%	11.2%	15.3%	11.0%	16.12%	19.2%	15.21%
Fixed Assets	73,409	47,227	47,504	42,481	35,478	30,154	28,110	24,446	20,739	18,676	
% Inc-Dec	55.44%	0.58%	11.82%	19.74%	17.6%	7.27%	15.00%	17.8%	11.05%	13.20%	16.95%
Profitability											
Earnings/Share	2.06	2.97	1.98	1.67	1.58	1.38	1.20	0.85	1.19	0.73	1.56
Return on Assets	4.58%	8.60%	6.05%	5.39%	6.13%	6.13%	5.94%	4.81%	7.52%	5.37%	6.05%
Return on Equity	12.10%	19.30%	14.50%	13.70%	15.00%	14.50%	14.20%	11.10%	17.40%	12.20%	14.40%
Shareholder Equity	81,645	75,842	64,951	57,867	50,698	45,016	40,075	35,666	32,787	28,259	51,281
Ret. on Capital	-15.27%	58.96%	14.29%	4.87%	13.56%	17.11%	37.24%	-13.13%	51.78%	2.98%	17.24%
Ret. on Inv. Cap.	7.55%	13.74%	9.80%	7.85%	9.77%	9.37%	8.78%	6.64%	11.74%	7.91%	9.52%
Activity											
Turnover											
Total Asset	1.60	2.08	2.01	1.86	1.89	1.91	1.85	1.65	1.72	1.50	1.81
Fixed Asset	4.52	6.96	6.25	6.11	6.20	6.40	5.97	5.29	5.87	4.90	5.85
Leverage											
Long Term Debt	44,083	23,072	26,049	23,375	22,235	20,977	21,247	21,368	12,537	13,108	
L.T. Debt/Asset	0.21	0.15	0.18	0.17	0.19	0.21	0.23	0.27	0.18	0.21	0.20
L.T. Debt/Equity	0.54	0.30	0.40	0.40	0.44	0.47	0.53	0.60	0.38	0.46	0.45
Times Earned Int.	2.81	6.09	3.86	4.82	5.58	6.06	5.52	4.72	5.93	5.92	5.13
Debt to Equity	1.48	1.02	1.27	1.41	1.29	1.24	1.26	1.20	1.16	1.16	1.25
Liquidity											
Current Ratio	1.90	2.00	2.00	1.70	1.90	2.10	2.10	2.50	1.90	2.00	2.01
Working Capital	53,447	47,344	44,113	35,838	32,575	32,135	29,194	28,410	20,244	17,087	
Cash Flow	-17,720	15,220	180	1,307	4,677	4,093	3,317	-6088	1,808	126	

Table 16.5
Key Financial Ratio Comparison

Solvency	Midwest Chemical 1981	Midwest Chemical 1982	Change(%)	Industry 1982
Quick Ratio	1.26	1.18	-6.35	1.20
Current Ratio	2.00	1.87	-6.50	2.30
Current Liability to Net Worth	.63	.77	22.22	0.48
Current Liability to Inventory	1.48	1.36	-8.11	1.20
Total Liability to Net Worth	1.02	1.48	45.10	0.69
Fixed Assets to Net Worth	.62	.90	45.16	0.30
Efficiency				
Collection Period (days)	50.41	61.77	22.53	40.00
Days Payable (days)	34.60	57.40	65.89	30.00
Inventory Turnover (days)	56.29	67.86	20.55	37.63
Total Asset Turnover (times)	2.08	1.60	-23.08	1.95
Fixed Asset Turnover (times)	6.96	4.52	-35.06	9.46
Assets to Sales	0.48	0.62	29.17	0.40
Sales to Net Working Capital	6.94	6.21	-10.52	6.90
Accounts Payable to Sales	0.06	0.08	38.34	0.06
Selling Exp & G&A to sales (%)	21.69	23.66	9.08	20.00
Profitability				
Return on Sales (%)	4.13	2.86	-30.75	5.00
Return on Assets (%)	8.60	4.58	-46.74	10.20
Return on Net Worth (%)	29.00	16.00	-44.83	18.00
Return on Invested Capital (%)	13.74	7.55	-45.05	14.40
Return on Shareholders' Equity (%)	19.30	12.10	-37.31	14.70
Return on Invested Capital (%)	13.74	7.55	-45.05	9.52
Debt Management				
Debt	0.52	0.61	17.30	0.41
Capitalization	0.27	0.40	48.15	0.14
Debt to Equity	1.02	1.48	45.10	1.20
Interest Coverage (times)	6.12	4.62	- 24.51	- -
Burden Coverage (times)	3.34	2.40	- 28.14	- -

*Source: Industry Norms and Key Business Ratios, 1982–83 (New York: Dun & Bradstreet Credit Services, 1982), p. 65.

in rank order of gross sales (with 1982 gross sales shown in millions), include:

• Lubrizal Corporation ($812.20)
• Naleo Chemical Company ($643.90)
• Ferro Corporation ($595.80)

Table 16.6
Comparison of Midwest's 1982 Operating Performance with Industry Competitors

Earnings Data	Midwest 1982	% of Net Sales	Nalco 1982	% of Net Sales	Loctite 1982	% of Net Sales	Inter. F&F* 1982	% of Net Sales	Witco 1982	%of Net Sales
Net Sales	331,800		643,863		216,450		447,889		1,305,418	
Cost of Sales	228,019	68.72%	322,204	50.04%	94,203	43.52%	232,757	51.97%	1,086,981	83.27%
Gross Profit	103,781	31.28%	321,659	49.96%	122,247	56.48%	215,132	48.03%	218,437	16.73%
S G & A Expen.	78,496	23.66%	189,565	29.44%	91,811	42.42%	82,107	18.33%	129,567	9.93%
Oper. Earnings	25,285	7.62%	132,094	20.52%	30,436	14.06%	133,025	29.70%	88,870	6.18%
Interest Exp.	5,486		5,102		6,837		4,683		14,339	
Inc. Tax. Exp.	8,290		44,730		10,180		38,130		20,322	
Other (net)	2,016		24,146		-2,359		27,052		24,367	
Net Earnings	9,493	2.86%	58,116	9.03%	15,778	7.29%	63,160	14.10%	29,842	2.29%

*International Flavors and Fragrances.
Source: *Moody's Industrial Manual,* Volume 1 (New York: Moody's Investor Service, Inc., 1984).

Table 16.7
Comparison of Midwest's 1981 Operating Performance with Industry Competitors

Earnings Data	Midwest 1981	% of Net Sales	Nalco 1981	% of Net Sales	Loctite 1981	% of Net Sales	Inter. F&F* 1981	% of Net Sales	Witco 1981	%of Net Sales
Net Sales	328,682		666,591		213,912		451,088		1,291,878	
Cost of Sales	226,117	68.80%	332,799	51.69%	97,950	45.25%	232,757	51.97%	1,087,920	83.34%
Gross Profit	102,565	31.20%	333,792	51.84%	115,962	53.57%	218,331	48.75%	203,958	15.62%
S G &A Exp.	71,316	21.70%	181,332	28.16%	95,491	44.12%	81,814	18.27%	102,416	7.85%
Oper. Earnings	31,249	9.51%	152,470	23.68%	20,471	9.46%	136,517	30.48%	101,542	7.78%
Interest Exp.	5,107		3,084		5,094		3,444		14,679	
Inc. Tax Exp.	12,410		61,660		2,616		38,827		29,783	
Other (net)	145		6,517		2,384		28,123		18,500	
Net Earnings	13,587	4.13%	81,209	12.61%	10,377	4.79%	66,123	14.79%	38,580	2.96%

*International Flavors and Fragrances.
Source: *Moody's Industrial Manual,* Volume 1 (New York: Moody's Investor Service, Inc., 1984).

Table 16.8
Midwest/Competition Ratio Analysis Comparison for 1982

INDICATOR	MIDWEST	ADHES[2] SEAL	NALCO[1]	LOCTITE[1]	WITCO[1]	INTER.[1]* F&F	GREAT[1] LAKES
Return on Sales	2.9%	5.0%	9.0%	6.9%	2.3%	14.1%	9.4%
Return on Assets	4.6%	10.2%	12.5%	7.9%	4.5%	14.6%	8.1%
Return on Share. Equity	12.1%	17.9%	16.6%	12.8%	9.2%	18.8%	13.6%
Return on Invest. Capital	7.6%	14.4%	16.5%	11.3%	6.7%	18.8%	9.7%
Quick Ratio	1.2	1.2	1.8	1.8	1.6	2.4	1.2
Current Ratio	1.9	2.3	2.3	2.4	2.2	4.2	2.3
Debt Ratio	51.5%	41.1%	24.0%	37.1%	44.9%	15.6%	55.2%
Collection Period (Days)	60.9	40.0	58.0	66.8	48.5	64.6	76.8
Sales to Inventory	7.8	9.7	13.2	6.2	13.5	3.7	4.9
Acc. Payable to Sales	10.8%	5.9%	7.7%	5.6%	10.5%	3.6%	10.8%
Assets to Sales	62.4%	39.1%	75.9%	88.4%	50.7%	96.3%	115.6%
Cogs to Sales	68.7%	71.4%	50.0%	41.7%	82.5%	52.0%	71.3%
Earnings Per Share	$2.06	--	$1.62	$1.59	$2.10	$1.73	$1.13
% Chg EPS 81-82	-30.6%	--	-19.8%	51.4%	-23.9%	-4.4%	-9.6%
% Chg Sales 81-82	0.9%	--	-3.4%	3.7%	1.0%	-0.7%	12.8%

* International Flavors and Fragrances

Sources: 1. *Moody's Industrial Manual* (New York: Moody's Investor Services, Inc., 1984), pp. 2908–2909, 2985; 2. *Industry Norms and Key Business Ratios, 1982–83* (New York: Dun & Bradstreet Credit Services, 1982), p. 65.

Table 16.9
Selected Inflation Rates

	1979	1980	1981	1982	CPI Change 1979-82 (%)
United States	217.4	246.8	272.4	289.1	32.98
Canada	221.0	243.5	273.9	303.5	37.33
France	259.1	294.2	332.7	373.1	44.00
Germany	166.9	175.8	186.9	196.8	17.91
Italy	328.5	398.0	472.4	549.4	67.24
United Kingdom	359.0	423.6	473.9	514.7	43.37
Japan	261.3	282.3	296.2	304.1	16.38

Source: United Nations, *1984 Statistical Yearbook* (New York: United Nations, 1984).

Table 16.10
Selected Growth Rates

	1979	1980	1981	1982
United States	110.7	108.6	111.0	103.1
Canada	109.8	108.1	109.0	97.4
France	107.0	106.0	103.0	101.0
Germany	107.0	107.0	105.0	102.0
Italy	108.7	114.7	112.1	109.6
United Kingdom	107.0	100.0	96.0	98.0
Japan	113.7	118.9	120.1	120.6

Source: United Nations, *1984 Statistical Yearbook* (New York: United Nations, 1984).

Table 16.11
Exchange Rates for Various Countries in which Midwest Operates (units of foreign currency per U.S. dollar average exchange rates for each calendar year)

	UNIT	1975	1981	1984 (Projected)
Austria	Schilling	16.64	17.21	20.002
Belgium	Franc	36.06	42.49	58.024
Canada	Dollar	1.0228	1.21	1.3482
New Zealand	Dollar	.7567	1.19	1.6083
France	Franc	4.047	5.83	9.3879
W. Germany	Mark	2.347	2.44	2.8465
Japan	Yen	291.4	234.46	243.68
Mexico	Peso	12.49	24.55	185.48
Brazil	Cauzeiro	10.00	93.45	2850.3
Costa Rica	Colon (1974)	6.57	20.04	47.241
Nicaragua	Cordoba	7.026	10.00	9.943
El Salvador	Colon	2.50	2.50	2.4734
Guatemala	Quetzel	1.00	1.00	.9894
Honduras	Lempera	2.00	2.00	1.9787
Lebanon	Pound (1974)	2.30	4.380	7.7862
Netherlands	Guilder	2.406	2.72	3.4543

Source: Federal Reserve Bank, Cincinnati, Ohio.

Table 16.12
U.S. Exports and Imports in the Chemical Industry

	Exports	Imports	Ratio Imp./Exp.
1966	$ 2.6 billion	$ 957 million	0.068
1974	$ 8.8 billion	$ 3.9 billion	0.443
1975	$ 8.7 billion	$ 3.7 billion	0.425
1976	$ 9.9 billion	$ 4.7 billion	0.475
1985 (projected)	$21.7 billion	$14.5 billion	0.668

Source: United Nations, *1984 Statistical Yearbook* (New York: United Nations, 1984).

- Raychem Corporation ($534.90)
- Dexter Corporation ($522.20)
- International Flavors and Fragrances ($447.90)
- Midwest Chemical ($331.80)
- Petrolite Corporation ($302.60)
- Betz Laboratories, Inc. ($254.70)
- Grow Groups, Inc. ($228.70)
- Loctite Corporation ($216.50)
- Crompton & Knowles Corporation ($213.30)
- Stepan Company ($208.40)
- Great Lakes Chemical Company ($169.70)
- Learonal, Inc. ($142.80)
- Lawter International, Inc. ($180.00)
- Products Research and Chemical ($157.30)

Also, in selected market areas twelve diversified companies were competitors, as are twenty-one industrial chemical firms. Overall, there were over sixty-five companies competing in the chemical industry in 1982, and among these were some well-known companies: Procter & Gamble, Unilever, Great Lakes, Union Carbide, DuPont, Allied, W. R. Grace, Dow, and Imperial. Competition was, in a word, intense.

Another important area to be examined is anticipated and projected growth in the economy as a whole and in the specialty chemical industry in particular during the next few years. After a relatively poor year economically in 1982, the economy showed some signs of improving in early 1983. The U.S. real GNP increased at an annual rate of 3.1 percent in the first quarter of 1983.[4] It is expected to grow at a rate of 4.5 percent for the entire year.[5] The GNP in Britain, France, Italy, West Germany, Japan, and Canada is expected to grow at a slower pace than in the United States.[6]

Industrial production is also expected to increase slightly.[7] The speed of recovery is indicated in capacity utilization data, but the operating rate is still far too low to have much effect in the capital goods sector.

After average prime interest rates of 12.67 percent in 1979, 15.27 percent in 1980, 16.27 percent in 1981, and 14.83 percent in 1982, the prime interest rate projection for 1983 is around 10 percent, but there is a growing threat that the Federal Reserve may tighten credit which then would send the interest rates even higher.[8] Long-term interest rates are already at mid–1982 levels in 1983. If the interest rates increase and money supply decreases, the recovery will be much more uncertain than anticipated. Along with possibly continued high interest rates, average short-term unemployment is forecast at 10.2 percent.[9]

Inflation is projected by the Warton Econometric Forecasting Association to decrease slowly. They project an average rate of 5.8 percent for the 1980s, a 4.2 percent rate for the 1990s, and a 3.4 percent rate by the year 2000.[10]

All of these data on general economic conditions project positive growth, though modest and subdued, during the 1980s, both for the United States and Europe. The projected economic future for the specialty chemicals industry, specifically the adhesives and sealants area, must also be examined in conjunction with the projections for the economy as a whole.

The five-year growth projection for the chemical industry as a whole is that it will grow at a rate of about 14 percent.[11] The adhesives and sealants portions of the chemical industry are expected to enjoy an 8 percent annual growth rate in the value of shipments through 1995.[12] Adhesives are expected to gain in market share from 31 percent in 1979 to 55 percent in 1995 because they have several advantages over traditional fasteners.[13]

With this background information in hand, it is now possible to generate some additional financial projections. It should be carefully noted, however, that certain assumptions are based on data previously presented and discussed; therefore, much qualitative judgment is involved in the manipulation of the resultant quantitative output. The financial projection presented in Tables 16.13 through 16.17 are therefore only a few of a multitude of various scenarios that could be presented.

When Midwest's real sales growth is corrected for inflation, it grew at a rate of approximately 7 percent from 1973 to 1982. With an inflation rate close to 6 percent projected for the remainder of the 1980s, a 6 percent financial sales growth projection is shown in Table 16.13. Assumptions made in this projection are that sales would grow at a compounded annual rate of 6 percent, the cost of sales would remain at an average rate of 68 percent of sales, selling and administration expenses would continue at an average rate of 22 percent of sales, income taxes would continue to average 46 percent per year, dividend payments would continue to average 18 percent of net earnings, and long-term debt would stabilize for the remainder of the period at $44 million. Under this scenario, none of the newly proposed 1987 financial goals would be met.

One of the financial goals proposed by Midwest for 1987 is a doubling of sales for the five-year period starting at the end of 1982. To accomplish this, a compounded sales growth of 14.9 percent per year would have to be reached. For ease of calculation, Table 16.14 has been developed using

Table 16.13
Financial Projection for 6 Percent Growth (dollars × 1,000)

	1981	1982	1983	1984	1985	1986	1987
Sales	328,682	331,800	351,708	372,810	395,179	418,179	444,023
Cost of Sales	226,117	228,019	239,161	253,511	268,722	284,845	301,936
	68.80%	68.72%	68.00%	68.00%	68.00%	68.00%	68.00%
Gross Profit	102,565	103,781	112,547	119,299	126,457	134,045	142,187
Selling & Admin.	71,316	78,496	77,376	82,018	86,939	92,156	97,685
	21.70%	23.66%	22.00%	22.00%	22.00%	22.00%	22.00%
Operating Profit	31,249	25,285	35,171	37,281	39,518	41,889	44,402
Interest Expenses	(5,107)	(5,486)	(9,000)	(9,000)	(9,000)	(9,000)	(9,000)
Other Income/(Exp)	594	(2,610)	- 0 -	- 0 -	- 0 -	- 0 -	- 0 -
Earnings Before Taxes	26,736	17,189	26,171	28,281	30,518	32,889	35,402
Income Taxes	(12,410)	(8,290)	(12,039)	(13,009)	(14,038)	(15,129)	(16,285)
	46.42%	48.23%	46.00%	46.00%	46.00%	46.00%	46.00%
Net Earning	14,326	8,899	14,132	15,272	16,480	17,760	19,117
Dividends	2,100	2,343	2,544	2,749	2,966	3,197	3,441
	14.66%	26.33%	18.00%	18.00%	18.00%	18.00%	18.00%
Retained Earnings	12,226	6,556	11,588	12,523	13,513	14,563	15,676
Long Term Debt	23,072	44,083	44,000	44,000	44,000	44,000	44,000
Assets	157,997	207,196	218,784	231,307	244,821	259,384	275,060
Equity	75,842	81,645	93,233	105,756	119,270	133,833	149,509
Earnings/Sales	4.36%	2.68%	4.02%	4.10%	4.17%	4.24%	4.31%
Return on Assets	9.07%	4.29%	6.46%	6.60%	6.73%	6.85%	6.95%
Return on Equity	18.89%	10.90%	15.16%	14.44%	13.82%	13.27%	12.79%
Return on Inv. Capital	14.48%	7.08%	14.48%	10.20%	10.09%	9.99%	12.42%

a 15 percent sales growth. Assumptions made in developing this scenario included increasing sales 15 percent per year, using an average cost of sales of 68 percent for each year, improving selling and administrative expenses by reducing them to 20 percent of sales each year, continuing income taxes at the average rate of 46 percent per year, retaining dividend rates at 18 percent per year, and increasing long-term debt by approximately $60 million through acquisitions and by using a constant average debt/equity ratio of 50 percent for each year. Using these inputs, each of Midwest's 1987 financial goals would be met except for return on invested capital. All assumptions in the final column in Table 16.14 (1987*) are identical to the 1987 data column except that selling and administrative expenses have been increased to 22 percent of sales. When this is done, then 1987 financial goals for return on equity and return on invested capital cannot be met. This is why it is important for Midwest to reduce its selling and administrative costs in its effort to reach its financial goals.

From 1978 to 1982, Midwest's sales did not increase at a rate of 15 percent per year, but sales were closer to an 11 percent compounded rate of increase. Since Midwest's average growth rate slowed down, a third financial projection has been made (see Table 16.15) for a sales growth of 10 percent per year, which is probably a more practical and realistic goal for

Table 16.14
Financial Projection for 15 Percent Growth (dollars × 1,000)

	1981	1982	1983	1984	1985	1986	1987	1987*
Sales	328,682	331,800	381,570	438,805	504,626	580,320	667,368	667,368
Cost of Sales	226,117	228,019	259,468	298,388	343,146	394,618	453,810	453,810
	68.80%	68.72%	68.00%	68.00%	68.00%	68.00%	68.00%	68.00%
Gross Profit	102,565	103,781	122,102	140,418	161,480	185,702	213,558	213,558
Selling & Admin.	71,316	78,496	76,314	87,761	100,925	116,064	133,474	150,157
	21.70%	23.66%	20.00%	20.00%	20.00%	20.00%	20.00%	22.5%
Operating Profit	31,249	25,285	45,788	52,657	60,555	69,638	80,084	63,401
Interest Expenses	(5,107)	(5,486)	(9,000)	(11,034)	(13,582)	(16,511)	(19,880)	(19,880)
Other Income/(Exp)	594	(2,610)	-0-	-0-	-0-	-0-	-0-	-0-
Earnings Before Taxes	26,736	17,189	36,788	41,138	60,555	69,638	80,084	63,401
Income Taxes	(12,410)	(8,290)	(16,923)	(18,923)	(27,855)	(32,034)	(36,839)	(29,165)
	46.42%	48.23%	46.00%	46.00%	46.00%	46.00%	46.00%	46.00%
Net Earnings	14,326	8,899	19,866	22,214	32,700	37,605	43,245	34,236
Dividends	2,100	2,343	3,576	3,999	5,886	6,769	7,784	6,162
	14.66%	26.33%	18.00%	18.00%	18.00%	18.00%	18.00%	18.00%
Retained Earnings	12,226	6,556	16,290	18,216	26,814	30,814	35,461	28,074
Long Term Debt	23,072	44,083	48,967	58,075	71,482	86,900	104,631	104,631
Debt/Equity	30.42%	53.99%	50.00%	50.00%	50.00%	50.00%	50.00%	50.00%
Assets	157,997	207,196	223,486	241,702	268,516	299,351	334,813	334,813
Equity	75,842	81,645	97,935	116,151	142,965	173,800	209,262	209,262
Earnings/Sales	4.36%	2.68%	5.21%	5.06%	6.48%	6.48%	6.48%	5.13%
Return on Assets	9.07%	4.29%	8.89%	9.19%	12.18%	12.56%	12.96%	8.18%
Return on Equity	18.89%	10.90%	20.28%	19.13%	22.87%	21.64%	20.67%	16.36%
Return on Inv. Capital	14.48%	7.08%	13.43%	12.75%	15.25%	14.42%	13.78%	10.91%

* Same assumption as for 1987, except selling and administrative expenses are increased from the reduced 20.00% of sales to Midwest's previous average of 22.5% of sales

272

Table 16.15
Financial Projection for 10 Percent Growth (dollars × 1,000)

	1981	1982	1983	1984	1985	1986	1987	1987*
Net Sales	328,682	331,800	364,980	401,475	441,626	485,788	534,368	534,368
Cost of Sales	226,117	228,019	250,362	270,996	298,098	327,907	360,698	360,698
	68.80%	68.72%	68.60%	67.50%	67.50%	67.50%	67.50%	67.50%
Gross Profit	102,565	103,781	114,618	130,479	143,528	157,861	173,670	173,670
Selling & Admin.	71,316	78,496	83,296	98,325	107,054	116,440	124,433	106,874
	21.70%	23.66%	22.82%	24.50%	24.24%	23.95%	23.28%	20.00%
Operating Profit	31,249	25,285	31,322	32,154	36,474	41,441	49,237	66,796
Interest Expenses	(5,107)	(5,486)	(5,400)	(5,350)	(5,325)	(5,275)	(5,200)	(5,200)
Other Income/Exp.	594	(2,610)	(1,800)	(1,000)	(800)	(400)	000	000
Earnings Before Taxes	26,736	17,189	24,122	25,804	30,349	35,766	44,037	61,586
Income Taxes	(12,410)	(8,290)	(10,176)	(11,870)	(13,961)	(16,452)	(20,257)	(28,234)
	46.42%	48.23%	42.19%	46.00%	46.00%	46.00%	46.00%	46.00%
Minority Interest	(739)	(303)	(700)	(500)	(800)	(1,000)	(1,400)	(1,400)
Earn. Before Extra Items	13,587	8,596	13,246	13,434	15,588	18,314	22,380	31,862
Extraordinary Items	000	897	-0-	-0-	-0-	-0-	-0-	-0-
Net Income	13,587	9,493	13,246	13,434	15,588	18,314	22,380	31,862
Dividends	2,100	2,343	2,384	2,418	2,806	3,296	4,028	5,786
	15.45%	24.68%	18.00%	18.00%	18.00%	18.00%	18.00%	18.00%
Retained Earnings	11,487	7,150	10,862	11,016	12,782	15,018	18,352	26,076
Long Term Debt	23,072	44,083	48,923	55,547	62,023	65,392	68,000	68,000
Debt/Equity	30.42%	53.99%	50.00%	50.00%	50.00%	50.00%	50.00%	50.00%
Assets	157,997	207,196	232,433	269,057	269,100	275,456	283,550	283,550
Equity	75,842	81,645	97,945	111,094	124,046	130,785	136,000	136,000
Earnings/Sales	4.13%	2.86%	3.63%	3.35%	3.52%	3.77%	4.19%	5.96%
Return on Assets	8.59%	4.58%	5.70%	4.99%	5.79%	6.65%	7.89%	11.24%
Return on Equity	17.91%	11.63%	12.57%	11.92%	13.52%	11.63%	16.46%	23.43%
Return on Inv. Capital	18.74%	7.55%	9.02%	8.06%	8.38%	9.34%	10.97%	15.62%

* Same assumptions as 1987 except selling and administrative expenses are reduced from 22.28% of sales to 20.00% of sales

273

Midwest. This scenario assumes that sales would increase at a rate of 10 percent per year, selling and administration expenses would vary but average close to 23.75 percent of sales per year, the income tax rate would remain constant at 46 percent per year, dividends would be paid out at a rate of 18 percent of net income each year, long-term debt would increase by more than 50 percent through acquisitions, and the debt/equity rate would remain constant at 50 percent per year. Under these conditions none of the 1987 financial goals would be met and would all require revision downward. Column 1987* was developed using the same assumptions that were used for the 1987 column except that the selling and administration costs were reduced to 20 percent. By reducing the selling and administrative expenses to 20 percent, all of the financial goals except doubling of sales or achieving $1 billion in sales would be met.

Since one of Midwest's financial goals is to attain $1 billion in sales by the end of 1987, a financial projection to see how this might be achieved was developed in Table 16.16. This scenario is what might be classified as a forced situation in that the two end data years of 1982 and 1987 were generated before the in-between years. It was first assumed that all of the 1987 financial goals would be met. Starting with $1 billion in sales, it was then easy to generate the 1987 requirements for net earnings, equity, assets, and long-term debt. With these numbers determined, it was further assumed that the cost of sales would be 68 percent of sales, selling and administrative costs would be 20 percent of sales, and dividend payments would be 18 percent of net earnings. To accomplish all of these goals would require almost doubling long-term debt possibly through additional acquisitions. In spite of this, the long-term debt-to-equity ratio dropped to 33.33 percent in 1987, almost back to its 1981 level. If, however, the long-term debt-to-equity ratio is increased to 50.00 percent, as in 1982, then long-term debt would almost triple to $111 million (as shown in column 1987*). In either case, to take this route to achieving $1 billion in sales would require the acquisition of another $80 million to $100 million worth of new business. A few possible candidates might include:

Company	1982 Sales ($M)[14]
Essex Chemical	169
Findley Adhesives	75
Franklin Chemical Industries	39
Peter Cooper	70
Piedmont Label	15
Pratt and Lambert	156
Products Research and Chemical Corporation	65
Transparent Products Corporation	30
Troy Chemical	25

Table 16.16
Financial Projection for $1 Billion in Sales (dollars × 1,000)

	1981	1982	1983	1984	1985	1986	1987	1987*
Sales	328,682	331,800	413,755	515,952	643,392	802,310	1,000,000	1,000,000
Cost of Sales	226,117	228,019	281,353	350,085	437,507	545,570	680,000	680,000
	68.80%	68.72%	68.00%	68.00%	68.00%	68.00%	68.00%	68.00%
Gross Profit	102,565	103,781	132,402	165,867	205,888	256,740	320,000	320,000
Selling & Admin.	71,316	78,496	93,095	113,509	135,112	164,474	200,000	200,000
	21.70%	23.66%	22.5%	22.0%	21.0%	20.5%	20.0%	20.0%
Operating Profit	31,249	25,285	39,307	52,358	70,773	92,266	120,000	120,000
Interest Expenses	(5,107)	(5,486)	(15,869)	(18,994)	(23,048)	(25,082)	(26,058)	(26,058)
Other Income/(Exp)	594	(2,610)	-0-	-0-	-0-	-0-	-0-	-0-
Earnings Before Taxes	26,736	(17,189)	23,438	33,364	47,725	67,144	93,942	93,942
Income Taxes	(12,410)	(8,290)	(11,026)	(15,208)	(21,996)	(31,054)	(43,942)	(43,942)
	46.42%	48.23%	47.04%	45.88%	46.08%	46.25%	46.78%	46.78%
Net Earnings	14,326	8,899	12,412	18,056	25,729	36,090	50,000	50,000
Dividends	2,100	2,343	2,234	3,250	4,631	6,496	9,000	9,000
	14.66%	26.33%	18.00%	18.00%	18.00%	18.00%	18.00%	18.00%
Retained Earnings	12,226	6,556	10,178	14,806	21,098	29,594	41,000	41,000
Long Term Debt	23,072	44,083	50,116	57,089	64,968	73,933	83,333	111,111
Debt/Equity	30.42%	53.99%	49.75%	43.92%	39.96%	36.28%	33.33%	50.00%
Assets	157,997	207,196	244,331	299,934	360,350	426,596	500,000	500,000
Equity	75,842	81,645	100,829	129,993	163,883	203,783	250,000	222,222
Earnings/Sales	4.36%	2.68%	3.00%	3.50%	4.00%	4.50%	5.00%	5.00%
Return on Assets	9.07%	4.29%	5.08%	6.02%	7.14%	8.46%	10.00%	10.00%
Return on Equity	18.89%	10.90%	12.31%	13.89%	15.69%	17.71%	20.00%	22.50%
Return on Inv. Capital	14.48%	7.08%	8.22%	9.65%	11.24%	12.99%	15.00%	15.00%

* Same assumptions as for 1987, except long term debt/equity ratio has been increased to 50.00%

Table 16.17
Adhesive Sales/Market Share Projections for Midwest's Goal of $1 Billion in 1987
(in millions of dollars)

	1982	1983	1984	1985	1986	1987
Total Domestic Adhesives Market	3800	4000	4200	4400	4600	4900
Domestic Sales	168	217	278	357	460	595
International Sales	87	100	115	122	152	175
Total Sales	255	317	393	489	612	769
Domestic Market Share	4.42%	5.40%	6.12%	8.11%	10.00%	12.14%
% Share Increase	---	2.22%	2.26%	2.25%	2.33%	2.14%

Assume: • 77% of Midwest's Total Sales are in adhesive related products

• In 1982, 66% of Midwest's Sales in Adhesives are Domestic

• There is a 5% Domestic Market Growth Rate

• There is a 15% Growth Rate In International Sales

A final scenario is shown in Table 16.17, which projects the market share Midwest must acquire if it wants to reach $1 billion in sales in 1987. This projection assumes that 77 percent of Midwest's sales are in adhesive-related products, 66 percent of its volume is domestic, the domestic adhesives market is expected to grow at approximately 5 percent per year, and Midwest will be able to increase foreign sales by 15 percent per year. If Midwest hopes to achieve $1 billion in sales by this route, it would have to improve its domestic market share from 4.42 percent in 1982 to 12.14 percent in five years; this is approximately 2.25 percent improvement per year. This is not a very likely prospect in light of past performance and intensive external competition.

Another way to improve financial performance would be to drop the 5 percent philanthropic contribution. Financial analysis shows that this would improve earnings as a percent of sales only fractionally and could actually reduce earnings if employees or outside sources took a negative view of the loss of what has been a deeply ingrained policy of Midwest. Unhappiness and displeasure with the dropping or reduction of this long-standing policy could result in a loss of customers and/or reduced efficiency of employee operations so that production, administration, and sales cost would actually increase to offset any financial gains initially anticipated.

The extrapolation, extensions, and scenarios developed in this section of the analysis provide a bank of financial information that can be drawn upon and further analyzed with other information during the remainder of the microanalysis, the evaluation portion, and the corrective action part of the case.

Functions of Management/Functional Area Analysis

Corporate Planning

	Strengths	**Weaknesses**
PLANNING	Strong growth in international areas with decisions to identify and develop growth opportunities in world markets.	Conflicting growth goals. Considerable cost in developing foreign plants.
	Identification of products, services, or market segments that allow success.	Little emphasis on Asia.
	Identification of "good fit" in foreign markets.	No cost breakdown of international operations.
	Directing attention to politically stable economies.	No management development program.
	Consultant groups for developing strategic plan.	No manpower study.
	SWOTI opportunity-finding concept exists.	No studies of future costs of raw materials, energy, overall operations, and so on.
	Implementation and use of "Special Opportunities" and "Pioneer" groups.	No projections of future market segment growth.
	Depth and breadth of product line.	No study of chemical industry forecasts.
	"Going where the competition isn't."	No study of present and projected allocation of manufacturing plants.
		No contingency planning.

		No determination of future long-term capital needs from outside sources.
		Lack of MIS plan.
		District managers responsible for profit without control over costs.
ORGANIZING	Responsible directly to the president.	Lack of management committee.
	Strategic business units with profit responsibility.	Structure does not support SBU intentions.
	Fifteen SBUs with marketing, sales manufacturing, and so on.	Unstructured international operations.
	Long-range plan involving R&D, human resources, finance.	International organization does not represent magnitude of operation.
	Director of corporate planning exists.	District managers are responsible for profit without control over costs.
	"Special Opportunities" and "Pioneer" groups exist.	Small MIS in use for the total organization. It does not generate information for benefit of overall company.
	Centralized planning and control.	Lack of structured and formal strategy for managerial development.
	Central MIS system.	
	Decisions made at all levels.	
	Combination of cyclical, contracyclical, industrial, and consumer market products.	
DIRECTING	Environmental/ecological considerations.	Improper basis for profit sharing plan.
	Orientation toward employees.	Promotion without experience or training.
	Profit sharing program.	Lack of coordinated training throughout the company.
	Human resources department.	MIS only supporting some plants.

	Thrift savings plan.	Not promoting company toward greater marketing efforts; marketing not stressed.
	Clinical dependency and employee counseling programs.	Head of department has finance and international background only; little background in market, sales area.
	Community affairs councils (5 percent of pretax profits).	Specific financial goals may not be attainable.
	No terminations of ARC personnel.	
	Career and personal development.	
	Promotion from within.	
	National coordination of sales training in some divisions.	
	MIS system to support sales.	
CONTROLLING	Market share, market growth planning system provides some mechanism to monitor performance.	No overall plan for controlling costs in international area.
	Mechanism provided to respond to change.	Sales goals need to be more specific.
	Control centralized; responsibility decentralized.	Staff promotion and growth needs more control.
	Willing to use outside expertise.	Overemphasis on attaining financial goals may stifle other opportunities.

The functional area of strategic corporate planning provides support and overall direction for Midwest's operations. Overall, this area is in good shape. Over the years Midwest has established and implemented strategic long range plans (SLRPs). Its latest effort in this area is seeking out new opportunities, aligning them with company goals, and setting priorities and checkpoints for controlling its plans. The SWOTI technique provides a very proactive framework for identifying existing and future problems and opportunities and provides alternatives for dealing with them effectively. In setting corporate goals, however, Midwest needs to check the overall consistency of its goals. Its goals of doubling sales every five years and reaching $1 billion in sales by 1987 conflict. Achieving the first goal would not help achieve the second. Also, one area where Midwest has not provided adequate planning is in the area of management training. A program needs to be established that prepares individuals with a background and education allowing them to be effective managers as they move up through the organization.

Midwest is strongly aware of its responsibility to its employees and communities. The company has always been very people-oriented with gifts for employees such as Thanksgiving turkeys and Easter hams to show management's appreciation for service and contributions. It also provides the employees with a bonus check at the end of the year which is a pro rata share of that year's profits. Midwest has shown interest in its employees by supporting career and personal development and promoting from within. Its commitment to employees is evident in its agreement not to terminate any ARC employees. Other examples of Midwest's emphasis in this area are its human resources department, its savings thrift plan, and its clinical dependency and employee counseling programs. Midwest could improve its efforts in career path planning and training and could modify its employee incentive programs to be less standardized and more directly related to performance of operating units and individuals.

Midwest has demonstrated its commitment to the community with an active involvement in community affairs councils to which it devotes 5 percent of its pretax profits. It has shown its awareness of environmental concerns with its development of nonpolluting water-based coatings and contact adhesives, which conform to OSHA regulations in furniture manufacturing. The company also promotes the reuse or recycling of cleaning chemicals and preserves wetlands and wildlife habitat on its facility in Ohio.

By decentralizing its operational structure, Midwest has made an organizational move in the right direction. This provides a stronger means of evaluating and controlling overall operations. Also, SBUs provide an effective means for Midwest to deal with the many unique situations affecting different products and industries. However, the SBUs are not organized by major product groups as intended. Implementing fifteen SBUs is excessive for efficient and effective operations and control. Also, Midwest's R&D efforts are not aligned to support the SBU structure effectively. While decentralizing its operations, Midwest intends to keep its planning and control centralized. However, it lacks a management committee structure to support this.

Midwest has not made an effort to organize—and thereby effectively control and direct—its international operations. Politically and economically unstable areas, such as Latin America, provide a totally different problem for management than the other geographic regions. Midwest's international organizational structure does not sufficiently represent the magnitude and importance of international operations.

Midwest is just getting started in the area of MIS. Its central computer does provide the foundation for continuing efforts. Systems have been implemented to support sales, finance, and the plants, although there has been only limited participation. The size of the MIS department will not support the overall organization. Long-range planning in this area is needed to enhance Midwest's ability to support and integrate all functional areas of the company.

R&D and Engineering

	Strengths	**Weaknesses**
PLANNING	Expanded, improved, and centralized laboratory facilities.	Product development may not be cost effective.
	Special opportunities group.	Little long-range planning.
	Hiring of additional Ph.D.s.	Overemphasis on continuous new product development.
	Emphasis on securing and maintaining technical leadership.	No obvious, clearly planned link between R&D and customer needs to support new financial goals.
	Developing new products and applications.	
	Close customer relations.	
ORGANIZING	R&D vice president reports directly to the president.	Decentralized approach leads to "reinventing the wheel"
	Plans in place to centralize research facilities.	Centralized R&D causes loss of some valuable close customer contacts.
	Industry groups near centers of activity.	
	Flexibility with customers in new product development; R&D personnel go into accounts to work with plant personnel.	
	A "Special Opportunity" group is in operation to focus on long-term projects for entire company.	
	Seven percent of employees are technical R&D people.	

	A "Plug It" employee incentive program generates new ideas at all levels of employment throughout all functional areas.	
DIRECTING	Improved communications link at U.S. plants.	Efforts focused more on product development than on basic research.
	Increased efforts to reduce duplications.	Efforts concentrated in wrong markets.
	Technical service specialists assigned to specific problems to increase customer satisfaction.	All plants not yet in the communication network.
	R&D personnel directed to work in customers' plants to solve their problems.	Decentralized laboratories.
CONTROLLING	R&D vice president reports directly to the president.	High R&D expenses.
	Patented technology.	All plants not yet connected into the communication network with R&D.
	Improving communication network among plants.	Approximately 7 percent of workforce involved in R&D; duplication of effort and keeping track of projects is difficult.

Research and development is a very important area to Midwest. The company places great emphasis on securing and maintaining technological leadership. With Midwest's strategy of entering new markets, new products and technology are important in achieving sales growth. Midwest's R&D group also provides support to sales by sending representatives into sales accounts along with manufacturing chemists and plant personnel to implement new processes or to troubleshoot problems.

Midwest emphasizes R&D in many ways. It is centralizing its R&D organization, which includes the construction of a $12 million facility. Consolidation of R&D should make Midwest more effective in the development of new products and applications and should reduce the likelihood of duplication of efforts, which occurred in the decentralized structure. Midwest is also attempting to improve its new product development by hiring several Ph.D.s into its technical group and by encouraging individual creativity among all members of its technical staff. The "Plug It" program helps generate new ideas, and the "Special Opportunities'' group, which includes both marketing and production personnel as well as scientists, deals with state-of-the-art technology advancements.

Manufacturing

	Strengths	**Weaknesses**
PLANNING	Various locations of plant and technical service centers result in fast delivery and reduced shipping costs.	Marketing/sales personnel do not participate in production scheduling.
	Specialists in chemical products (adhesives, sealants, coatings, etc.).	Capacity utilization not prepared to meet peak demands because no inventory of finished products exists.
	Simple manufacturing process and equipment.	Various departments require different technologies and types of equipment within the same facility.
	Product mix evens out the uneven market demand.	Large inventory exists.
	Planning for rapid growth.	Production not steady.
	Cost-control system improving.	No automated manufacturing methods.
	Inventory (raw material) control in place.	
	International plants added only after a sales base is established.	
ORGANIZING	Location of plant and technical service centers close to customer.	No steady production.
	Skills to produce highly technical product.	No standard products.
	Well-defined responsibilities.	Duplication of efforts in various plants.
	Manufacturing is organized within SBUs.	No formal training program.
	Nonunion workforce.	Exposure to Latin American economic and political instability.
	Efficient, experienced, and capable plant personnel.	High wages paid for low-quality work in some areas.

	Data processing capabilities available to different plants.	Excessive promotion from within, particularly in critical areas, results in poor management.
DIRECTING	Well-defined technically oriented products.	High raw material inventory.
	Knows the need of the marketplace.	Simple machines not most efficient.
	Excellent product quality.	Lack of formal training, hence inexperience at supervisory management level.
	Strong R&D.	
	Extensive depth and breadth of products.	
	Orientation to satisfy customer needs and desires.	
	Cost reduction programs in place through participatory "trim it" program.	
	Simple production processes.	
	Production scheduling done by plant and district managers.	
	Self-owned truck fleet allows for lower shipping costs.	
	First-class manufacturing facilities acquired with ARC.	
	Inefficient manufacturing facilities being replaced and new manufacturing techniques being introduced.	
CONTROLLING	Quality control inspection insures high-quality products.	Inexperience and lack of training at supervisory level.
	Short lead time of three to four days in the manufacturing processes.	Simple machinery does not accurately control processing.
	Low level of finished product inventory.	Degree of automation not well defined.
	Cost control.	Production is not steady.
	Experienced workforce.	Large raw material inventory exists.

Controlled shipping due to self-owned delivery system.	Costs of new products not fully controlled.
Financial feedback supplied through SBUs.	Structure of research and development costly.
	Much overlap in seeking ideas for new products.

Midwest's manufacturing operations are carried on in many plants throughout the world. There is concern that the plants in Latin America countries are exposed to political and economic instability. However, during a civil uprising in Nicaragua, Midwest replaced damaged, inefficient manufacturing facilities with new warehouses, and a Central American helped Midwest resume business. With the acquisition of ARC, Midwest also acquired excellent manufacturing facilities in Europe.

Most of Midwest's manufacturing processes are neither capital intensive nor labor intensive. Midwest sometimes pays high wages for low-quality work, but most of its production personnel are highly skilled and well qualified. However, some managers lack appropriate management skills because they were promoted from within the company and because of a lack of management training programs.

Production scheduling is done jointly by plant and district managers. The input of both production and sales personnel allows for more effective scheduling. Midwest's three to four days of lead time maintains low inventories of finished goods, but a large raw material inventory is required to be able to assemble products quickly.

Also, Midwest owns a fleet of delivery vehicles, which allows for prompt delivery and control of shipping costs.

Finance/Accounting

	Strengths	**Weaknesses**
PLANNING	Newly installed strategic planning process and annual budget system.	Lack of information about competition.
	Clear financial reports.	Lack of contingency planning.
	LIFO system.	No formal sales and advertising budget.
	Director of planning and corporate development for the strategic planning function.	Optimistic goals may lead to overextending financial position.
	Outside consultant to help in the planning process.	No evidence of capital budgeting to prioritize and maximize use of limited funds.

	Investment philosophy for acquisitions and internal growth.	Conflicting goals.
	Performance appraisals.	Lack of currency hedging program.
	Relatively sound financial position.	Little emphasis on improving financial ratios.
	Innovative.	Political instability in Central America needs more positive attention.
	Cost and inventory control programs.	
	Diverse product line.	
	Good breadth and depth in product line.	
ORGANIZING	Vice president reports directly to the president.	Fixed costs in plant and equipment.
	Corporate financial plan in effect.	High inventory level and low inventory turnover.
	Well suited for growth markets.	Special markets to be served.
	Developing overseas operations for long-term growth and profitability; plant expansion into new geographic locations.	Major portion of international sales from economically unstable Latin America.
	Sound financing philosophy.	
	R&D centralized to cut costs.	
	Profit center emphasis.	
	SBUs use corporate goals to determine their own goals.	
DIRECTING	Planned operating budgets.	Earnings not impressive.
	Timely financial data available for review.	No contingency planning.
	Budget plan/review permits project process review.	Formalized sales and advertising budget.
	Good sales growth.	High inventory of raw material.
	Investment for expansion and growth.	
	Money well spent on R&D.	

Nonunion employees.

Cost reduction and productivity improvement programs.

Start of MIS utilization.

CONTROLLING Manufacturing costs are tracked.

Lack of concern for competition, competitive products, and their costs.

Timely financial reports.

Some operations in politically unstable areas.

Budgeting processes, plans, and reviews continuously in progress.

High inventory levels exist, increasing costs.

Financing of acquisitions done on a reasonable basis.

Efficiency needs improving.

Steady growth of sales.

Wide variety of products not cost effective.

Sound financial status, although improvements are needed.

Spread over a large geographic area not cost efficient.

High-quality products at competitive prices.

Financial ratios and implications require closer observation and corrective action.

High debt ratios.

Currency exchange rates require more attention.

Little use or application of MIS.

Growth is a primary goal of Midwest. Sales increased every year from 1972 to 1982, with an anticipated $1 billion in sales and increased net earnings of 5 percent in 1987. These and additional financial goals, such as 10 percent return on assets, 15 percent return on invested capital, and 20 percent return on shareholders' equity, have never been achieved previously by Midwest. Table 16.4 reveals that sales have not even doubled in the last five years but have averaged closer to a compounded 11 percent growth per year; return on sales has averaged 3.34 percent over the past ten years with a high of 4.37 percent in 1974 and a low of 2.86 percent in 1982; return on assets has averaged 6.05 percent over the past ten years with a high of 8.60 percent in 1981 and a low of 4.58 percent in 1982; return on shareholders equity has averaged 14.40 percent over the past ten years with a high of 19.30 percent in 1981 and a low of 11.10 percent in 1975; return on invested capital averaged 9.52 percent from

1973 through 1982 with a high of 13.74 percent in 1981 and a low of 6.64 percent in 1975. Figures 16.1 through 16.5 and Tables 16.2 through 16.4 show that Midwest will have to grow and improve efficiencies of operation at unprecedented rates to achieve these goals. Even if Midwest were to double its sales by 1987, it would reach only $664,471,000, which is $335,529,000 short of the $1 billion sales goal. This is a tremendous amount of growth to expect out of the opportunities and innovations portions of Midwest's SWOTI program.

Midwest's international operations have occurred at some expense, such as the considerable costs of establishing its three adhesive plants in Australia and repairing its damaged facilities in Nicaragua.

Other expenses, such as those in sales and administration, rose 10.1 percent from 1981 to 1982, including costs incurred by establishing SBUs, quality management, and strategic planning programs in the United States. A major expense in 1982 was the acquisition of ARC for $27 million, which included $13 million of assumed liabilities. R&D expenses in 1982 were also up 9.1 percent from 1981.

On the brighter side, the 1980 "Trim It" program succeeded in reducing operating expenses to improve profits in 1981.

The year 1981 was profitable and brought the largest net earnings increase since 1974. Return on sales was 4.13 percent, return on equity was 19.3 percent, return on assets was 8.6 percent, and return on invested capital, which is identified as capital stock plus retained earnings plus surplus reserves plus bonds, was 13.74.

The year 1982, however, brought a less promising financial picture. Although sales were up 1 percent, net earnings declined 30 percent. Net earnings included an extraordinary gain of $897,000,000, or 19 cents per share, for the sale of land.

Studies of Midwest's various returns and operating performance in 1981 and 1982 show that in most instances Midwest's cost of sales was higher percentagewise than that of its competitors, and its gross profit, operating earnings, and net earnings were less than those of its competitors.

A quick reexamination of the data presented in the tables and figures earlier in this chapter and the impact of these data on Midwest and its 1987 goals and objectives will help highlight some of the problems Midwest must overcome if it is to achieve these goals. These data also shed light on Midwest's financial soundness. It should be noted that all ratios involving debt considerations confirm a dangerously high debt level at Midwest and possible difficulty in maintaining debt payments.

The burden coverage ratio dropped 28.1 percent from 3.34 times in 1981 to 2.40 times in 1982, indicating that a large portion of the earnings must be used to pay debt service. This is one piece of evidence of Midwest's high level of debt.

The current and the quick (sometimes referred to as the acid test ratio) liquidity ratios help determine the ability of the firm to pay its current liabilities when due. Midwest's current ratio dropped 6.5 percent, from 2.0 in 1981 to 1.87 in 1982. The industry average is 2.3, and a level of 2.0 or higher is usually considered safe for paying off current liabilities. Midwest's low level does raise some concern. The quick ratio, which is more stringent than the current ratio because it removes less liquid inventory from current assets in the calculation, also dropped 6.5 percent from 1981 to 1982 but still remained at the fairly healthy figure of 1.18; a ratio of 1.0 or greater is usually considered reasonable. The main concerns here are that both ratios dropped from 1981 to 1982 and both ratios are below industry average. In general, the ratios indicate a borderline ability to pay off current liabilities on time.

In analyzing the above liquidity ratios, it is evident that both the current assets and liabilities increased, but the current liabilities increased faster than the current assets. An increase in accounts payable and the days outstanding of accounts payable are causes for increasing current liabilities. Midwest's average days payable outstanding ratio increased almost 66 percent from 34.6 days in 1981 to 57.4 days in 1982; this is well above the industry average of 30 days. Further examination of the ratios also indicates that Midwest's collection period on its bills increased 22.5 percent from 50.41 days in 1981 to 61.77 days in 1982, far in excess of the 40-day industry average. The decreasing liquidity ratios coupled with the increasing days payable outstanding and the increasing collection time ratios indicate that Midwest was beginning to encounter a cash flow problem. Other than in 1981, Midwest's positive cash flow was never too high, and in 1982 it dropped to a negative $17,720,000.

Financial leverage ratios help determine the amount of debt a firm is employing relative to equity. It shows a firm's ability to raise debt and the ability of a firm to pay its debt when due. Midwest's debt-to-asset ratio increased 17.3 percent, from 52 percent in 1981 to 61 percent in 1982, when the industry average was 41 percent. This is a significant increase and well above the industry average. This increase in debt-to-asset ratio indicates that Midwest's strategy to expand by acquisition is largely financed by debt. For example, the purchase of ARC in 1982 was largely debt financed. Midwest assumed $13 million in liabilities to purchase ARC, which itself added 12.1 percent in liabilities to Midwest's balance sheet. In general, the high debt-to-asset ratio indicates a future difficulty in paying debt when due or borrowing more money for additional expansion or acquisition.

Midwest's capitalization ratio increased from 27 percent in 1981 to 40 percent in 1982; this is an increase of over 48 percent and is well above the industry average of 14 percent. This also indicates Midwest's financing of acquisitions through long-term debt. The fact that the capitalization ratio increases at a much higher rate than the debt-to-asset ratio indicates that long-term debt, and not current liabilities, is being used to finance acquisitions. This is generally considered positive.

Midwest's debt-to-equity ratio also increased significantly from 1981 to 1982 from 102 percent to 148 percent and is much higher than the industry average of 120 percent. This high debt-to-equity ratio could have a negative impact on Midwest's stock prices, which in turn could preclude the future use of stock issue to finance further acquisitions and expansion.

The interest coverage ratio, as well as the burden coverage ratio discussed earlier, helps evaluate a firm's capacity to meet interest payments by showing the number of dollars earned for each dollar of interest due; the higher the ratio the better. Midwest's interest coverage ratio fell almost 25 percent from 6.1 in 1981 to 4.62 in 1982. This significant decrease again confirms the high level of debt taken on by Midwest.

Efficiency ratios help determine management's performance in managing and controlling assets, as well as providing insight into how much capital is required to support sales. The collection period ratio and the days payable ratio, discussed earlier, are efficiency ratios in that they both indicate Midwest's worsening efficiency because both of the ratios increased considerably from 1981 to 1982. Of major concern to Midwest is the increasing time required to make trade payables, which is another indicator of increasing cash flow problems. This could tarnish Midwest's reputation as a customer to suppliers if this situation is not improved. Also, late-payment penalties could increase cost.

Total asset turnover decreased 23 percent from 2.08 in 1981 to 1.60 in 1982, with an industry average of 1.95. This indicates an inefficient use of company assets. Because Midwest's asset turnover is less than the industry average, competition could start to undercut Midwest's prices.

The fixed asset turnover ratio helps examine capacity utilization and the quality of efficiency of fixed assets. This ratio decreased 35 percent from 6.96 times in 1981 to 4.52 times in 1982. The industry average was 9.46 times or almost double Midwest's 1982 ratio, indicating that Midwest had excess capacity. Most of Midwest's competitors serve only regional markets, thus they do not need as many manufacturing facilities and can use their facilities more efficiently. This somewhat explains the higher industry average. Midwest's decrease in fixed asset turnover is significantly larger than the decrease in total asset turnover, further emphasizing its overcapacity of fixed assets.

The inventory turnover ratio helps determine how well inventory is controlled and managed. Inventory turnover, in days, increased 20.55 percent from 56.29 days in 1981 to 67.86 days in 1982; the industry average was 37.63 days. The increasing time for inventory turnover indicates increased inventory carrying costs. Midwest's slower inventory turnover represents an area of competitive disadvantage for Midwest.

When examined in total, all of the efficiency ratios at Midwest point to a general lack of efficiency when compared against industry averages. Marked improvements in all of these areas would be necessary if Midwest were to move toward reaching its 1987 financial goals.

In addition to decreased efficiency, Midwest's profitability ratios decreased substantially (30 percent to 45 percent) from 1981 to 1982, and in every instance Midwest's 1982 profitability ratios were considerably below the industry average. Midwest's significant decrease in return on assets and its shortfall against the industry average also indicate high expenses and a lack of efficiency at Midwest. The marked decrease in return on equity is yet another indication of Midwest's financing its assets with debts.

A summary of these financial ratio analysis findings indicates that Midwest has the following problem areas: a high debt level, inefficient use of capital, excess capacity in fixed assets, and cash flow problems. However, there is no evidence that Midwest is seriously trying to compensate for or take advantage of worldwide variations in currency and inflation rates. This situation and many other problems could be solved by international expansion of the MIS network and computerizing the finance side of the business.

In addition, international centralization of all financial transactions could not only hedge against exchange rate risk but could also cut tax expenses. By centrally sourcing all the company's funds, the controller could move funds out of high-tax countries before repatriation. Also, the controller could control on a daily basis the risk of loss due to changing exchange rates. On the other side of the coin, the company could possibly make money on changes in the exchange rate. These profits are taxable in most countries, so the profitable exchanges could be carried out in countries with lower taxes while loss exchanges could be carried out in high-tax countries. The result would be avoiding high income taxes and earning more tax credits for losses. Such cash management could be carried out with the use of MIS among various countries.

The state or canton of Neuchatel in Switzerland could serve as a location for such tax breaks. Neuchatel and Switzerland both offer tax advantages on the federal and state level. The overall tax rate in 1982 for Switzerland's federal government is 7.6 percent, and Neuchatel taxes foreign income at 3 percent. Thus the complete tax by Neuchatel is approximately 11 percent. As compared with other countries' tax structures, Neuchatel stands out. For instance, West Germany has a composite tax of nearly 75 percent on income generated in the country and repatriated. To avoid this tax, funds could be transferred to Switzerland via modem because West Germany and Switzerland have a tax treaty within the EEC that permits repatriation without taxation. Therefore, the composite tax drops from 75 percent to 11 percent before being sent back to the United States to be taxed at approximately 34 percent. This tax rate permits for a tax credit of 11 percent, leaving only 23 percent due to the United States. Overall, having a financial center in Switzerland—particularly Neuchatel—would save 52 percent of Midwest's profits passed through its office, as well as offering hedging advantages.

Additional financial information, illustrated earlier in Tables 16.13 through 16.17, shows that it is theoretically possible for Midwest to achieve its lofty 1987 financial goals if everything goes perfectly from 1982 through 1987, with orderly acquisition growth, consistent market share improvement, reduction in selling and administrative costs, and so on. Based on Midwest's past history, world conditions, and increasing competition, this rosy scenario does not appear to be the most logical outcome.

Financial projections, shown in Table 16.13 through 16.15, show other possible growth patterns. The 6-percent growth pattern shown in Table 16.13 appears excessively conservative based on Midwest's past performance. The 15-percent growth pattern shown in Table 16.14 is a remote possibility for Midwest if the company scales back on some of its other financial goals. The 10 percent growth pattern shown in Table 16.15 appears to be the growth pattern closest to what Midwest achieved in the past and is capable of achieving from 1982 to 1987, again with some other reduced financial goals. However, to achieve $1 billion in sales growth strictly through market expansion, as shown in Table 16.17, requires almost tripling Midwest's market share in five years against an array of competent competitors.

Reaching the $1-billion goal, or any other level of expansion, through increased market share alone or through acquisitions is not a feasible or realistic approach. A combination of the approaches discussed above, along with much improvement in efficiencies within the company, are needed.

Marketing/Sales

	Strengths	**Weaknesses**
PLANNING	Good depth and breadth in the product line.	No detailed plan, with only limited forecasting.
	Worldwide marketing area.	A wide variety of products.
	Good distribution system.	Lack of advertising and promotion by product lines.
	New product ideas and innovations constantly developed.	Marketing services at the corporate level.
	Customer service orientation results in new business and good customer relations.	Little emphasis on underestimating competitors' response and strength.

Product planning and philosophy exists throughout the company.

Market research not organized.

Marketing services exist at the corporate level.

Lack of coordination with manufacturing.

Systems-oriented strategic planning process to seek out new opportunities.

Short-term profitability not stressed.

Social responsibility considered with all customers and employees.

Scarcity of experienced marketing personnel.

Commission plan for salesman motivation.

Little indication of planned expansion into the Asiatic areas of Japan, Korea, Thailand, and so on.

Market research continuously in progress.

Conflicting sales goals.

Long-term growth vs. short-term gains seriously considered.

Limited planning exists on what to do in politically unstable Latin America.

Product line technological leadership.

Synergy in acquisitions and product lines.

Market share matrix system in operation.

Products comply with OSHA regulations, energy and environmental concerns.

Emphasis on going where the competition isn't.

Expansion of European volume.

The acquisition of ARC.

Movement into counterrecessionary product lines.

ORGANIZING

Plants and service centers located to meet customer needs.

Sales personnel shared with different SBUs.

Technically organized sales force.

Some marketing personnel with sales background.

	Increasing amounts of information available from data processing.	Availability of experienced marketing personnel.
	Systems-oriented strategic planning process.	No formal marketing department.
	Close coordination between marketing/sales and technical functions due to SBU organization.	Manufacturing organization not consulting with sales and marketing.
	Complete, large, modern laboratories internationally.	Current marketing services primarily at the corporate level.
DIRECTING	Reputation for excellence and performance.	Compensation plan does not promote new products.
	Technical expertise is customer oriented.	Marketing director has no technical marketing background.
	Customer service is localized.	No marketing budget.
	Continuous growth.	Some divisions have no marketing personnel.
	Sales growth doubled every five to six years.	Weak advertising and promotion.
	Technically trained sales force.	Inexperienced and untrained marketing people.
	Promotion of multiple ways to use many products.	
	Good product distribution.	
	"Plug It" employee incentive program initiated by the marketing service department to encourage employee participation.	
CONTROLLING	High-quality products.	Midwest sometimes wants to expand into new market areas that it has not thoroughly examined.
	Competitive pricing.	Competitors' strategy not closely monitored.
	Short distribution channels close to the customer.	Scarcity of trained or experienced marketing personnel.

Sales force reacts quickly to customer needs.

No marketing programs by division.

Customer service feedback.

Lack of budgets for marketing, advertising.

"Plug It" incentive program is monitored.

Product innovation burn-out.

Well-defined corporate plans.

No specific criteria for continuous product development.

Market areas increased on a programmed basis.

Some markets located in unstable countries.

Limited number of applications for products.

New products.

Well-defined strategy of going where the competition isn't.

Leadership position with a dominant share of the market.

Market segmentation.

Sales compensation based on performance.

The past success of Midwest was accomplished in an atmosphere of limited emphasis on marketing. Past success was attributed to technical expertise, high-quality products, and customer service. Starting in the late 1970s, however, Midwest attempted to strengthen its marketing efforts.

An early strategy of "going where the competition isn't" holds true through the period of this examination. Midwest refined its strategic market strategy plans to: (1) expand the volume of European operations; (2) focus on the European markets as a number-one priority in international business; (3) shift current emphasis of European business toward industrial adhesives; and (4) integrate and crosspollinate American and European products (synergy). The acquisition of ARC kept with these strategy plans. ARC's 1981 sales in Europe nearly doubled those of Midwest in Europe for the same time period. Another benefit of acquiring ARC was that their product strengths directly complement those of Midwest. Midwest also had a strategy for entering new markets to establish a sales base, add manufacturing facilities as needed, and build to a position of profitability as quickly as possible. Short-term losses were initially experienced by this, but the philosophy worked well in developing future markets.

Due to the recessional economy's effect on sales, Midwest has shifted its emphasis to improving profitability through operating efficiency, cost reductions, and emphasis on profitable markets and products. Midwest began to focus its efforts on market segments where market share could be gained through product innovation, better service, or added value. The SBU reorganization assists these efforts since SBUs integrate targeted marketing industry specialization and technical service. Control is maintained through a market growth–market share matrix system, a systematic process to monitor performance, established in 1977. The SBU concept has also improved the direction of Midwest's salesforce. The SBU salesforces are made up of specialists who have only one focal point—the SBU manager—to contact for product and technical information. By specializing, the company gains in-depth rather than cursory knowledge of each of its products.

In all areas of the company, a reputation for product excellence and performance, customer-oriented technical expertise, and localized service are recognized strengths. In addition, Midwest's product/market diversification, increased sophistication of R&D facilities, domestic and international acquisitions, product/process innovation, systems-selling approach (i.e., sale of product and its application equipment), and countercyclical consumer products are all important factors in maintaining the company's leadership position. The company's attitude of flexibility toward current events has also helped to keep its products in line with OSHA regulations, energy conservation, and environmental concerns.

Internally, the company has established employee programs to further its marketing efforts. The "Special Opportunities" group was organized for the purpose of identifying projects that will likely have the greatest impact on Midwest's future sales and earnings. The "Plug It" program was established to encourage employees to submit ideas for new products. The "Pioneer" group bolsters coordination between marketing and research, thereby speeding up the process by which new products are introduced to the market. Finally, the "Trim It" program challenges employees to contribute cost reduction suggestions in order to improve profitability.

Midwest's marketing function is centralized in the corporate management by a senior vice president in charge of marketing and industry group sales.

Despite all of the above strengths, the organizing function of marketing management has some serious drawbacks. The scarcity of experienced marketing personnel has resulted in some divisions operating without any marketing staff. Others have marketing personnel whose background is sales. Due to the projected corporate growth, a sense of urgency arises to solve this problem. Furthermore, with the reorganization into SBUs, the primary responsibility for marketing services should be shifted from the corporate level to the individual SBUs. Another potential problem exists with regard to the salesforce compensation program, which was implemented to concentrate efforts on products that have provided high profits. Unfortunately, this method risks overlooking the potential of new products.

Human Resources

	Strengths	**Weaknesses**
PLANNING	Strategic planning process.	No managerial training program.
	Business units involved in planning.	No personnel development and training for future growth.
	Training middle management in developing strategic plans.	Lacks clearly defined recruitment policy.
	"Plug It" program promotes employees' participation in new product ideas.	No well-defined incentive plan for success.
	Technical training program exists for the salesforce.	No emphasis on any particular area except R&D.
	Employee savings program.	Cost consciousness not a major point of concern.
	Emphasis on product quality and social concerns and responsibility.	Lack of coordination between manufacturing and sales.
	Top management dedicated to growth, quality, innovation, and concern for the employee and society.	Overemphasis on promotion from within can hurt proper and adequate staffing of new critical areas.
	Responsiveness to changes in the marketplace; change is planned as and when needed.	No uniformity in pay scales. Some people are overpaid for the work they perform.
	Promotion from within encourages personnel to excel.	
ORGANIZING	Well-defined responsibilities.	Organization still being developed; now reports to law and administration.
	Newly developed SBUs with well-defined market segments.	Lack of coordination between different SBUs and manufacturing facilities.

Most promotions are from within. This is a strength and a weakness.

Scarcity of well-skilled personnel in management positions because most promotions are from within.

Large number of qualified personnel.

Training of marketing/sales personnel done by division management; training varies from good to inadequate.

Top-level managers well turned to the market and needs of employees.

Little organized management training within the company.

Outside consultants hired if necessary.

Scarcity of trained marketing personnel.

Responsiveness to changes in the marketplace; organization is changed as and when needed to achieve long-term objectives.

Labor is nonunionized.

Experienced, successful management at the corporate level.

Manufacturing process is not labor intensive.

Decentralized operating management with strong centralized planning and control, encourages employees to work together as a team.

DIRECTING

Budgets are reviewed.

Not enough direction from above in case of problems.

Pleasant and harmonious work environment.

Plants spread over a wide geographical area.

Good relations among management.

Lack of qualified personnel at the plant level.

Emphasis on product quality.

No formalized, structured training program for management.

Many well-defined long-term goals and objectives.

High wages paid for low-quality work in some cases.

Strong social program involvement.

	Technical training of sales personnel.	
	Strong centralized planning and control at the corporate level.	
	Well-staffed human resources department.	
	Free counselling program available to all personnel.	
	Savings program for all employees.	
CONTROLLING	Formalized budgeting process.	No well-defined lines of authority because of new organization.
	Emphasis on quality products with customer feedback.	Cost controls in some areas not effective.
	Social programs emphasized and monitored.	Lack of qualified and trained personnel to monitor all personnel functions fully.
	Cost controls.	Policy of promotion from within, in some instances, results in supervisors who lack management experience and skills.
	Independent profit centers.	
	Well-defined responsibilities in most areas.	
	Long-term plans and goals, with adherence to achieving them closely monitored.	
	Decentralized decision making while maintaining centralized control helps build managers who are capable of making decisions and controlling operations.	

Human resources dependency is a function of management practices and procedures. Corporate philosophy is to share the benefits of growth with all constituencies, customers, shareholders, employees, and the community. The company has demonstrated its philosophy with various employee benefits and perks discussed earlier. Midwest has developed community affairs councils, employee groups that distribute funds to local communities where the company has offices. Midwest also devotes 5 percent of its pretax profits to these accounts. Midwest has encouraged its employees to become involved in local affairs and projects. By giving employees time off and by holding workshops, the company has garnered worker support for such projects as a sheltered workshop in Germany and youth ice hockey in Canada. Midwest has also focused on the problems of battered women and abused children.

Promotions from within have created a need for continuous upgrading of skills and evaluation of personnel, but without a formal, structured program for the development of management, which in some cases results in poor performance. Also, Midwest has not developed a performance award attached to various benefits and programs.

Midwest's organizational structure has undergone a change over the years. It takes time to completely organize SBUs with lines of authority and responsibility. In fact, a total of fifteen SBUs can be excessive and confusing; the number should be reduced. Midwest's labor force is non-union, but in spite of this, high wages are paid in some areas for low-quality work.

Interface

	Strengths	Weaknesses
PLANNING	Strategic planning process implemented in 1978.	Strategic planning process and training program for managers not fully implemented.
	Director for planning and corporate development reports directly to the president.	Weak marketing services, not coordinated with other departments.
	Assistance from outside consultants.	Weak or lacking marketing strategy for various product areas.
	SBUs organized along product lines.	Decentralized structure not well defined and in the evolutionary stage.
	Decentralized structure with centralized control.	No clear lines of communication throughout the organization.
	Annual budgeting system complemented by strategic planning process.	New financial goals and how to achieve them not explained or coordinated for achievement with various functional areas.

MIS being introduced.

Customers and company work closely together.

Plant managers work with district managers to establish production scheduling.

Self-owned fleet of trucks for fast, low-cost delivery to customers.

ORGANIZING	Organization being changed to meet future growth.	Training of personnel and development of skills leave much to be desired.
	Salesforce well organized to serve customer needs.	Aggressive cooperation among functional areas nonexistent.
	Director of planning and corporate development coordinates company functional area and customer interface.	Lack of qualified personnel at different levels of management.
	R&D and engineering centralized to develop new ideas and products and eliminate duplication.	Line of authority and responsibility not clearcut.
	"Special Opportunities" and "Pioneer" groups organized on crossfunctional lines to bring new product and service ideas to the marketplace.	Engineering strengths and capabilities not present at the plant level to solve immediate problems.
	Organizational change to SBUs help functional-areas and customer interface.	Lack of experienced marketing personnel to interface with R&D, engineering, manufacturing, and other functional areas.
DIRECTING	There are well-defined profit centers with responsibilities.	Lack of clearcut interrelationships between different levels.
	Company planning methods are sound.	New corporate structure in the development stage.
	Long-range plans well defined.	Lack of trained and qualified personnel.
	An annual budget system ties the company functional areas together.	Political problems in certain areas where subsidiaries exist.

	Qualified new SBU managers.	Over one-half of the employees are in foreign countries and of foreign nationality, which presents communication problems.
	SBU directors report directly to the president.	No management development program.
	New communication network for the technical service chemists.	MIS not fully implemented in all areas.
CONTROLLING	Budgeting process helps coordinate functional area activities.	Unstable political situation in certain parts of the world.
	Product quality controlled at all stages.	Different social vales in different geographic areas which must be addressed.
	Director of planning and corporate development coordinates and monitors progress.	Qualified personnel shortage.
	Well-laid-out SBU profit centers along product lines are monitored for adherence to budget.	Lack of cost control in inventory planning.
	Cost-reduction plans in effect.	Excess of inventory.
	"Special Opportunities" group responsible for prioritizing research projects.	Operation and administration costs not controlled as well as they should be.
	"Pioneer" group responsible for coordinating new product development.	MIS department not yet large enough to coordinate and monitor various company activities.

Midwest has placed great emphasis on securing and maintaining technological leadership. It has emphasized superior technology, quality, and customer service and relationships. Marketing was put on the back burner but has worked on the corporate level. Middle management's strategic planning process should also improve with the help of the consultant from the American Management Association. During 1981, the separation of six divisions into fifteen SBUs helped to alleviate the anomaly as one general manager supervised operations and oversaw marketing, sales, and production. These factors should contribute to controlling and directing the company's operations effectively.

Also, Midwest's promotion and recruitment policies are not well-defined and need more attention. Promotions from within could affect the quality of management's decision-making capability.

Continued interface improvement between all functional areas is necessary for success. Management training, hiring of more highly qualified personnel from the outside in specialty areas, and an increase in the size and functions performed by MIS are also required for growth.

MIS

	Strengths	Weaknesses
PLANNING	Centralized computer system.	MIS capabilities not fully utilized.
		No integrated planning process for expansion of MIS.
		No integration of MIS into the strategic planning process.
		No strategic information yet supplied by MIS.
ORGANIZING	MIS provides information to salesforce only.	Only six people in the department.
		MIS not listed on organization chart.
		MIS does not provide for operations research or for strategic or tactical planning.
DIRECTING	MIS information for the salesforce only.	Company is accounting oriented rather than information oriented; MIS must be integrated into an information role.
		MIS does not provide for operations research or strategic or tactical planning.
CONTROLLING	MIS generates financial and sales reports and does invoicing.	MIS not used for operational information, manufacturing, R&D strategic or tactical planning, or financial analysis or control.
		MIS not a part of the entire company operation.

The centralized and small MIS has only been used for financial and sales reports and invoicing. Salespeople have had access to properties and formula uses that should increase sales in existing products. To take full advantage of MIS, its use and operations must be expanded. It must be used for total company integration and coordination. It must be made a part of the total planning process and internal and external interface. It should be directed by a vice president of MIS operations.

The Force Field: A Summary of the Most Frequently Cited Strengths and Weaknesses

	Strengths	Weaknesses
PLANNING	The location of plant and technical service centers are well distributed to maximize customer satisfaction.	The decentralized planning structure is new and not very well developed.
	There is a strategic planning process and annual budget system in effect.	There is a lack of information about competition.
	Director of planning and corporate development exists at the vice president level.	There are no formal sales and advertising budgets.
	Outside consultants help in the planning process.	Capacity utilization is not optimized.
	Midwest is in a relatively sound financial position.	Large inventories exist in some areas.
	Top management is committed to the planning process.	Manufacturing is not automated.
	There is decentralized operation with centralized control.	Recruitment and promotion strategy is not clearly defined.
	There is a planned investment philosophy for acquisitions and internal growth.	There is a lack of personnel training and planning for the future.
	Midwest is highly oriented toward social responsibility.	There are no contingency plans.
	Performance appraisals are used in evaluating employees.	Marketing services are only at the corporate level.
	R&D and innovative capabilities are strong.	There is inadequate historical profit data available.
	There are cost and inventory control programs in effect.	There is not a well-developed marketing, advertising, or pricing philosophy.

Well-implemented production methods and processes are in operation.

Costs are not adequately measured or controlled.

There is excellent breadth and depth in the product line.

There is no plan to address cultural differences.

Sales personnel are well trained.

Unstable Latin American operations are not adequately addressed.

"Special Opportunities" and "Pioneer" groups exist for generation of new ideas and indirect marketing research.

No plan exists for expansion into the rapidly growing Asiatic market.

The "Plug It" program helps generate innovative ideas.

No plan exists for meeting the proposed 1987 financial goals or to improve financially stressed areas.

Midwest is responsive to changes in the marketplace.

A savings plan and other employee benefit programs are in operation.

Quality products are emphasized.

There is strong focus on market segmentation.

Expansion into more stable European markets is in progress.

ORGANIZING

Manufacturing plant and technical service centers are strategically located close to customers.

SBU organizational structure is in early stages of development.

There are promotions from within.

There is a lack of coordination between different SBUs and manufacturing facilities.

There is a strategic planning process with a director for planning and corporate development.

There is a scarcity of personnel properly trained in MIS.

There is a large pool of qualified personnel with technical backgrounds.

There is a lack of management training programs.

Top-level managers are well tuned to the needs of customers and employees.

Most training is on-the-job training; some is good and some is poor.

Outside consultants are hired if and when needed.

Midwest is responsive to changes in the marketplace; the organization changed as and when needed to achieve long-term objectives.

Midwest is acquisition oriented with an eye toward synergy of operations.

SBUs have been introduced into company operations.

There is product line responsibility through SBUs and profit centers with centralized control.

R&D and engineering are centralized to develop new ideas and products.

"Special Opportunities" and "Pioneer" groups have been formed to help generate ideas across functional lines.

There are experienced and capable production personnel.

MIS has been installed.

There is no vice president in charge of sales or marketing.

There are no well-defined lines of responsibility in many areas.

Many plants are not close to sources of raw materials.

There is a lack of marketing in all divisions and a sharing of personnel between areas.

MIS is small, understaffed, and limited in operation.

DIRECTING

Quality products are emphasized and produced.

There are profit centers with well-defined responsibilities.

An annual budgeting system is in operation.

Customer service is a key to success.

There is technical training for the salesforce.

Well-developed distribution channels exist; Midwest operates its own truck fleet.

There could be more qualified people at all levels of operation.

R&D is not market oriented.

There are no marketing personnel in some divisions.

There is a lack of management and marketing training.

There is no sales budget or clearly defined sales requirements.

There is a lack of contingency planning.

There are well-defined corporate goals.

There are political problems in Latin American countries, which are not adequately addressed.

A budgeting process and control system exist.

Sales personnel are shared among different SBUs.

A financial reporting procedure exists, and financial reports are generated.

MIS is inadequate for directing operations or supplying much needed strategic information.

There is a lack of overall communication and feedback.

CONTROLLING

Product quality is controlled.

There is a lack of qualified MIS personnel.

Steady growth is emphasized.

There is a lack of market research to follow competitors' moves and financial data.

Midwest is in a relatively strong financial position and can control steady growth.

Different divisions have their own market programs and strategies.

Marketing service exists at the corporate level.

There is a lack of sales and advertising budgets.

Midwest has its own distribution channels.

Management personnel training is inadequate.

Production plants and customer service operations are strategically located.

Inventories, pricing, collection times, and so on are not adequately monitored and controlled.

There are inventory and cost controls procedures in place.

There are no effective performance measurements.

The manufacturing process is fairly simple and well controlled.

The company is highly leveraged.

Sales personnel are well trained in company procedures.

R&D and engineering departments are strong.

Social awareness and social programs are well established.

Midwest has a leadership position in most areas in which
it operates.

Customer-oriented service
provides excellent product
feedback.

Improved laboratories are in
operation.

Profit centers and SBUs are
in operation.

PHASE III (PRESCRIPTIVE)

Case Narrative

Since the 1940s, Midwest has grown from a regional adhesive supplier
to a multimillion-dollar, multinational specialty company due to its commitment to creative product development and technical service, close
customer relations, and a focused marketing effort.

During the time period under examination—the early 1980s—Midwest
is a company in transition. As it moves into the next phase of growth,
greater emphasis is being placed on technology and marketing. The company has also been structured into SBUs, each of which focuses on specific
market opportunities through a targeted marketing and sales approach.
Stronger emphasis is being placed on developing new, sophisticated products so that the technical competency will allow the company to achieve
continued growth and maintain its competitive edge. Efforts are also underway to improve operating efficiencies by incorporating unique manufacturing techniques.

The company has formulated and expressed very ambitious long-term
growth plans and is taking action to achieve these objectives. Questions
have been raised about the compatibility and achievability of these goals
and objectives.

Serious doubt is raised about reaching $1 billion in sales by 1987, Mid-
west's bicentennial anniversary. The company made only $100 million in
sales in 1974 and passed $200 million in 1978. In fiscal year 1982, sales
were $331.8 million, but 1982 was a disappointment for the company,
interrupting as it did Midwest's record of rapid and sustained growth.
Midwest had some serious problems with its subsidiary in Costa Rica in
1982. A series of currency devaluations forced the company to raise prices
so that it would have the cash to pay for raw materials which it buys in
dollars. Prices went up to a level where customers would not buy paint
for the big painting season, which is in the fall there.

When Midwest became publicly owned, it was mainly a sales and service company. That orientation is changing in the early 1980s, as greater demands are being placed on R&D to come up with new products and to solve customers' problems; thus, a new centralized R&D facility is being built.

The marketing structure has also been changed. Midwest's historical strengths were in field sales, with a large number of salespeople calling on many customers. The emphasis is now being shifted toward true marketing efforts.

The specialty chemical industry has become more sophisticated and technical, and Midwest has had to adjust to this. The company established its fifteen SBUs to handle specific product areas. Each has a business manager who is completely responsible for profit and is responsible for offering the right kind of product, for technical service, for knowing the machinery used in that industry, and for knowing new developments or trends in that industry. The formation of the "Pioneer" commercial development groups and the "Special Opportunities" groups is another step toward gaining much better marketing information and shortening the time between research and introducing the actual product in the field. The effect of this effort means more sales growth in areas already established as well as the development of new areas.

Some future growth will have to come from acquisitions. The ability to make increasingly intelligent acquisitions will be one of the byproducts of the company's reorganization into SBUs.

The goal of $1 billion in sales by 1987 was formalized in the early 1980s.

Midwest has been accustomed to high-growth business in the past, but overall it is felt that achieving $1 billion in sales within a five-year period is overzealous and an improbable goal. Even if this goal were reached, other areas would most likely suffer to the overall detriment of the company.

In this period of examination, the U.S. economy is showing some signs of improving. The GNP increased at 3.1 percent during the first quarter of 1983 and is expected to grow at a rate of 4.5 percent through the rest of the year. Industrial production is also expected to increase slightly. The speed of recovery is indicated in capacity utilization data, but the operating rate is far too low to have much effect on the capital goods sector. The prime interest rate projection for 1983 is around 10 percent. Long-term interest rates are rising, which, if coupled with a diminishing money supply, would make economic recovery much more uncertain. Another economic shortfall is that unemployment is forecast at the high level of 10.2 percent. Inflation is also projected to decrease slowly.

The economic forecast in Europe for 1983 and 1984 is brighter than in the past, but the GNP in Europe for 1983 and 1984 is expected to grow at a slower pace than in the United States.

All the data mentioned above does reflect positive growth during the early 1980s, both in the United States and Europe, though at a subdued rate.

The growth rate of the market in which Midwest has participated is steadily increasing. R&D has been most profitable in mature and slow growth markets because a rapid rate of new product introductions depresses ROI. Midwest spent 2 percent of its sales on R&D compared to the chemical industry average of 2.9 percent. One of Midwest's competitors, Loctite, spent 2.6 percent of its sales on R&D. In order to maintain product leadership and gain market share, however, Midwest has to spend much more on R&D, which depresses profits.

More specifically in Midwest's interest is the five-year growth projection for the chemical industry; it is expected to grow at a rate of about 14 percent from 1982 to 1987. The adhesives and sealant industry is projected to have an 8 percent annual growth rate in the value of shipments through 1995. Compared to these rates, though the chemical and adhesive industries will grow at a rate of 14 percent and 8 percent respectively over the next five years, Midwest wants to realize an annual growth rate of 24.7 percent to achieve its $1 billion goal by 1987. This would be extremely difficult without some major acquisitions, which would require financing either through debt or equity. Midwest's high debt precludes additional borrowing during the time of analysis.

Another improbability is achieving the 5 percent of sales earning rate by 1987, which would require a phenomenal growth rate in earnings of 39.5 percent per year.

Despite its lofty goals, Midwest is poised for long-term growth. It boasts diversity of product lines, a reorganized marketing structure, presence in Europe and Latin America, emphasis on R&D, and commitment to management and employees.

However, Midwest is not without problems and could face some growing pains, such as an increase in debt-to-equity ratio, which increased from 30.4 percent in 1981 to 54 percent in 1982. The increase in 1982 was primarily due to acquisition of ARC, the purchase of a hot melt manufacturing plant in Atlanta, and the construction of an office building and laboratory facilities. To grow in the future at its intended rate, the company would have to increase its debt by further acquisitions.

International sales represented 32 percent of the sales in 1981 and 34 percent in 1982. By 1987, Midwest is shooting for a 40/60 split between foreign and domestic sales, with European sales accounting for 52 percent of all international revenues. Meanwhile, sales in Latin America as a percentage of international revenues are projected to fall to 33 percent due to the political climate there.

The company has encountered a high degree of competition in the marketing of its products. Because of the large number and variety of its products, Midwest has competed with several large national firms as well as many smaller, local independent firms. In the marketing of sealants and coatings, the larger competitors generally have greater research and development. The competition is not going to sit idle and let Midwest nibble away at their share of the market.

However, Midwest has wanted to take advantage of some of the growth markets. Some of these are the increased use of adhesives in the automotive industry, the nonwoven market, and the window market. It is usually best to seek relatively high market share in high-growth markets, which is what Midwest plans to do, but usually large sums of money must be spent on marketing and R&D. According to general findings of PIMS (profit import of market strategies) research, ROI diminishes with high levels of market and R&D expenditures, but businesses (like Midwest) with broader product lines than their competitors and a lower investment intensity tend to have a higher cash flow (measured as a percentage of investment intensity).

Hence, if Midwest wants to grow at a rate of 24.7 percent, its profitability will be affected. Either the company could achieve its $1 billion in sales but with adverse effects on profitability, or the company could have extreme difficulty in achieving both $1 billion *and* a 5 percent return on sales.

One measure of Midwest's profitability—return on shareholders' equity—has been steadily inching up. Except for the odd jumps in 1974 to 17.4 percent and in 1981 to 19.3 percent, it has stayed between 11.1 percent and 15 percent. Thus, the chances of achieving 20 percent return on shareholders' equity, which is also one of the company's objectives, may also be difficult.

Based upon the above factors, Midwest's objectives of achieving $1 billion in sales and a 5 percent return on sales were not compatible. It will be very difficult to "grow" both of them at the required rates. The growth rate of 24.7 percent will require excessive cash flow and will have an effect on earnings in the long run. Cash flow within the company is already negative. More realistic goals would be to push the $1-billion target into the early to mid–1990s and reduce the levels of earnings as a percentage of sales as well as all of the other financial goals for 1987.

Midwest has always had a close working relationship with its customers. Salespeople and research chemists have worked in the plants with customers to resolve their problems. In many cases this has resulted in duplication of products, lack of true marketing, and poor interface between various functional groups within the company. Maintaining good customer relations has also meant building manufacturing plants in strategic locations for timely product delivery. However, it has also created inventory problems and sometimes excess capacity problems.

Promotion from within has been a large plus for Midwest in most instances. It has promoted loyalty and a knowledgeable workforce. On the other hand, the company has had no management training program, it has paid higher wages than necessary in some areas, and it may not have promoted efficiency and effectiveness among workers.

MIS has been implemented, primarily to assist in sales. It has not been fully staffed or utilized to coordinate all functional areas and operations within the company. This is required if Midwest is to continue to grow and remain competitive.

With this background in mind, the president and chief executive officer, Adam Andrews, admits that it will not be easy to achieve such goals, and he expects more acquisitions to be made to get there. Although this will increase Midwest's debt, Andrews, in a personal interview, said, "But growth is major with our company because it stimulates the mental apparatus for individual performance. People don't grow by doing the same thing day in and day out. . . . You have to continue to develop new plans and new products. That's why we have to be growth oriented. If the company isn't growing, the people aren't growing."

Corrective Actions and Impact of Corrective Actions

A few recommendations for corrective action can be made that would help Midwest achieve greater growth and profitability and eventually bring the company close to all of its long-term objectives.

Restate Corporate Policy and Financial Goals. Midwest should switch its corporate policy from specific to general financial goal pronouncements for the following reasons:

- Stockholders' disappointment if publicly announced goals are not met could result in decreased market value of stock.
- Competitors, suppliers, and customers do not need to have this competitively sensitive information.
- Lower-level managers could feel closed out of the decision-making process, which could lead to organized opposition and a souring of attitudes.
- Salary reviews based on performance would be more difficult to justify if merit raises are given despite lackluster goal attainment.
- Public corrections and restatements will not have to be made at a later date, reducing the credibility of top management.

Precise measurements and goals should be made in selected circumstances, but general goals can help form cohesiveness in a diverse organization and enable employees to identify with the goals to form a common bond.

Specific goals should be used in the planning process but only in conjunction with the budgeting process and by select personnel, not broadcast to the entire workforce. Specific goals should also be reviewed frequently, and contingency plans should be formulated to achieve these specific goals.

Financial goals should also be reduced to more realistic levels. Based on the previous history of Midwest, the financial analysis undertaken earlier, Midwest's numerous internal problems, the unsettled political climate in certain regions, and the projected subdued growth prospects for the economy, the following financial goals could be recommended for Midwest:

	Midwest goal	Recommended goal
Average sales growth per year	15%	13%
Earnings/sales	5%	4%
Return on assets	10%	8%
Return on invested capital	15%	15%
Return on equity	20%	17%

These recommended goals are more conservative, will not overstrain Midwest's finances, but will still demand innovation and improvements in all areas of Midwest's operations.

Improve Financial and Operational Problems. Midwest's long-term debt-to-equity ratio is in excess of 50 percent. Most lending institutions are reluctant to lend additional funds with a ratio this high; they prefer this ratio to be in the area of 30 percent to 35 percent. Its high ratio would impede Midwest from further immediate borrowing of funds for additional acquisitions. Midwest may have to finance acquisitions from 1982 to 1987 through equity, although selling stocks would negatively affect the stockholders' equity and reduce the owners' control in the company. Another drawback is that a poor equity market could exist at that time.

In addition to Midwest's high debt level, there are also several other financial and operational problem areas that require attention. These include inefficient use of capital, excess capacity in fixed assets, and cash flow problems. The company's inefficient use of capital and its operational problems show up in the high burden ratio, the high cost of sales, the long collection period, the long accounts payable time, the excessive inventory turnover time, and the high selling and administration expenses. Lack of improvements in all of these areas, at least to equal the industry averages, will probably prevent Midwest from achieving its goals. Poor cash flow must also be corrected if continued growth is to occur. The strongest *positive* impact of the negative cash flow and high debt is that it makes Midwest a less desirable candidate for takeover by some other company. Midwest could also prevent takeover by being a strong, aggressive, well-run company with a high stock price; this can best be accomplished by improving all the discussed problem areas.

Cash flow can be improved by increasing net income. Net income, in turn, can be improved by reducing long-term debt (interest expenses should decrease), decreasing the cost of sales, improving inventory turnover time, improving poor utilization of facilities, eliminating duplication of R&D efforts, improving the collection times of accounts receivable, elimination of paying high wages for poor quality work, improving training programs, and reducing selling and administrative expenses. Improved earnings would, of course, also improve Midwest's possibility of reaching its financial goals.

Hire a Foreign Exchange Money Handler. Midwest should immediately hire an aggressive, experienced foreign trader. This position, reporting to the CEO as a staff function, would be responsible for:

- credit analysis of foreign governments
- credit analysis of foreign customers
- political analysis of foreign governments
- macroeconomic analysis—foreign and domestic
- review of foreign receivables and capital expansion plans
- placement of foreign investments
- analysis of foreign payables
- hedging foreign currency exposure against the U.S. dollar

This position would have to be entrusted with the authority to handle currency transactions quickly within parameters set by top management. A standard salary plus commission structure is common for this type of position. This generally encourages profitability for both the trader and the company.

The trader would help determine if changes in geographical focus would benefit or harm the company because of exchange rates and political scenarios in the countries involved. The trader's input should also be considered by the planning committee for the corporation as well as by the boards of various multinational subsidiaries.

Expand Marketing and Sales Objectives. Midwest should expand its marketing and sales objectives to include untapped geographical, industrial, and consumer markets for which it has already existing technology.

Entry into the Chinese market is suggested, with its target market of over 800 million people. The Chinese attitude toward capitalism has become more favorable, so official acceptance of a Midwest subsidiary could be easy to obtain. In addition to labor availability, this area of the world is becoming more conscious of consumerism. Midwest's quality products might gain immediate acceptance. Expansion into other Pacific Rim countries should also be examined.

Serious consideration should be given to reducing operations in Latin America and expanding them in Europe. Examination should be made of expanding further not only in western Europe but in eastern Europe and even the Soviet Union. Also there should be more emphasis on attaining synergy between America and Europe. Continued expansion in Europe and Asia and less emphasis in Latin America should thus reduce risks and encourage steady growth within Midwest.

Industrial applications of adhesives appear to be limited. Horizontal integration into the abrasives industry through a new line of high performance resin and vitrified grinding wheels should be carefully examined. Midwest has almost all the technical expertise and raw materials required to enter this market. Since Carborundum, a leading firm in this field, was folded by its parent company Kennecott, machine tool manufacturers have struggled to find a suitable replacement, a role that Midwest could fill. Solvents and coolants may also be viable line expansions.

The consumer market seems to have been all but ignored by Midwest. Product line expansions could include decorative, protective paints to compete directly with products such as Rustoleum. Single-application glue containers (similar to mustard and ketchup packets) could be sold by retail or to manufacturers of do-it-yourself projects, such as furniture. This would expand Midwest's contracyclical business lines and help stabilize sales and earnings during business cycles. Limiting the scope and mission of Midwest products could only result in limiting sales of existing product technology. In other words, Midwest's market-driven strategy must be accompanied by a reexamination of the corporate mission statement. Not all of the opportunities for growth are in already existing technical lines. Some may be in completely new and unique areas compared to current products and direction.

In addition, there should be increased communication between market research and product development. It is fruitless to develop a product for which there is no market or to market a product that would take years to develop.

The expansion of the market research department as well as the "Special Opportunities" and "Pioneer" groups could also help Midwest explore market opportunities more fully.

Vertical Integration. Midwest should also consider vertical integration by purchasing one or more of its suppliers. Not only would this lead to stabilization and improvements in both availability and cost of raw materials, but it could also lead to increased sales. The new supplying subsidiary should also be allowed to produce and market raw materials to its existing customers. Such synergies could be beneficial to Midwest's bottom line as well. The new subsidiary could bring with it new distribution channels and R&D expertise. Back-office functions could be consolidated at headquarters, bringing it net reductions in salary and administrative costs. This should result in a reduction of the 68 percent cost of goods sold as well as help reduce selling and administrative expenses.

An analysis of Midwest's suppliers, suppliers' competitors, and their target markets should be undertaken by a team from market research, purchasing, and financial planning. Midwest should then develop contingency plans for acquisitions so that action is taken quickly as opportunities present themselves.

Care must, however, be taken during vertical integration not to overexpand. In good economic times, vertical integration would give Midwest control over its supplies and costs, but in poor economic times, 100 percent vertical integration in any area would put a financial strain on the company because all fixed costs would still have to be paid. A solution to this problem, practiced by some other companies, is to supply and control a portion of the product through vertical integration but to continue to purchase part of the product supply on the outside. With this system in position, Midwest could drop its outside suppliers during tight economic periods.

Develop a New Market Plan and Reduce the Number of SBUs. Midwest should develop a strategic market plan that would have each SBU develop its own strategic market plan, which would be reviewed by upper management for consistency with corporate objectives and goals. Such a plan should involve five areas:

- Define the business.
- Determine the mission or role of the business.
- Formulate functional strategies.
- Establish budgets.
- Implement management and marketing training programs.

In addition, the SBUs and R&D should utilize the marketing research department before a product is developed and produced to determine if a market exists for it.

Emphasis should also be placed on reducing the number of SBUs to a maximum of five, with smaller sub-SBUs beneath them. To achieve the necessary in-depth understanding of fifteen SBU plans is unnecessary and a possibly unmanageable load on the shoulders of too few people at the top. This is similar to a problem GE faced in the late 1970s—corporate review of SBU plans suffered from an overload of too many SBUs. It is recommended that Midwest incorporate a solution similar to that used by GE: create a sector structure that represents a macrobusiness of industry areas. The sector executive in turn serves as the spokesperson for that industry and is responsible for supplying management direction to the sub-SBUs, which were called group SBUs, division SBUs, and department SBUs at GE; on the proposed Midwest organizational chart in Figure

16.6, lower level SBUs are shown simply as a single group, sub-SBUs. The five main SBUs should focus heavily on developing opportunities that transcend the main SBU lines but still remain within the scope of the main SBUs. The Midwest corporate executive office can then focus its review on the strategic plans of the five SBUs and the development of new sub-SBUs within the main SBUs' scope. The sub-SBUs will in turn act as normal SBUs and develop new business areas by expanding into contiguous product-market areas. Implementation of this concept could give Midwest better control over its SBUs, help develop new product areas, and expand existing product areas.

Expand MIS. Another major recommendation to help Midwest achieve greater profit margins and reduce costs would be the total development of MIS. Ideally, a real-time MIS should be able to meet as many objectives as possible and simultaneously reduce costs for the firm. Excessive inventories, selling and administrative costs, collection times, and bill payment times must all be improved through closer monitoring and tighter controls implemented through an expanded MIS. In addition, MIS can provide more accurate and up-to-date information needed to operate the company, help in strategic and tactical planning, permit access and evaluation to all chemical formulas with the possibility of eliminating any duplication, improve manufacturing and supply process, and aid management in making decisions. The following are the major steps in developing a management information system (the percentages at the right are total amount of time, which is based on past research):

Feasibility Study

Exploratory survey, including current system analysis	12%
Basic system design	15%
Equipment selection	10%

System Implementation

Preparatory work of new system:

• Training all personnel	8%
• Flowchart, including decision tables	10%
• Programming, desk checking, and system testing	10%
• Program compiling and testing	20%

Operation of New System

Parallel operations for checking new system	5%
Final conversion to new system	10%

Two to three years completion time	100%

Improve and Upgrade Human Resource Policies. Midwest must define and improve personnel policies and practices. First, it must implement a

Figure 16.6
Suggested Organizational Chart

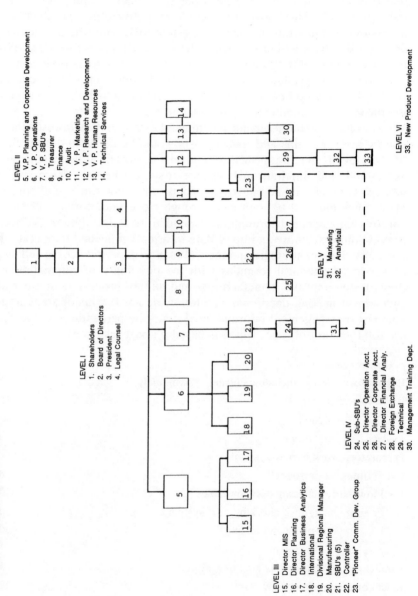

LEVEL I
1. Shareholders
2. Board of Directors
3. President
4. Legal Counsel

LEVEL II
5. V.P. Planning and Corporate Development
6. V. P. Operations
7. V. P. SBU's
8. Treasurer
9. Finance
10. Audit
11. V. P. Marketing
12. V. P. Research and Development
13. V. P. Human Resources
14. Technical Services

LEVEL III
15. Director MIS
16. Director Planning
17. Director Business Analytics
18. International
19. Divisional Regional Manager
20. Manufacturing
21. SBU's (5)
22. Controller
23. "Pioneer" Comm. Dev. Group

LEVEL IV
24. Sub-SBU's
25. Director Operation Acct.
26. Director Corporate Acct.
27. Director Financial Analy.
28. Foreign Exchange
29. Technical
30. Management Training Dept.

LEVEL V
31. Marketing
32. Analytical

LEVEL VI
33. New Product Development

management training program utilizing both inhouse job rotation and training and outside educational seminars and classes. Technically skilled personnel need to stay current as developments are made in the industry. Line personnel need improvement in management and personal communication skills. In order for promotion from within to work, management depth and skills must be encouraged. Personnel from outside the company should be hired when special skills are in short supply.

Second, Midwest must implement a formal personnel evaluation program. Job responsibilities need to be made more clear to both management and the employee. Job descriptions should be assigned a level of difficulty for the salary administration program. Evaluations for merit increases and cost of living adjustment (COLA) should be standardized and based on performance. Staff and supervisors should be rated on achievement of goals (modified management by objectives, or MBO), whereas manufacturing personnel should be evaluated on the performance of their assigned duties for future promotability.

Third, in areas where special talents or skills are needed (such as Ph.D.s in R&D) and where outside people would improve operations considerably, Midwest should make provisions for hiring from outside the company as well as promoting from within. It should generate a job description or definition of requirements for the position being offered, and if no internal personnel have the qualifications, the needed talent should be acquired from outside.

All of these improvements should more than pay for themselves through improved operations.

Expand and Improve Worldwide Sales Effort. Midwest should review and improve its worldwide sales effort and strategies. Incentives must be used to encourage the sale of new products as well as older, more profitable ones. In addition, the strategy of employing all company-paid outside salespeople is questionable.

Sales calls grow more expensive annually. Customer service may actually improve in areas where sales coverage is limited or sparse. Local distributors are generally thought of first when a purchasing agent is in need. The following is recommended: (1) expand sales through utilization of manufacturers' representatives, and (2) expand sales through industrial distributors and supply houses. These strategies are quite common in industrial settings. They expand distribution channels while reducing salary and administrative expenses.

A more aggressive advertising campaign is also recommended in order to achieve a greater market share. Midwest's strategy has seemed to be "the product sells itself." Trade magazines would be an excellent means of reinforcing brand recognition through advertising and articles. Trade shows for customers are also an excellent outlet for industrial customers. Consumer brand recognition seems to be minimal, so an effort should be

made to publicize Midwest's product line at the consumer level through
do-it-yourself publications and even on television.

Specialized advertising through selected media will increase name recognition and thus help sales and earnings.

Review Charitable Contribution Practices. Midwest should review its
charitable contribution practices as a function of the financial planning
process. As the company grows, its 5 percent philanthropic donation
automatically increases. Because Midwest suffers from a negative cash
flow, it is recommended that a charitable trust be set up so that contributions can be leveled out between high earnings years and low earnings
years. Midwest should neither decrease its 5 percent contributions to
charity nor increase it to 10 percent as permitted in its corporate plans.

Midwest should analyze the impact of its donations in all parts of the
world by amount and by organization. Midwest should emphasize medical
and educational donations that are sorely needed and that may accentuate
Midwest's interest in the people in the areas it serves.

In reviewing charitable contributions it is recommended that Midwest
also implement the following procedures for managing contributions:

- Align gifts with products and goals.
- Put some distance between corporate contributions effort and the CEO.
- Choose the right organizational structure.
- Pick a manager for these donations.
- Treat grant seekers like customers.
- Set long-term budgets for contributions.
- Prepare for opposition.

After the above steps have been taken, Midwest should then consider the
next six rules:

- Do not run the contributions program as a public relations program.
- Do not automatically renew grants to programs.
- Do not get too involved in grantees' day-to-day operations after donations have
  been made.
- Do not try to please everyone.
- Take a chance on an unconventional cause.
- Do not work in isolation.

Following these procedures and recommendations will insure contributions that will be beneficial to both Midwest and the recipients.

Acquisitions. For continued growth Midwest must consider additional
acquisitions. This is necessary whether an attempt is made to reach the

$1 billion goal or normal, steady growth of 10 to 15 percent per year is desired. Candidates for acquisition must be carefully selected if they are to help Midwest financially rather than hurt it. Four high-sales candidates recommended for consideration are: Essex Chemical, Pratt and Lambert, Product Research and Chemical Corporation, and Nordson Corporation. Highlights of these four companies are shown below:

High Sales Acquisition Candidates

Essex Chemical	$169M (1982 sales)

Product line

Pharmaceuticals

Industrial Chemicals

Refrigerant gases

Sealants, adhesives, and coatings for autos and appliances (industry leader)

Retained earnings	$13M
Book value plant and equipment	$67M

Accelerated new product development and introduction

Pratt and Lambert	$156M (1982 sales)

Product line

Paints

Architectural finishes

Coatings (high-growth area)

Net worth	$21M
Retained earnings	$31M
Book value	$40M
Net income (1983)	$6M

Product Research and Chemical Corp.	$65M (1982 sales)

Product line

Sealants for insulated windows (industry leader)

Pipe coating for natural gas process (good innovation and reputation; England)

Book value	$28M

Nordson Corp.	$126M (1982 sales)

Product line

Application equipment for thermoplastic adhesives and sealants, paints and power paints, and industrial solvents and coatings

Foreign sales are 55 percent of total sales

Book value of plant and equipment	$27M
Retained earnings (stable)	$67M
Net income (1983)	$10M

Acquisition of any of these four candidates would be a large bite for Midwest to take but would certainly help its product line. Unfortunately, due to Midwest's high debt, it is improbable that Midwest could borrow the amount of money it would take to finance such an acquisition. Limited funds could be raised through the equity market if the market was right. Improved financial ratios and a higher stock price would help make Midwest stocks more desirable and bring Midwest higher returns. Since all preferred stock is owned by Edward Andrews, who bought the Midwest franchise in the 1920s, and each share carries eighty votes compared to one vote for each common stock, he controls 21.3 percent of the voting power in the company from preferred stocks alone. When his common share holdings are added to this, his voting power is increased to approximately 22.4 percent. This means that Midwest could sell a fair number of additional unissued common shares and still retain a reasonable amount of control over the company. Any acquisition of major size would, therefore, probably have to be financed by a combination of increased debt financing and equity financing, both of which in the short run could deter Midwest from reaching its 1987 financial goals.

Spinoffs. Midwest should examine spinning off some of its less profitable product lines in an effort to focus its business direction. Products aimed at consumer markets would be good candidates, and divesting some of its Latin American business should be seriously considered.

Mergers. A merger would probably not result in the type of financial maximization that Midwest is seeking. Therefore, this business combination should not be considered as an alternative for Midwest.

Joint Ventures. Joint ventures are excellent ways to enter markets with good potential but where barriers of some sort (political, economic, technological) exist. This is a good way for Midwest to expand in the risky Latin American markets and also gain entry into eastern European and Pacific Rim areas, while at the same time minimizing its exposure.

Company Reorganization. Although Midwest has been served well by its current organizational structure, certain changes should be made in order to maximize growth. Figure 16.6 illustrates a recommended organization. Key areas of change are in human resources, marketing, operations, SBUs, R&D, and MIS.

Important to Midwest's future growth are well-qualified and highly motivated employees. To ensure proper attention in this area, a human resources department should be established, directly under a vice president. This department would weed out unqualified and unmotivated employees.

But the initial focus should be to determine management and employee training requirements. By drawing upon internal field experience, employing outside expertise, and selectively promoting from without and within the organization, Midwest can upgrade its workforce and properly prepare its managers to meet the challenges set before them. Critical to this effort is the establishment of a management training division reporting directly to the human resources department.

To expand, Midwest requires a focused marketing effort. For this reason a marketing department should be established at corporate headquarters with a vice president directing the overall effort. Dedicated marketing units should be added to the reduced number of SBUs and the Pioneer commercial development groups (PCDGs). As stated earlier, the number of SBUs should be reduced to five with sub-SBUs under them. The PCDGs should be moved under the authority of R&D with a dotted line liaison from the SBU and PCDG marketing units to the marketing department. This arrangement should permit Midwest to fully exploit new product development and permit the company to expand quickly into new markets.

By decreasing the span of control, Midwest will be better prepared to address new marketing opportunities as they become available, permitting the firm to become more dominant and increasing its leverage within its technology areas.

The finance department should be left intact. However, we recommend the establishment of an ad hoc "acquisition task force" chaired by the finance department and staffed by key management representatives to seek out, examine, and evaluate possible spinoff areas, acquisitions, vertical integration prospects, joint venture candidates, and improvement of financial problem areas.

A management training department should be established as a part of the human resources department. This training department should draw upon field expertise to train the current managerial staff. Incompetent managers should be dismissed as part of this process. Promotion from within must be adhered to so as to build morale and keep talented individuals within the company. However, talented personnel must be hired from outside the company to invigorate management with new ideas.

As part of the training program and in conjunction with marketing, sales incentives should also be redesigned to support the total market mix. Efforts should be expanded in Europe and Japan and other Asiatic countries to market adhesives, powder coatings, and new products. Incentives should be available for all product lines, not only the most profitable.

MIS should be located directly under the vice president of planning and corporate development. At a later time it might be desirable and advisable to let it stand alone directly under its own vice president. This department should be expanded as discussed earlier. MIS should be used in the entire strategic and planning process; financial and accounting data analysis, evaluation, and control; marketing research, analysis, and control; sorting, integrating, and consolidating all chemical formulas and having them available for instant recall; in R&D, engineering, and manufacturing for continued expansion and consolidation of R&D, CAD/CAM, MRP, JIT inventory control, and so on; and any other areas where MIS can be advantageously used. In other words, MIS should be fully developed to become an integral part of the entire business operation and increase active interface among all internal and external areas. Although not shown as such on the organizational chart, this will require dotted-line relationships among all major participating areas.

The foreign exchange money handler should be placed under the controller and should handle all of the company's money exchange transactions.

Summary of Corrective Action Recommendations

This section summarizes the corrective actions to be taken by Midwest to improve its corporate strategy, which are displayed in a recommended time sequence format. The time activity format is a simple bar chart (see Table 16.18) and covers the period from 1983 through 1987. Since many of the activities listed on the chart continue throughout the five-year period, the bar chart lends itself well to this type of presentation. To interpret Table 16.18, the following key should be used:

Activity: A short description of the activity to be accomplished.

Solid bar: Time period of full-time operation on the activity.

Dashed bar: Time period of periodic follow-up operation on the activity.

▲: Short-term activity point or special activity implementation point.

NOTES

1. World Bank, *World Development Report, 1987* (New York: Oxford University Press, 1987), pp. 202–203.

2. Ibid.

3. Philip Chenier, *Survey of Industrial Chemistry* (New York: John Wiley & Sons, 1986).

4. Dale W. Sommer, "Strength Below the Surface—Investments One Potential Place," *Industry Week* 217, no. 5 (May 30, 1983): 69.

5. "Discovery Brings the Summit," *Business Week*, no. 2792 (May 30, 1983): 27.

6. Sommer, p. 69.

7. Ibid.

8. Ibid.

9. "Average Unemployment Rate Forecast for 1982," *Business Week*, no. 2771 (December 27, 1982): 50.

10. "A Soaring Economy Will Produce a New Country," *U.S. News & World Report* 94, no. 18 (May 9, 1983): 23.

11. "Early Stirrings of Improvement," *Business Week*, no. 2773 (January 17, 1983): 59.

12. "Adhesives, Sealants, to Gain Larger US Market Share," *Rubber and Plastics News*, April 13, 1981, p. 50.

13. Ibid.

14. *Standard & Poor's Register of Corporation Directors and Executives*, volume 1 (New York: Standard & Poor's Corp., 1985).

Table 16.18

Recommended Time Activity Chart for Midwest for 1983 through 1987

ACTIVITY	1983	1984	1985	1986	1987
Corporate policy of financial goals					
•Switch to general financial goals					
•Reduce level of specific financial goals					
Improve financial & operational problems					
•Reduce debt to equity ratio					
•Improve facilities usage					
•Improve inventory levels					
•Improve collection times					
•Improve accounts payable time					
•Improve selling and administration expenses					
•Improve cash flow levels					
Foreign exchange money handler					
•Conduct money handler search					
•Hire experienced money handler					
•Set up foreign exchange office					
•Put office into continuous operation					
External marketing and sales objectives					
•Search for new market segments					
–existing technology, existing markets					
•Search for new market segments					
–existing technology, new markets					
•Expand consumer market					
•Reexamine mission statement and revise when needed					
•External market research					
•Improve communication and interface with other functional areas					

ACTIVITY	1983	1984	1985	1986	1987
Vertical integration					
•Examine possible vertical integration areas					
•Examine vertical integration candidates					
•Vertically integrate if advantageous to Midwest					
Develop and implement new market plan with a reduced number of SBU's					
•Develop strategic market plan					
•Reduce number of SBU's					
•Implement and carry out new market plan					
Expand MIS					
•Conduct usage, application, and feasibility study					
•Implement new applications					
•Place expanded MIS in full operation					
Improve and upgrade human resources policies					
•Develop management training programs					
•Implement management training programs					
•Develop personnel evaluation program					
•Implement new hiring and promotion program					
Expand and improve worldwide sales effort.					
•Expand advertising effort					
•Utilize alternate sales sources					
Review charitable contribution policies					
•Establish charitable funds review committee					
•Review allocation practices					
•Review funds recipients					
•Establish charitable trust					
•Allocate charitable funds					
Acquisitions					
•Evaluate acquisition conditions					
•Evaluate acquisition impact on company					
•Make acquisitions when advantageous					
Other business combinations and alternatives					
•Evaluate areas of Midwest for potential spinoffs					
•Implement spinoffs if advantageous					
•Evaluate possible joint ventures					

Table 16.18 (Continued)

ACTIVITY	1983	1984	1985	1986	1987
•Implement joint ventures when advantageous					
•Evaluate equity financing					
Company reorganization					
• Restructure organization					

Conclusions and Recommendations

17

Conclusions and Recommendations

Throughout the 1980s, the creative energies of organizations were often focused upon change in areas concerned with financial gain. During this period, over a trillion dollars were spent on merger, acquisition, and leveraged buyout activity. Ten million manufacturing jobs were eliminated, and seventeen million new jobs were created. Obviously no aspects of corporate life are protected from the forces of change. Not only were the 1980s dynamic and, for many, traumatic, but they may well have been a mere warmup for the 1990s.

NEW AREA OF COMPETITION

A new competitive arena, tougher and even more complex than in the past, now lies on the horizon. Japan, now more powerful than ever, and Europe, soon to be anchored by a united Germany, will not grant the United States an inch. The combined impact of the European Economic Community and Japan, along with a stronger more competitive Korea, Taiwan, and other Pacific Rim nations, places the United States on a playing field that may not be too level.

Foreign competitors are the beneficiaries of nationally funded research and development in many key areas of technology. Other foreign firms enjoy tariff and legislative protection of their markets from foreign competition, and others are directly subsidized by their governments. Whatever their competitive advantage, and no matter how bitterly U.S. businesspeople may complain about a lack of fairness, there is only one viable solution: American businesses must be strong and competitive. Thankfully, our free enterprise system presents few barriers to solid productivity improvement. Barriers that do exist tend to be within the management structures and systems of organizations. Innovation, risk taking (both financial and behavioral), and bold actions are the essence of positive, competitive progress.

THE NEED FOR KNOWLEDGE

Corporate self-confidence, which leads to desirable competitive progress, flows from knowledge of the true status of structure, people, and systems. From such knowledge emanate correct attitudes, which in turn lead to correct direction and positive avenues of change. Such knowledge is enhanced by a certainty of conditions within an organization. Seldom are corporations as good, or as bad as a quick overall analysis might indicate. Unfortunately, decades of rigid functional specialization have left businesses with few managers, even in the more senior positions, who truly have a comprehensive, "high-terrain" view of overall status and conditions.

THE NEED FOR MULTIPLE MEASURES

The corporate operational analysis procedure and the Midwest example provide a comprehensive blueprint for knowledge attainment. Knowledge of an entity as complex as this typical organization does not come easily. The human heart is in many ways parallel to the organizational system. The medical profession has been struggling to develop a safe and solidly differentiating test to identify whether a heart and cardiovascular system are healthy or dangerously ill. The best answers to date come from not one test but from multiple measures looking at the heart, key arteries, and the entire system as a whole. In like manner, the better evaluations of an organizational system come from multiple areas of evaluation that, in total, provide a complete answer.

STAY THE COURSE

We can make no stronger recommendation to users of the corporate operational analysis procedure than to "stay the course" of the system as presented in the prior chapters. Feedback from successful users, both U.S. and foreign firms, suggest that while a temptation to shortcut some steps does exist, often the most useful insights develop from areas that can be overlooked in an abbreviated application of the procedure.

The most difficult aspect of staying the course in terms of analysis of the more complex organization is the seeming lack of progress during the early stages of an examination. There are dozens of questions that are addressed in the early stages, including the inevitable question, "Isn't there an easier way?" The answer is an unequivocal "No." A wise man of India was once asked by his young charge, "Master, how could one ever eat an elephant?" The reply was, "My son, one eats an elephant as he would a dove: one bite at a time." The task of comprehensive corporate and organizational analysis can appear as foreboding as attempting to consume an elephant, but taken one bite at a time, according to plan, the task is manageable.

Without adherence to a plan, the functional areas of most interest to those directing the analysis or investigation will probably receive a disproportionate degree of attention. This tendency of "mirror focus" is reflected in the trend of change that occurred at Chrysler and later at General Motors as both firms in the 1960s elected chief executives from accounting and finance rather than from production. Today, however, both Chrysler and General Motors are led by executives noted for new model development and production rather than accounting and finance. Years of losing to German and Japanese auto firms led by engineers transmitted a message that leadership tends to focus and excel in its own area of functional specialization.

The key objective in corporate operational analysis is balance rather than excessive focus upon any single functional area. Only through a balanced approach to analysis will positions of strength and weakness be identified, which lead to the key variables identified in the force field analysis. Here, at least, focusing on identified areas of weakness can activate the creative abilities of the corporate staff as avenues of corrective action are considered and developed.

ANTICIPATING THE IMPACT OF CHANGE

As decision makers come to agreement concerning the nature of desired changes, a critical question to ask is, "Does this removal of fat cut into the muscle of the organization?" A prime example of organizational change that led to this problem is the 1986 LBO of Safeway Stores. Buyout specialists Kohlberg Kravis Roberts & Company acted as the advisory team and led the investigative group that bought controlling interest in Safeway. In mid–1990, researchers from the *Wall Street Journal* reported on a two-month investigation of postbuyout decisions and actions, which revealed enormous human costs and unintended side effects. In the wake of cost-cutting moves, some 63,000 managers and workers were cut loose from Safeway primarily through store sales and layoffs. When Safeway itself selected a group of its own employees to speak to the researchers on behalf of their company, not one of them praised the buyout decision.[1] Evidence from in-depth analysis of Safeway operations through April 1990 did not entirely support the argument made by management that the LBO made Safeway a healthier institution. A consensus opinion is that the chain cut plenty of muscle with the fat from its holdings, its labor forces, and also in terms of deferred capital improvements that could not compete against demands of the all-consuming debt.[2]

Analysis of the route taken by Kroger Co. grocery chain in avoiding a nearly identical LBO offer by the KKR group reflects the value of analysis of the impact of change. Kroger avoided the LBO route, choosing instead to offer shareholders a hefty dividend and employees a significant ownership stake in what remains a public company. With employees able to evaluate objectives and the change necessary to attain them, a far different pattern of decisions emerged. These changes were far more balanced in terms of personnel, suppliers, and financial needs. Kroger, as of May 1990, supported some 60,000 more workers than Safeway, it increased its charitable cash contributions to $3.6 million in 1989, up from $2.1 million in 1987, while Safeway trimmed its corporate cash giving to $2.7 million in 1989 from $3.2 million in 1986.[3]

Kroger, while being more humane and motivating to its employees and more supportive to its communities, maintains the same operating profit per employee as Safeway. Of even greater importance is the probable long-term future of Kroger as compared to Safeway. By taking a more balanced, less financially myopic view, Kroger holds a strong position for competition in the 1990s. It enjoys the benefits of a less stressed, more motivated workforce strongly supported by a well-designed logistical system. Community support, strong in the past, continues unabated.

The message that flows from the review of these two corporations strongly supports the need for impact analysis. Major change in policies that control the human assets, supplier relations, and community relations have a depth and breadth of impact that must be considered in the short, intermediate, and long run. No organization can fail to consider loyalty, service, and image when considering change. Also, should firms disregard the laws controlling the economy, it is a near certainty that corrective legislation will be passed that will limit competitive freedom in our society.

MIS AND THE DECISION PROCESS

MIS plays a vital role in the corporate operational analysis procedure for purposes of evaluation of the masses of data generated by the organization. Without question, spreadsheet analysis and similar software programs are of value in the determination of corporate strengths and weaknesses. Material requirements planning, manufacturing resources planning, and computer-aided process planning (CPP) can be critical strengths and weaknesses to a company. The quality of software activities is possibly the most difficult area of evaluation within an organization.

Part of the problem lies in the individualistic aspects of a software package. Program glitches can be a major disaster. For management to determine the transferability of its internally generated software would require basically unattainable levels of understanding.

In the final analysis, the critical question management needs to address is, "Does the organization have MIS or a decision support system (DSS)?" In all probability elements of both are built into the data analysis process. Has application software been designed in an interactive model that can be readily accessed to enhance problem solving and analysis? Such systems for solving unstructured problems take considerable development time and are more often found in specialized areas, such as marketing or medical application. Computational constraints of DSS, plus the reality that a majority of the information which must be considered is qualitative rather than quantitative, limit the application of MIS and DSS in the broad, all-encompassing areas of analysis. For planning purposes most database information will be of value. In all but the most limited of situations, data from standard MIS configurations must be treated as only one stream of information that cannot stand alone. For those organizations with DSS, some areas of analysis in the procedure may be completely answered through interrogation of the corporate DSS. Unfortunately, such cases are the exception rather than the rule. In time, software will probably be developed that answers a majority of questions posed in the procedure. Such programs will allow a nearly complete, annual audit of organizational status where desired, with even more frequent limited-focus surveys becoming a practical reality.

CONDITIONS FOR CREATIVE CHANGE

An intuitive manager is attuned to the basic conditions of his or her organization. Understanding the conditions of fundamental management processes of planning, organizing, directing, and controlling provides a launch pad from which vehicles cloaked with creative power may be inserted into the organizational system. No single approach will dependably make a manager intuitive and creative, but much of what has been recommended and detailed in this book will stretch capabilities and stimulate through knowledge the development of viable, creative courses of action.

A FINAL OBSERVATION

Corporate operational analysis cannot be reduce to one simple formula. This procedure is intended to develop modes of thinking that come into play as, layer by layer, the operational processes of the working organization are placed under the spotlight of scrutiny. With patience and practice a learning curve can develop that will significantly speed the application of this procedure and, ultimately, improve the odds of developing winning decisions related to both strategic change and the retention of established operations.

The primary purpose of this book is to encourage comprehensive consideration of all key factors as the evaluation is conducted. Miracles are not promised, but assurance is given that the dedicated user will not be unpleasantly surprised by events and consequences that were not considered. Not being taken by surprise allows untold mental energy to be conserved at the opportune time and allows one to focus on problem solving with creative, productive mental insight.

NOTES

1. "Safeway LBO Yields Vast Profits but Exacts a Heavy Human Toll," *Wall Street Journal*, May 16, 1990, pp. A-1, A-8.
2. Ibid., A-8.
3. Ibid.

Selected Bibliography

Anderson, Jerry W., Jr. *Corporate Social Responsibility: Guidelines for Top Management*. Westport, CT: Quorum Books, 1989.

Blau, Peter M., and W. Richard Scott. *Formal Organizations: A Comparative Analysis*. San Francisco: Chandler Publishing Company, 1962.

Christopher, Robert C. *The Japanese Mind: The Goliath Explained*. New York: Linden Press, 1983.

Cyert, R. M., and J. B. March. *A Behavioral Theory of the Firm*. Englewood Cliffs, NJ: Prentice-Hall, 1963.

Daniels, John D., and Lee H. Radebaugh. *International Business, Environment and Operations*, 5th ed. Cambridge, MA: Addison-Wesley, 1989.

Deardon, John. *Computers in Business Management*. Homewood, IL: Dow Jones–Irwin, 1966.

Drucker, Peter F. *The Effective Executive*. New York: Harper & Row, 1967.

Gibson, Charles H., and Patricia A. Freshhoff. *Financial Statement Analysis; Using Financial Accounting Information*, 2d ed. Boston: Kent Publishing Company, 1983.

Hayes, Robert H., and Steven C. Wheelwright. *Restoring Our Competitive Edge*. New York: John Wiley & Sons, 1984.

Herzberg, Frederick. *Work and the Nature of Man*. Cleveland, OH: World Publishing Company, 1966.

Hofer, Charles W., Edwin A. Murray, Jr., Ram Charan, and Robert A. Pitts. *Strategic Management*. St. Paul, MN: West Publishing Company, 1980.

Kash, Fremont D., and James E. Rosenzweig. *Organization and Management*, 4th ed. New York: McGraw-Hill, 1985.

Keegan, Warren J. *Multinational Marketing Management*, 2d ed. Englewood Cliffs, NJ: Prentice-Hall, 1980.

Litterer, Joseph A. *The Analysis of Organizations*, 2d ed. New York: John Wiley & Sons, 1973.

March, James G., ed. *Handbook of Organizations*. Chicago: Rand McNally, 1965.

Melcher, Bonita H., and Harold Kerzner. *Strategic Planning Development and Implementation*. Blue Ridge Summit, PA: Tab Professional and Reference Books, 1988.

Milkovich, George T., and William F. Glueck. *Personnel, Human Resources Management: A Diagnostic Approach*, 4th ed. Plano, TX: Business Publications, 1985.

Morgan, Gareth. *Images of Organization*. Beverly Hills, CA: Sage Publications, 1986.

O'Brien, James A. *Information Systems in Business Management*, 5th ed. Homewood, IL: Irwin, 1988.

Odiorne, G. S. *Management by Objectives: A System of Management Leadership*. New York: Pitman Publishing, 1965.

Ohmae, Kenichi. *The Mind of the Strategist*. New York: McGraw-Hill, 1982.

Pearce, John A., II and Richard B. Robinson, Jr. *Strategic Management*, 2d ed. Homewood, IL: Richard D. Irwin, 1985.

Porter, Michael E. *Competitive Strategy*. New York: The Free Press, 1980.

Ryans, John K., Jr., and William L. Shanklin. *Strategic Planning: Concepts and Implementation*. New York: Random House, 1985.

Sayles, Leonard R. *Leadership*. New York: McGraw-Hill, 1979.

Schmenner, Roger. *Making Business Location Decisions*. Englewood Cliffs, NJ: Prentice-Hall, 1982.

Starr, Martin K. *Managing Production and Operations*. Englewood Cliffs, NJ: Prentice-Hall, 1989.

Steiner, George A. *Top Management Planning*. New York: Macmillan, 1969.

Sumanth, David J. *Productivity Engineering and Management*. New York: McGraw-Hill, 1984.

Szymanski, Robert A. *Computers and Information Systems in Business*. Columbus, OH: Merrill Publishing Company, 1990.

Terpstra, Vern, and Kenneth David. *The Cultural Environment of International Business*. Cincinnati, OH: South-Western Publishing Company, 1985.

Tugendhat, Christopher. *The Multinationals*. New York: Random House, 1972.

Wilkins, Mira. *The Emergence of Multinational Enterprise: American Business Abroad from the Colonial Era to 1914*. Cambridge, MA: Harvard University Press, 1970.

―――. *The Maturing Multinational Enterprise: American Business Abroad, 1914–1970*. Cambridge, MA: Harvard University Press, 1974.

Name Index

Subject Index

cies and strategies, 86–93; segmentation, 83
Markov analysis, 74
Marks and Spencer department store, 103
Marriott, 193
Master schedule management, 98
Materials requirements planning (MRP), 64–65, 99
Matrix departmentation, 150
McDonalds, 195
Mergers, 170–176, 322; conglomerate, 170; defined, 170; horizontal, 170; vertical, 170. *See also* Acquisitions
Merck, 155, 195
Micro analysis, 214, 256–277
Microcomputers, 166
Midwest Chemical Products Company, Inc. case, 219–245, 268
Minnesota Mining and Manufacturing (3M), 28
Minority business legislation, 58
Mission of company, 12
Mitsubishi Electric Corporation, 197
Motivation, 154
Multinational business, 191–207, 310, 319; environment, 200–204; exchange rates, 203; exports, 191; franchises, 191; growth, 193–198; imports, 191; joint-ventures, 191; licensing, 191; markets, 198–200; operations, 192; tourism, 191; transportation, 191; travel, 191; turn-key operations, 191. *See also* Multinational cultural environment
Multinational cultural environment, 201–204; economics, 202; education, 202; financial, 203; group affiliation, 201; language, 202; marketing, 203; religion, 201; technology, 204

Nalco Chemical, 225, 265
Nasco, 195
National Adhesives, 225
National Aeronautics and Space Administration (NASA), 163

National Environmental Policy Act, 54
National Institute for Occupational Safety and Health (NIOSH), 55
Nestlé, 193
Nippon Life Insurance Company, 193
Nippon Mini Computer, 195
Nordson Corporation, 321
Nucor Corporation, 152

Objectives: company, 12; defined, 15
Occupational Safety and Health Act, 54, 55
Occupational Safety and Health Administration (OSHA), 55, 251, 296
Occupational Safety and Health Review Commission (OSHRC), 55
Olivetti and Philips, 197
Operations information systems, 134–135; automated office systems, 135; electronic data processing (EDP) systems, 135; process control systems, 135; transaction processing systems, 135
Organizational interface, 162
Organization charts, 149–150
Organisation Commune Africaine et Mauricienne, 200
Organization: culture, defined, 144; design, 150; formal, 148; informal, 148; structure, 143–159; talent, 155
Organization of African Unity, 200
Ostfriesland (battleship), 167

Pacific Rim, 52, 198
Packaging, 86, 250
Payout/payback method, 110
Peter Cooper, 274
Petrolite Corporation, 269
Philanthropy. *See* Social responsibility
Philip Morris, 153
Piedmont Label, 274
Planning, 11–21, 242–243, 253–254, 277–279; intermediate range, 11, 17, 18; long-range, 11; policies, 17;

About the Authors

JERRY W. ANDERSON, JR., is professor of management and past chairman of the Department of Management and Information Systems at Xavier University in Cincinnati, Ohio. He is the author of *Corporate Social Responsibility*, published by Quorum in 1989, as well as numerous journal articles.

JOHN B. CAMEALY is associate professor of management at Xavier University in Cincinnati, Ohio, and heads his own consulting firm, Executive Development Research.